Old Schuylkill Tales

A History of Interesting Events, Traditions and Anecdotes of the Early Settlers of Schuylkill County, Pennsylvania

By Ella Zerbey Elliott

Published by Pantianos Classics

ISBN-13: 978-1-78987-571-3

First published in 1906

Contents

Preface iv

Part One - The Early Settlers 5

Part Two - Oldest Towns of Schuylkill County 21

Part Three - History of Coal and Canal 50

Part Four - History of Pottsville 78

Part Five - History of Early Churches 102

Part Six - Interesting Local Stories 119

Part Seven - Other Tales 144

TO THE SCHUYLKILL COUNTY HISTORICAL SOCIETY THIS WORK IS
RESPECTFULLY DEDICATED BY THE AUTHOR

Preface

The "Old Schuylkill Tales" may not claim the dignity of a history, yet the brief and impartial records of historical events are correct. Those who have read other early histories will find scant reference in them to the early incidents of the lives of the first settlers. The tales are true stories with, perhaps, in some cases, the substitution of fictitious names for those of the principal actors in them, that the, sometimes, super-sensitiveness of their descendants may be satisfied. Some few digressions too, as part of the storyteller's art are pardonable, but the material has all been gathered by the compiler from the lips of the old settlers themselves or their descendants. It is with the view of perpetuating these stories as little pleasantries of the early days that the author presents them to the public.

Those who have attempted to merge general historical facts with local incidents know what difficulty is encountered in preserving a consecutive chronological arrangement of the events. The consequent irrelevant lapses that will occur in the embodiment of such history and narratives, the latter of which, to assume an attractive and readable form, must necessarily be dressed in a style resembling, more or less, fiction. It should, however, be borne in mind that truth is stranger than fiction and that the rich vein of folk lore in Schuylkill County has not yet been sounded to its depths, there are still rich treasures to unearth.

The writer is indebted to Bayard Taylor's and Beidelman's Histories of Germany and the Pennsylvania Germans, the Pennsylvania Archives and Rupp's History of Counties, for data; to the Weekly Schuylkill Republican, C. D. Elliott publisher and founder, for some of the facts, and to many individuals who did all in their power to furnish the substance for the body of the work. With the hope that the tales will be received in the spirit for which they were intended, the author submits them to an indulgent and generous public.

— E. Z. E.

Part One - The Early Settlers

The Pennsylvania Germans

Where They Originated

The Pennsylvania Germans whose ancestors were exiled from their homes in the beautiful valley of the Rhine and Neckar by furious religious and political persecution are yet, after a lapse of many generations, bound by invisible ties to the land which has been consecrated and hallowed by the same blood which courses in their veins.

The early history of Germany and the frequent quarrels between the Romans and the German tribes is a familiar one. The Franks, Goths, Saxons and Alemanni finally became merged into one tribal relation and these occupied the lower course of the Shelt, the Emeuse and the Schwalm Rivers, west and in the lower Rhine region.

The Palatinate was formerly an independent state of Germany, and consisted of two territorial divisions, the Upper or the Bavarian Palatinate and the Lower or Rhine Palatinate. The story of the Rhine Pfalz is one of great interest. In that country dwelt the ancestors of the Pennsylvania Germans, two centuries before persecution drove them from it. Nature was lavish to that valley. For more than a thousand years the Rhine was the prize for which the Romans, Gauls, and Germans contended. There is no region of country on the globe that has witnessed so many bloody conflicts as the Palatinate on the Rhine. The Romans struggled for more than five centuries to subdue the various German tribes, only to leave them unconquered, and after the Romans withdrew the rich prize was coveted by European nations. The Germans of the Rhine provinces suffered from the French as late as the Franco-German war, and the crimes committed in the Palatinate in consequence of religious intolerance, fanaticism, and political persecution are unparalleled in the history of human savagery.

For thirty years the Palatinate was frequently ravaged by contending armies and the country became the theatre of war and a continuous conflict followed until peace came at the end of the thirty years, and the Palatinates were saved to Germany, but at what a fearful cost. The people were no longer compelled to worship God at the point of the sword, but their persecutions were not yet to end. The worst cruelties were yet to be inflicted on them. Passing over the period of religious persecution which shows the chief reasons for the emigration of the Palatinates to America we come to the date that led up to the grand Exodus of German Palatinates to Pennsylvania.

As early as 1614 three European travelers started from a point on the Mohawk River not far from Albany, New York, and proceeded up the Mohawk

Valley about thirty miles, after which they came south to the Delaware River. Henry Hudson is believed to have been the first white man that came within the present limits of Pennsylvania, which was ruled over by the English.

In 1681 the British government made a grant to William Penn which included the boundaries of Pennsylvania, and one of his first acts was a treaty with the Indians, whom he recognized as the rightful owners of the soil. Penn made three visits to the Palatinate in Germany, and being a proficient German scholar, spoke the German language and had no difficulty in inducing the Palatines to settle in his province in Pennsylvania.

Many who had no money for their passage were carried by masters of vessels who depended upon them to work out the price of the passage in a term of years. This species of servitude had all the features of chattel slavery. The system of selling emigrants was vigorously protested against by the German Quakers or Mennonites. The German settlers occupied all the counties south and east of the state along Chester and the lower end of Bucks county.

New York received a large German emigration in 1710. The Schoharie Settlers had internal difficulties and many left New York under the guidance of John Conrad Weiser and his son Conrad and settled in Pennsylvania. In 1739 Christopher Saner began to publish a German newspaper at Germantown. Copies of it in existence now are considered invaluable as an encyclopedia of information. The Germans tilled their land, and Sauer's paper taught them to believe that the English were seeking to put restrictions on them as great as those which they had borne in the old country, and the English feared that the Germans would make the province a German province.

It was about 1754 when the largest influx of German immigrants came to this section of country, in what is now Berks, Schuylkill, Dauphin and Lebanon counties. The early settlers of the lower part of Schuylkill County, then a part of Berks, were mainly from the Palatines or the next generation of those who came from there. When the first blood was shed at Lexington, the Germans espoused the cause of the American patriots on behalf of freedom. In May, 1776, before the adoption of the Declaration of Independence, Pennsylvania reported that five full companies enlisted from the Germans for immediate service Every officer of this battalion was a German. It took the field and rendered conspicuous service during the early part of the war The German Battalion participated in the battle at Trenton in 1776 and sustained Washington at the ill-fated fields of Brandywine and Germantown and spent the terrible winter of 1777-1778 with him at Valley Forge. The deeds and sufferings of this German Battalion are a proud memorial of the part the German soldiers took in the Revolutionary War.

There is a belief among some people that the Hessian Mercenaries brought over by the British government to fight the Americans remained here after the war was over and that their descendants constitute a part of the element of Pennsylvania Germans in this section to-day. This is erroneous. These men were under contract to return after the war was over. A few perhaps remained and made good citizens, but there was an intense hatred in some localities against the so-called Hessian soldiers. Some of it still lingers with the present generation. It should be remembered, however, that the Hessians were forced into the British service by the poverty stricken German princes, who sold them to the British like so many slaves. Their service was not voluntary. Many of the Hessians deserted in large numbers, and found refuge among the German colonists in Pennsylvania and New York. Thirty dollars a head was offered in Europe by the British government for hireling soldiers to fight against the Americans, but the rulers of Holland and Russia refused to entertain the proposition.

The so-called "Pennsylvania Dutch" language is a misnomer; there is no such thing. The Dutch are designated in Germany as Hollandisch and their language is Holland Dutch. These people came from Holland immediate and settled mainly in New York. Unthinking people are apt to confuse the term German and Dutch. The ancestors of the Pennsylvania Germans who came from the upper and lower Rhine regions spoke a dialect that is known as Pfalzisch and the people at the time of the great emigration from there were known as German Palatines. The dialect of the Pennsylvania Germans is an inheritance from these ancestors and, barring its English infusion, is substantially the same as when first brought over. Pennsylvania German has deteriorated through borrowing from the English. It is now a mixture of bad German and worse English, but the Rhine Palatinate and Rhine Pfalzisch still remain. The literature still in existence among local families, the German Bible, German prayer book and Hymnal in the central counties of Pennsylvania, a number of them in Schuylkill, show that the parent speech has not been forgotten.

In the region in Switzerland embraced in the Canton of Gresous, the Pfalzisch dialect still exists that was used several centuries ago. The Pfalzisch dialect spread all over south Germany and the Pennsylvania German and the south German dialects agree in many particulars. No Schuylkill County descendants of German ancestry need be ashamed of the Pennsylvania German dialect.

Early History of Schuylkill County

Schuylkill County was formed by Act of Assembly, passed March 1, 1811, from portions of Berks, Lancaster and Northampton Counties. In 1818 a small area was added from Columbia and Lehigh. The county has an area of 840 square miles, with an average length of 30 miles, and an average width of 24 and a half miles. The county was named after the Schuylkill river. The word Schuylen is a Swedish one and means to hide.

The tract on which Orwigsburg is located belonged to Lancaster county. In 1752 that part of the State was ceded to Berks County. Rev. Henry Melchior Muhlenberg narrates the history of the German captives, who were taken by the Indians during the years from 1755 to 1765.

Johannes Hartmann lived in the forest, on a spot near where now stands St. Paul's Lutheran Church, Orwigsburg. The records of Zion's Kirche, (the "Red Church") in West Brunswick township, one and a half miles southeast of Orwigsburg, tell of the firing in 1755 by the Indians of the first log church just completed by the settlers; the massacring of the people and the laying of their homes in ashes. Those who could escape — among them Henrich Adam Ketner and his wife Katharine, who came there in 1755, — fled across the Blue Mountains into Berks county; subsequently returning with others they built the church and re-established their homes afresh. It was at this date that a frightful massacre occurred at the site of what is now Orwigsburg.

Daniel Deibert, born in 1802, published an early history of his forebears, who lived near the spot. William Deibert came from Germany to Philadelphia early in the eighteenth century, when his son Wilhelm was three years old. The latter with his brother Michael, when they came to manhood's estate, left their parents in Bern township, Berks county and in the year 1744 took up 300 acres of land in Manheim township, Schuylkill county, now known as the Peale and Filbert farms. Nearly at the same time, the Deibert narrative states, "a few years earlier than my grandfather settled here, another German family came from Europe, the head of which was Johannes Hartmann and settled where Orwisburg now stands." Daniel Deibert's father, John, subsequently bought 144 acres of land in West Brunswick township, just below the old White Church, in the valley, which farm is still in the possession of the Deibert family and one of the most beautiful and prosperous in the county. Daniel Deibert tells how, when he was a child four or five years of age, his father and mother, while clearing the land, took the cradle and the three children with them and that he, the eldest, would keep the locusts and other insects from the baby in the cradle, while the elders worked. His grandfather, William, frequently told him stories of how the Indians molested the early settlers.

Christian Deibert a son, was married to Mary Elizabeth Miller, daughter of Andrew and Elizabeth Miller, nee Stout, and was a sister of Hannah Miller, who married Andrew Schwalm. A subsequent chapter is devoted to the romantic courtship and "mad ride" of Elizabeth Stout, their mother, wife of Andrew Miller. Christian and Mary Elizabeth Deibert lived on the Deibert homestead near Orwigsburg for many years.

The Hartmann family had two boys and two girls. They were a pious and religious family. One day in the fall of 1755 the father and his eldest son were to finish their sowing. Mrs. Hartmann took their youngest son. Christian, to John Finscher's mill, near the P. & R. Railway and the Mine Hill Railway crossing, where Schuylkill Haven now stands, to have some grist done. When the father and the three children were eating their dinner a band of Indians, fifteen in number, headed by Hammaoslu (the tiger's claw) and Pottowasnos (the boat pusher) came and killed Hartmann and his eldest son, plundered the log house and set it on fire, carrying the two girls with them as victims into the forest.

When Mrs. Hartman and her son returned from the mill they found their home and out-buildings burned to the ground. The charred bodies of Hartmann and his son and a dog were discovered among the ruins, where they had been thrown into the fire by the mad savages, who performed in ghoulish glee the funeral dance around the flaming pile; but of the girls there was no sign.

They murdered the family of a man named Smith and took with them their little girl three years old. The girls were barefoot and their feet became sore. The eldest of the Hartmann girls grew lame and became very sick when they tomahawked her. They wrapped the feet of the two other girls with rags and took them to their camp in the forest. Some hunters found the body of the eldest girl and buried her.

Several times, years after, children were reclaimed from the Indians. On such occasions Mrs. Hartman went to see whether she could hear of her daughter. Once she went as far as Pittsburg, but could hear nothing. Thus nine years passed away when word came that a great many captive white children had been taken from the Indians, and were in charge of Col. Bouquette, at Carlisle. Mrs. Hartmann journeyed thither at once. The children spoke nothing but the Indian language and she did not recognize her child among them. Sad at heart she was about again to return home, when the Commander asked her if there was no hymn or lullaby which she remembered to have sung to her little girl during her infancy.

After some hesitation the mother began to sing "Allein und doch nicht ganz allein bin ich," ("Alone and yet not all alone am I") when a grown up swarthy complexioned Indian girl broke out from among the ranks and fell on her neck and kissed her. What a joyful meeting that was. The captive Sauquehanna (the White Lily), and with her, Koloska (the short-legged Bear), Susan Smith and a sister of Martin Woerner, who lived on a farm at what is now Landingville, all returned home with their friends.

The mother's affection for her child, Regina, was returned at once by the freed captive, hut it was not until Magdalena Hartmann had conveyed the exile to the brow of a hill, near which had stood their lowly home, that memory fully returned, and she exclaimed "washock!" "washock!" "The green tree," "the green tree;" her memory had returned and she gave one evidence after another of the awakened recollections of the past and her mother's teachings.

John Finscher's mill, built in 1744, was burned and the family murdered about a year after the Hartmann massacre. From 1755-65, Indian massacres were frequent and the early settlers were obliged to often flee for their lives. Daniel Deibert says, "my grandfather William and his brother, Michael, saved their lives by fleeing over the Blue Mountains to their father's home in Bern township." They buried their farming implements, but in their haste did not mark the place and on their return could not find the cache. When the Schuylkill canal was dug they finally found their treasures, which had been supplemented in the interim with others. There have been rude cooking utensils found on the Peale and Filbert farms, Indian arrows and pottery, which shows that Indians lived in that locality.

It is claimed by the descendants of Peter Orwig, that prior to the laying out of Orwigsburg in 1794-5, as recorded, one Gottfried Orwig and wife emigrated from Germany in 1747, and located upon a tract of forest land on what is now Kimmel's farm, and that Peter Orwig, was his grandson. If this claim is correct (there is no reason to doubt it) then Orwig settled in that locality before Hartmann or the Deiberts. It is probably true that there were others, too, in the vicinity, some of whom never returned after the Indian scare.

Among the Germans and Swiss who landed in New York in 1710 and settled in Livingstone Manor, there were twenty-three families who subsequently settled in the region of Tulpehocken, about fifteen miles from Reading. Among them were the families of Lorenz, John-Philip and Martin Zerwe or Zerbe, three brothers. On account of the bad treatment accorded them by the authorities in the dispossessing them of their lands, they left Livingstone Manor, N.Y., and settled in the Schoharie Valley, where they lived ten years. There, after making many improvements to their homesteads, they were deprived of them through a defect in the title.

After enduring many hardships and privations, they traveled across the country to the Susquehanna river, where they built rude rafts on which they drifted down the stream to where the Swatara creek empties into the river, at Middletown. They followed this stream to near where Jonestown now stands and distributed thereabouts, settling near "Reith's Kirche."

George Zerbe, Sr., who lived in Panther Valley frequently related the trials and difficulties these three brothers endured with others in New York State and their emigration to Pennsylvania. Their names, John Philip, Lorenz and Martin, occur among the list of taxables of male inhabitants over twenty-one years of age, 1711, in Livingstone Manor. He told of their nephew, Jacob Zerwe or Zerbe, whose name is also given in Rupp's "Thirty Thousand Immigrants' Supplement," as Jean Jacques Servier. They were all from Alsace and Lorraine, France, but subsequently removed to Switzerland, during the fierce struggles in the Palatines. Jean Jacques Servier came to America at the age of 29 in the ship Patience, Capt, Hugh Steel from Rotterdam, last from Cowes and qualified at Philadelphia, September 17, 1753.

In the list of taxables for the year 1772 in Pinegrove township, then a part of Berks County, appear the names of Benjamin, Daniel and Philip Zerbe, descendants of the three first named and in the record of Jacob's Church, 1799, occurs the name of Johannes Zerbe, a son doubtless, of one of the above. George Zerbe, Sr., first settled near the site of Port Clinton, subsequently removing to Bender Thai. Three sons, Henry, Daniel and George, were the fruit of this marriage. Daniel took up a claim near Cressona, George removed to West Brunswick township where he located a homestead. Henry worked on the building of the new Court House, where he contracted malaria from the effects of a sunstroke and died after a six weeks' illness of typhoid fever. He left one son, Henry M. Zerbe, of Lewistown, Mifflin County, the late head of that branch of the family. Daniel died when still a young man, leaving a widow. George Zerbe, Jr., lived to a ripe old age and left three sons and several daughters. He was the father of the late W. M. Zerbey, of Pottsville.

George Zerbe had a retentive memory and related the story of the murder by the Indians of the two children of Frederick Reichelsderfer and the burning of their cabin. The killing of Jacob Gerhart, two women and six children, two of the children escaping by hiding under the bed clothes. The massacre occurred in 1756. The story with others was told him by his father, George Zerbe, Sr. There were Indian troubles at the old mill at Landingville, built by Swartz in 1755, and also at the Boyer mill near Orwigsburg, built in 1770.

A George Zeisloff, his wife, a son of twenty, and one of twelve, and a girl of fourteen they scalped, and killed their horses, carrying off their most valuable effects. Sometime later the Indians again troubled the early pioneers and carried off the wife and three children of Adam Burns. They murdered a man named Adam Trump and took his wife and son prisoners, the woman escaping. In her flight she was pursued and one of the redskins threw a tomahawk at her which cut a deep gash in her neck. In 1775, near what is now Friedensburg, a neighbor from the Panther Valley went over to Henry Hartman's house and found him lying on his face in the doorway. He had been scalped by the Indians. Two men were found scalped on the State road to Sunbury and they were buried by the settlers who turned out to hunt the red fiends.

Defense Against The Indians

The avowed object of the French and Indian War was to wipe out every white settler from the face of the soil of Pennsylvania. The Journals of Commissary Young and Col. Burd tell of a visit of inspection made the Indian forts, in 1758, and accompanying facts of deep interest. This chain of forts consisting of a system of over forty block-houses, stockades and log forts, "with shelter for the women and children enclosed, reached from the mouth of the Delaware river to Fort Augusta, the outpost at Sunbury.

They afforded the settlers a refuge if they could reach them but many were killed enroute or died from exposure or privation. One woman, Mrs. Frederick Myers, who was ploughing was shot through both breasts and then scalped. Her husband was found in the woods some distance away, scalped. A detachment of soldiers from Fort Lebanon took a ladder and carried the man to his wife and the neighbors buried both. The man had the one year old baby in his arms which he tried to save and which though scalped lived.

The Finscher family who lived at the mill at Schuylkill Haven, were massacred and also the Heims at Landingville and Everhards, at Pinegrove. Sculps, or Scalps Hill, was so called owing to the number of scalps taken by the Indians in that vicinity. It is believed that more than one hundred persons in this county and in this immediate vicinity were killed by the Indians.

Fort Lebanon, between Auburn and Pinedale, was erected by Capt. Jacob Morgan, in 175G; Fort Franklin, by Benjamin Franklin, Philadelphia, in 1756, on Bolich's farm. West Penn Twp; Fort Diedrich Snyder on top of the Blue Mountain and Fort Henry at Pinegrove; these were the defenses of Schuylkill County: Fort Allen, near the Lehigh river, and Forts Norris and Hamilton, farther south, afforded protection for the settlers of the lower counties. Fort Lebanon was later known as Fort William. It was located on the farm of Lewis Marburger.

These forts were block-houses enclosed with a stockade of logs. They were fortified and some of them had subterranean passages for short distances for escape in case of defeat.

WILL MARK HISTORIC SPOTS

It is the object of the Schuylkill County Historical Society to erect markers on the historic spots of these old block forts and on the sites of the early Indian Massacres if the latter can be established. It has been so frequently asserted that, "as Schuylkill County was one of the later creations of counties in the State it had no history. That its early history belonged to the counties of which it was first a part." This is a mistake. The occurrences narrated belong to the locality in which they existed, and Schuylkill County is rich in historical lore; the error has been that the early settlers neglected to transcribe the facts. From time to time parties have come to the region from other parts with the avowed purpose of creating histories of Schuylkill County. While the data of the compilations (already on record in the archives of Pennsylvania) is correct, little that is original has been added to these works beyond the lives of individuals of a later period who have been prominent (and some of whom who have not,) in the business circles of the County. The histories have been compiled for advertising purposes and a certain sum secured the privilege of perpetuating the business or life history of a patron. It must not, however, be overlooked that many of the early settlers were husbandmen, or men not identified in pursuits that brought them prominently before the public. That the real makers of history in any locality cannot be those who merely visit it for purposes of gain, they must necessarily be of those who are identified with it, since much that is of interest is imparted and preserved only through scant written records and so largely through recollection and substantiated tradition.

Our mountain rocks, with engraved plates inserted will furnish markers for the sites of the Indian Forts, these Indian tales and the massacres. They should be erected as speedily as possible. It will not be many years before those who are still able to impart information on these subjects will have passed away. To mark all historic spots in the County and individually assist in every way possible those who are attempting to preserve our local history should be the aim of all who are able to assist in the matter.

EARLY REMINISCENCES

It is not altogether the aim or purpose of the writer to compile the data of the early chronological facts of the history of Schuylkill County, but rather to preserve the tales and reminiscences of the early settlers. To accomplish this properly it is necessary to draw upon recorded history to furnish the true facts as a foundation for the story teller's art and give the needed background for the word-pictures. Those who are familiar with these tales may, perhaps, complaisantly imitate the example of the good Vicar of Wakefield and his family when Farmer Flamborough aired his old jokes and they gave them their due of mirth again. As for the critics, anyone can criticise. These stories were not written for critics to quibble at, but with the view of perpetuating the narratives as little pleasantries of the early days. With the thought that — "A little nonsense now and then is relished by the best of men" (and some women too) and no further apology, they are presented to the reader.

HOW "OLD DRESS" SCARED THE INDIANS

The Indians in this section in the early days were a remnant of the Shawanese, Nanticoke and Delaware tribes. Three of the original six nations with whom William Penn made the treaty. The others being the Susquehannas, Hurons and Eries. There existed a continuous chain of Indian villages from the Delaware to the upper waters of the Susquehanna. One of the chain of war paths extended to Sunbury, where stood Fort Augusta, named in honor of a daughter of George the Second, who married the Duke of Saxony. Schuylkill County was not on the chain of war paths, but the savage marauders raided the locality as history shows.

Shamokin an Indian village stood on the present site of Sunbury, from which Shamokin afterward took its name.

The Indians that remained in this vicinity after the Indian War were not of one powerful tribe but included some Mochicans in addition to those indicated above. The Moravians farther southeast made strenuous efforts to Christianize the red man, Rev, David Zeisburger converted Shekilling, the chief of the Delawares, and the county paid for their scalps. The war of extermination waged against them so reduced their number that those that scattered beyond the pale of their tribal restrictions were considered harmless, but falsely as the settlers discovered to their undoing.

How "Old Dress" scared the Indians in the great Indian massacre just after the French and Indian War shows what a strategist can do if he has courage and is endowed with enough presence of mind. The Dress family lived in the Panther Valley (Bender Thal) on or near the farm now owned and occupied as a summer country home by Doctor B___, a leading Physician in the town of P___, about six miles northwest.

The Indians had been friendly at first, but since success was beginning to crown the efforts of the hardy pioneers, there were mutterings of discontent among them, and they had upon one or two occasions shown their hostility, but no real depredations had been perpetrated as yet.

Murders had been committed farther south, defenseless women and children were scalped or taken into captivity, their homes burned and their cattle driven away and the settlers were tortured beyond measure, but "Bender Thal" remained unmolested.

Word came one day that there was an uprising among the Indians and that they were headed for the Valley. The block stockade, Fort Lebanon, near what is now Auburn, had served upon several occasions as a place of refuge for the settlers when in danger of being attacked; and thither the now thoroughly frightened pioneers in "Bender Thal" made their preparations to flee.

The women and children were gathered together and placed in charge of Zerbe; and Kemerling and Markel gathered the cattle to drive them to a place of safety. The Dress family formed part of the little caravan that turned toward the fort,, but "Old Dress" was obdurate. He would not go.

He was the first settler to discover the rich farming land in that locality. He had spent several years in the "Thal" returning again and again to it and finally brought to it his wife and family. The Indians had given him the first kernels of com which he planted as seed and in turn he had shown them how to fashion the rude farming implements he used, the iron for which he brought from the Pott furnace on Maxatawny creek.

Once he had opened a great abscess for "Sagawatch" the chief of the mongrel tribe and dressed it with home-made salve. Not without some display of the necromancer's art, it must be confessed, for he knew he was powerless among them, and "Sagawatch" was cured. He had frequently treated their "boils" with which they were afflicted, the result of dirt and squalor and improper food, for they were a lazy set, and looking upon him as something of a medicine man, the Indians called him the "Little White Father;" and believed, some of them, that he had supernatural powers.

It was only the week before that an apparently friendly set had visited him. The mother had just completed the family baking in the huge Dutch oven back of the log cabin and on the plea of wanting a present from the "Little White Father" everyone of the large brown well-baked loaves of bread had found their way into a sack with other things they managed to lay hands on, and the good wife had another batch of bread to make. In the meantime the family subsisted on potato "buffers," (a species of hoecakes made of grated potato and flour and baked on the hearth) until the leaven had raised and the new bread was again baked.

Just a glance at "Old Dress" would show that he was not a man to be trifled with. Short, stout, broad of girth, and with sinewy muscles that stood out like whip cords, he was the picture of health and alert activity. His face was smooth and red and as has often been said of men who wear that type of whiskers, around the face from ear to ear underneath the chin, it was easy to be seen he was a man of determination. He wore his hair, which was scant, for he was partially bald, all combed up after the fashion of those days into a single tuft on the top of his head. This tuft from long practice stood up straight. If anyone could circumvent the Indians, the settlers knew he could. There was little time for parleying and the women and children with their leaders were soon out of sight.

Dress made his way hurriedly to the hillside and screened from view by some friendly bushes watched the approach of the redskins. They came some seated on their Indian ponies, the young braves running at the sides of the old men. Smeared with their war paint and with their war toggery on, beating their tom-toms and yelling like mad, they struggled up the defile.

He could not count them, although he at first tried. There was Sagawatch, too, the greasy villain and traitor. What could he do single handed against so many, with his one old flint lock musket and home-made cartridges and Marie not here to help load.

He fingered the tuft of hair, his top-knot which he knew would soon be hanging with the other smoking and gory scalps from the belts of the foremost of the band, and his mind was made up. Taking an extra hitch at his rusty brown linsey woolsey trousers and rolling up the sleeves of his yellow grey woolen shirt, he ran as hard as he could in the direction of the oncoming murderous crew and in full view of them to the crest of the near-by hill. Screaming and yelling at the top of his voice and wildly gesticulating with his long bare arms and pointing with his fingers: "Come on. Boys," he yelled. "Here are the Indians." (Cum Buva, dah sin Sie, Die Incha.) He screamed until he was purple with rage and told one imaginary party, with the wildest of signs and commands, to close up the defile and prevent their escape, the others should file up the left and right and surround them, and the rest should follow him. "Sagawatch" the murderous "tuyfel" could understand German, he knew, for he himself had taught him many words in the current vernacular. And then still screaming as loud as he could and doubly gesticulating, he ran down the hill with all his might toward the red warriors, who thought they were being attacked by at least a battalion of soldiers under command of "Old Dress," and they showed the white feather and turned tail and fled as fast as they could in the direction in which they had come.

All night "Old Dress" watched at the single window of the little log hut. His blunderbuss and old musket ready, he would sell his life as dearly as possible, if they returned; but they never did.

When the Kemerlings, Zerbes and the others returned, "Old Dress" was quietly sitting in front of his cabin mending an old fish net. The cattle had all been recovered by him from their impounding in the clearings in the mountain fastnesses and returned to their rightful owners. The cows had been milked, the cream was ready for the good wives to churn and everything was going on as usual. The Indians never molested the settlers again, and even to this day "Old Dress" is a hero to the descendants of the families of the early settlers of "Bender Thai."

ELIZABETH'S MAD RIDE

The Pennsylvania Germans, whose ancestors were exiled from their homes in the beautiful valley of the Rhine and Neckar by furious religious and political persecution, did not find life in their adopted home one on a bed of roses. The Miller and the Stout families originated in Alsace and Loraine. During the many fierce wars, in which these provinces were made a mere football by the contending forces of the Romans, Gauls and Germans, they migrated farther north to the Rhine Palatinate, which was then one of two divisions of an independent State of Germany. Again they migrated from the region of the Schwalm River to Switzerland from where they embarked for the United States of America in 1754.

The story of the Rhine Pfalz is one of great interest. There is no region or country on the globe that has witnessed so many bloody conflicts as the Palatinate on the Rhine. The Romans struggled for more than five centuries to subdue the Germans only to leave them unconquered and when the Romans withdrew, the rich valley was coveted by European nations. The crimes committed in the Palatinate in consequence of religious intolerance, fanaticism and political persecution are unparalleled in the history of human savagery. And this region continued to be the theatre of conflict after the great exodus of the German Palatines, which took place in the last half of the eighteenth century.

The German emigrants to New York who had suffered untold miseries with internal difficulties in the Schoharie Valley, with regard to the settlement of their lands and the titles to them, had again taken wing; and many of them turned under the leadership of John Conrad Weiser and his son, Conrad, to Pennsylvania. It was about 1754-1756 when the large influx of the Pfalzisch Germans came to Pennsylvania and settled in Berks County, which has since been subdivided into Berks, Dauphin, Lebanon, Schuylkill and parts of other counties. The Millers and the Stouts came over with the great exodus. The lands in the vicinity of the sites of Womelsdorf, Reading, Bernville, Tulpehocken and along the fertile Schuylkill Valley were soon taken up by the settlers. The families settled first near Tulpehocken, where both Andrew Miller and Elizabeth Stout were born, the former in 1756. The Stouts were represented in the five full companies that enlisted from the German settlers for immediate service after the adoption of the Declaration of Independence, in 1776, and the Millers, too, had sons that took the field and rendered conspicuous aid during the early part of the war, at the close of which the two families with several others removed to Bear Creek, east of what is now Auburn, between the Blue Mountain and the Summer Berg.

John Lesher, brother-in-law of John Wilhelm Pott, operated a forge and small furnace on Pine Creek and there was another near the site of Auburn, and here the men of the Miller and Stout families worked when not employed on their farms. The women occupied themselves with the milking of the cows, churning and making butter and raising the hemp from which was spun the flax that afterward made the coarse, soft linen that formed the bed sheets, towels and linen underwear of the families, some of which is still cherished among their descendants as the most precious of heirlooms. They also manufactured on rude looms the coarse homespun cloths, dyed them with home-made colors and fashioned them into the clothes their families wore. Those were busy times, but not unhappy ones.

No more beautiful country exists anywhere than that included in the tract from Bear Ridge and the Summer Berg to the Old Red Church below Orwigsburg. All around were primeval forests. The silvery Schuylkill uncontaminated by coal washings glistened in the distance. The roads through the forests were mere bridal paths and the first slow, gradual taming of the wilderness, the rolling hills to the edges of the Blue Mountain, the advance from the low log cabins, the scattered, scratch-farms to the first dwellings and farms of greater pretentions as the rich country grew in wealth and ambition, made a picture that excites the liveliest imagination.

It was past the noon mark on the sundial at the little low farm house on Bear Ridge, when Elizabeth Stout completed the chores for the morning. The milk in the spring-house was all skimmed, the log floor and huge hearth swept up with the birch broom, the linen bleaching on the meadow had been turned and wet anew, the blue delf china after the nooning was washed and spread on the great mahogany dresser. Elizabeth's deft fingers soon bound up her abundant brown hair with the snood that confined it; she slipped into her short bright brown cloth skirt, red pointed bodice with surplice of bright green, a concoction of colors she had made with home-made dyes and fashioned and copied the dress from the picture of a grand dame she had once seen.

Her sleeves just reached the elbow disclosing a pair of plump and shapely arms that would have been the envy of any city belle. Her stockings were bright red, knitted by her own nimble fingers. Her feet were encased in a pair of heavy shoes, for she must save the pretty low slippers adorned with the huge silver buckles that had remained among the few relics of the struggle under General Washington at Valley Forge and which were given her by her father. She had worn the buckles at various times on her bodice, at her waist, and now on her slippers, which were safely encased in the saddle bags together with a new cream cheese and some brodwurst tied firmly in snowy cloths and destined for a gift to the mother of the friend Elizabeth was about to visit.

She knotted a gay-colored 'kerchief about her bare neck and tied with its single plain black ribbon over her hair, the white turned back half hood and half sunbonnet or Normandy cap she wore; and adding the snowy white linen spencer for evening wear on her bosom and a few trinkets and necessaries to the little stock of clothing in the saddle bags, her preparations were complete. The black mare whinnied when she saw her approach with riding paraphernalia in hand and permitted herself to be caught without any remonstrance.

What a picture Elizabeth was. One that Joshua Reynolds would not have disdained to copy. Just eighteen and above medium height, well-developed and yet with not an ounce of superfluous flesh on her lithe form, well-rounded limbs and well-knit body. Large soft brown eyes, rosy cheeks, pearly teeth, smooth skin that the bright green and red in her raiment lighted brilliantly and harmonized with.

She was soon in the saddle and cantered off, waving her hand to her mother who sat at her spindle in a little building near the farm house, where the maid of all work was busily engaged in paring and stringing apples for drying and a little farther on her father with such scanty help as he could gather was with the yokels engaged in shocking the late corn.

A few miles of swift riding along the ledge brought her to the river which was soon forded. There were no wandering nomads to disturb the peaceful soliloquy of the traveler. The Indians were quieted down, at least for a time, and Fort Lebanon, the old log fortress of defense against the red-skinned marauders, looked deserted as she cantered by.

Nature was lavish to that valley. The huge mountains were dim with the Fall haze and looked blue and golden and red-tinted in the bright rays of the sun. The early sumacs had turned blood red and the golden maples painted the landscape with their dying beauty and brilliant splendor. The horse sped easily along the path and Elizabeth aroused by the beauty of the scene broke into the well-known Lutheran hymn "Ein feste berg ist Unser Gott," and sang the words to the close, the mountains re-echoing the song of praise of the German nut-brown maid. Then she dismounted and bathed her face in a running mountain stream. Shaping a cup from a huge wild grape leaf, she drank and gave the mare a loose rein that she, too, might slake her thirst. Drawing a small porcelain picture, that hung suspended about her neck by a narrow black velvet ribbon, from her bosom, she adjusted her white Normandy cap and taking a sly peep at herself in the limpid water, she kissed the picture and mounted the mare who neighed with delight at the prospect of once more starting toward the bag of oats she knew awaited her. The picture was that of Andrew Miller and they were betrothed.

The sun was already hanging low in the horizon when they entered the heart of the forest through which their path lay. The great oaks cast gigantic shadows over the entrance but the fragrant pines were well-blazed and the pathway plain and Elizabeth was a brave girl and there was nothing to fear; but she well knew that they must make haste if they would make the clearing near the mill below the Red Church before dark, where her friend Polly Orwig lived and where the corn husking would take place that evening. And where she expected to see her affianced, Andrew Miller, who had assisted at the raising of the new barn as was the custom in those days, and the husking was given in honor of the new building.

Elizabeth kept the mare at as brisk a pace as she could through the tangled underbrush and morass. She thought of Andrew how sturdy he was, surely of all the suitors for her hand she had the finest, the best looking man and the best informed. They had been lovers from their childhood, companions always but this brotherly affection had deepened into something more intense, something that fairly frightened her when she recalled how he had looked when he told her of all the girls around and about the country she was the handsomest. But her mother had told her, "it was a sin to think of one's looks," and had promptly removed the high stool from in front of the dresser, in the top of which was a huge looking glass, when Elizabeth attempted to see for herself if there was any truth in the assertion.

The shadows grew longer, the squirrels and rabbits scampered hurriedly across the path, the late birds had sought their nests, and the occasional screech of the panthers and other wild animals added not a little to her apprehensions about the lateness of the hour and the little mare seemed, too, to be disquieted and nervous. The superstitions of the country arose in her mind and she knew that they were nearing a little clearing in the forest where lived a German refugee who was accused of witchcraft and who was said to have the power of turning himself into a white cat and at times the wood was filled with a gathering of the felines, who would fill the air with their snarling and screeching.

Hark! there was the sound she had often heard described hut had forgotten about. A frightful yell. Surely the man would not hurt her. Had not her father carried him food in the ox sledge in the dead of winter that he might not starve and had he not always been kind to her when he came to borrow the few necessary things for his existence, which he never returned.

There it was again. Yes! and on that tree a white object with fiery green eyes. It was the witch, she dared not look again. There was a scream, a dull thud, she looked over her shoulder and saw a white cat perched on the haunches of the mare. Trembling with fear that each moment would be her last Elizabeth gave the mare the rein and leaning forward clasped her arms about her neck knowing full well that the little beast would do her best, she needed no urging and then she closed her eyes, prayed and prayed and waited.

On and on they sped. The soft green moss yielded to the hoofs of the mare and made the riding heavy. But Black Bess went as she never did before as if knowing her pretty mistress' life was the stake for which she was fleeing. From her nostrils came huge flecks of foam, her fetlocks and sides were wet with sweat and from her haunches dripped drops of livid red blood from the clawing of the white cat on her back.

Elizabeth could feel the hot breath of the creature but beyond an occasional unearthly yell and fresh clawing of the mare it made no effort to harm her. What a mad ride it was! Tam O'Shanter's was a mild one in comparison to it. Would the clearing never be reached? It seemed ages to the trembling girl and again she closed her eyes and prayed and feebly stroked the mare's ears.

At length she heard a soft snort in response. The clearing was in sight, like a silvery rift in the clouds, a light in the gathering darkness. The Old Red Church would soon be arrived at, and the witches hated churches and perhaps ____.

Just then a dark figure loomed up as they emerged from the wood. It was her betrothed, Andrew Miller, who came out to meet her. He caught the bridle of the exhausted and panting mare, the white cat gave a parting screech and disappeared in the wood and Elizabeth fell fainting into his arms. When she recovered he hinted at wild cats but the trembling Elizabeth would hear nothing of them. "Who ever heard of a wild cat acting that way?" said she. But being a sensible girl she consented to keep her adventure a secret until the morrow, for well she knew that the story of a witch so near would mar all the pleasure of the merry party.

The husking was a great event in a country bereft almost of entertainment for the younger people and it was the first one of its kind held in that part of the State. The trick of finding a red ear and then exacting a kiss from your partner was new to her and from the frequency with which Andrew exacted the forfeit she suspected him of having secreted some of the telltale Indian cereal on his person but he gave no sign. And the supper, how good it was and how hungry they all were and how they enjoyed it!

Elizabeth left for home in the bright sunlight on the morrow accompanied by Andrew who walked all the way by her side. But not without Elizabeth's having first confided to Polly the story of her adventure with the white cat. Polly, too, decided it was a witch but thought the witch meant her no harm but good luck, as the wedding was to take place at Christmas. And a witch the white cat has remained through successive generations as each in turn hands the narrative to the next.

Note: Andrew Miller and Elizabeth Stout were married December 25th, 1786. They raised a large family of boys and girls among whom was a daughter, Hannah, who was married to Andrew Schwalm in 1819, at Orwigsburg, and from whom are descended a large line of that name and other leading families residing in Old Schuylkill, Pottsville and elsewhere throughout the country. The John and Joseph Schwalm, Wm. E. Boyer, Frederick Haeseler and Wm. M. Zerbey families, are descendants of Andrew Schwalm and Hannah Miller. Elizabeth Stout was the great-great grandmother of the children of the present generation of the above mentioned. In the list of taxables, returned, "Reading, Berks County, about 1780, occurs the name of Andrew Schwalm, Tulpehocken. At that date the area from between the Lebanon Valley Railway to the Blue Mountain was known as Tulpehocken. This district has since furnished the dimensions for several townships in Berks and Lebanon Counties. The name Tulpehocken does not refer to the mere post office or locality as it now exists but included the area to Womelsdorf. Andrew Schwalm, Sr., was the father of Andrew Schwalm the above.

Part Two - Oldest Towns of Schuylkill County

McKeansburg has the honor of being the oldest town in Schuylkill County. The greater part of the town was laid out in 1803, and the remainder in 1809. The town was named after Governor Thomas McKean. Warrants for tracts of land were issued to the first settlers as early as 1750, the Webb family, who afterward sold their interest to Peter Orwig in 1790, being the original owners. Others followed, and a strong fight was waged to make this town the county seat. When Schuylkill was partitioned from Berks to Northampton, Orwigsburg had one of its citizens in the Legislature and succeeded in getting the Court House plum. Judge Daniel Yost, a native of Montgomery County, was made a Justice by Geo. Snyder in 1809. He became one of the first Judges of the Court of Common Pleas in 1811. He lived and died in McKeansburg, where he is buried. The grandfather of the late Judge D. B. Green lived there. The ancestors of Judge R. H. Koch, the father of Banker Jacob Huntzinger, Joshua Boyer and Dr. J. F. Treichler, one of the first physicians prominently known in the County, who was engaged in active practice for more than fifty years, were among the early settlers of McKeansburg. It is related that when the commissioners appointed by the Governor to examine the rival towns, Orwigsburg and McKeansburg, arrived at the former place a ruse was employed to gain the advantage. Peter Frailey, Daniel Graeff, John Kobb, John Drehr, Phillip Hoy and others induced the nearby owners of saw mills along the creek that ran along the Borough to dam up the water supply for a period. At a signal from the men, the blowing of a horn, the flood gates were hoisted and the Manhannan had such a supply of water that the commissioners concluded that it would be an excellent town for manufacturing purposes and Orwigsburg became the County seat.

Old Underground Passage

On what was the Heinrich Boyer homestead, near McKeansburg, where the heads of most of the families of that name, in different parts of the County, originated from, a valuable discovery was recently made. The early settler, Boyer, who settled here in 1754, whose log cabin stood for many years on the farm, had made a means of defense for himself and his neighbors against the Indians. He built and timbered an underground passage from the cabin to a tree some distance away, where there was an opening, for a means of exit and escape to safety. It was covered at the mouth with a brush heap to conceal it and was entered from the cabin by removing a log at the fire place. The picture of this cabin is a highly prized asset among the descendants of Heinrich Boyer.

View of Orwigsburg

ORWIGSBURG SECOND TOWN IN THE COUNTY

Orwigsburg was laid out in 1794 by Peter Orwig, bachelor, of Brunswick Township, then Berks County. A small pass book found among the effects of Christopher Loeser, Esq., gives the names of one hundred and forty-eight purchasers of lots, with the dates of the deeds to the same, all of which were recorded during the months of April, 1795, and April. 1796. Some of these lots were subject to ground rent and on this fact the claims of a lawsuit by the Orwig heirs and others is based. Schuylkill County separated from Berks and Northampton in 1811, but it was not until March 12, 1813, that Orwigsburg was regularly incorporated and became the County seat.

Of the older towns of the County the following is the data with that of other leading events:

McKeansburg, First Settlers......................................1750
" Town laid out..1803
Orwigsburg, First Settlers......................................1747-1755-1794
" Town laid out, Inc. 1794-5-1813
Pottsville, First Settlers..1780-1796-1802-4-6
" Town laid out, Inc. 1816-1828
Schuylkill Haven Incorporated..............................1841
" First Settlers...1775
Tamaqua laid out by Schuylkill Coal and Navigation Co....1830
Minersville, First Settlers...1793
" Laid out, Inc. ....1830-1831-'41

Port Clinton, laid out, Inc. 1828-1829
St. Clair, Incorporated..1844
Port Carbon. First Settlers...1826
Pinegrove, First Settlers..1816
" Laid out...1830

The "north of the mountain" towns are of mushroom growth as compared with the above and exist only since the upper basin of coal was opened. Different localities had their early settlers. Mahanoy City was incorporated in 1863, and its contemporaries in the upper valleys followed in its wake, during the next decade or two, and have since shown the most remarkable growth and spirit of enterprise and progress. Their incorporation is of too recent date to be included at this point.

SCHUYLKILL COUNTY FOLK-LORE

No country is richer in legendary folk-lore than that of the southern part of Schuylkill County. There were many quaint characters among the early pioneers. These frontiersmen were accredited with a phlegmatic temperament that the delightful imagery of poesy and imagination was not supposed to penetrate. Yet the old citizen of to-day will narrate the tales of his youth, stories rich with the folk-lore of the early days, the stories of his grandsires, that made his hair stand on an end, on occasions, and caused him many a sleepless night. He will tell you in one breath that there was nothing in them and with the next reiterate with Hamlet, that, "There are more things between Heaven and earth, Horatio, than are dreamt of in your philosophy."

Many superstitions existed among the early settlers of Schuylkill and Berks Counties. The New Englanders were not alone in their belief in witches. The same belief was rife in the southern part of this County, where several so-called magicians lived who were believed to be in league with the spirits, and who practised on the credulity of the country people for their own benefit. One of these was a man named Huntsicker, who claimed to have discovered the lost books of Moses in a spur of the Blue Ridge Mountains near where he lived.

PROLOGUE - SIXTH AND SEVENTH BOOKS OF MOSES

The Sixth and Seventh Books of Moses were translated from the Hebrew by Rabbi Chaleb from the Weimar Bible, and are dedicated to Magical Spirit-Art. It is claimed that these two books were revealed by God to Moses on Mount Sinai and subsequently came into the bands of Aaron, Caleb, Joshua, and finally to David and Solomon, and were then lost. In the original Hebrew, it says: "Thus spake the Lord of Hosts to me, Moses."

All the mysteries of conjuration through the seals of the Heavenly messengers that appeared to Isaac and Abraham, the Cherubim and Seraphim and ministering angels of God are given in these books, together with the seals of the angels of the planets, and with these seals, it is claimed, wonders can be worked. The spirits of the air and the spirits of fire are said to be under the command of the angels of the seven planets and of the sun. It is also claimed that:

The power of magic descended from the Israelites, when God spake to the people in dreams, so many of which are recounted in the Holy Scriptures, and which are republished in these lost books of Moses. The vision of Jacob and the ladder with the angels, how Jacob was told to practice a certain something that belonged to the art of necromancy in order to increase his herds, is given in full from the Bible story in Genesis. Other old Bible instances follow in succession, particular stress being given to the powers resembling magnetism which Moses possessed when he performed his wonders before Pharaoh. When he smote the rock in Rephidim and the waters gushed forth, and the spirit of clairvoyance and prophecy is set forth, that the Lord permitted Moses to convey upon the seventy elders. Further it is asserted that:

There were spurious magicians and prophets in those days but the school of these prophets, it was claimed, was inspired by God. The Kabala magic of the Sixth and Seventh Books of Moses was only performed by the assistance of God, by men who purified themselves by fasting and prayer and relied on Him. They must lead clean lives and must be perfectly healthy, but they could not tell of their Art to others, nor impart how it was done. They might tell right-minded, God-fearing people that they were not wicked but that they were assisted by God, who gave them the power to command the spirits of Evil that worked among men.

Note: — Anyone desiring to read further of the Sixth and Seventh Books of Moses will find a copy of them in the Library of the Schuylkill County Historical Society.

THE HUNTSICKERS

One morning in the early years of the last century, somewhere in the 'Twenties, smoke was seen ascending from the chimney of the deserted old log cabin near the Abram Albright farm in West Brunswick Township, about a mile and a quarter from Orwigsburg, the old County seat. The Peterpins who lived at the fork in the roads had not had such close neighbors for a long time and their interest was excited. During the day the "Fader" took occasion to walk over, something like a half mile away, to offer his services, if they were needed, in the moving, and to see who the newcomers were.

There were no visible evidences of moving or chattels about, except at the rude lit tie shed that did duty as a bam, where a black cow was tethered and a number of black chickens ran about responding to the feed thrown to them by a bent-up lame and very black negro, who was shambling about. "From the Long Swamp," said Father Peterpin, mentally.

Now the Long Swamp people were the aversion of the thrifty German settlers. A motley crew of a mongrel type of Indians, Negroes, and bad whites, some of them criminals, intermarried and living mainly by their wits, for they were too lazy to work. Sometimes several of them would appear to help in the harvest or planting, and when, subsequently, hay, corn, and fodder or even potatoes disappeared, it was always laid to the thieving Long Swampers, who had first sent out their scouts to work and to see where what they wanted was to be had and then came after it at night. The Long Swampers made baskets from the willows that surrounded the swamp and acted as fakirs at the battalions and vendues, but beyond this had no visible means of support. The remains of their deserted cabins may still be seen on the edge of the swamp.

The front door of the little cabin was opened and carefully shut by a plump, rotund little woman with a great peaked white cap with broad ruffles on her head. Her dress was pinned up over a finely quilted silk petticoat and her white lawn 'kerchief crossed on her ample bosom, betokened a refinement of dress not common to that part of the country. She wore a large seal gold ring on the middle finger of her right hand which she waved in welcome to Peterpin and said to him in a cultivated High German that "Herr Huntsicker was not at home. They had come to live there. She was glad to know that they had such kind and friendly neighbors as the Peterpins." From that time on they were known as "Der Herr und Die Fran Huntsicker."

The lame negro, whom no one had ever seen before, worked about the place, patched up the old roof, fixed up the barn. milked the cow, but how they had come there no one know. In the meantime, a quaint looking little old man would occasionally appear walking about the place, toward nightfall. His smooth-shaven face, yellow parchment-like skin, drawn tightly toward a large half-open mouth filled with big, even yellow white teeth and with bloodless lips. He was carefully dressed in smooth black small clothes with high cut vest, swallow-tailed coat, high collar, black silk hat, like the "Parrah" or the "Schulemaster," they said, and on the middle fingers of both hands he, too, wore a large golden seal ring. That was Herr Huntsicker. He seemed to be always searching for something in the ground or in the sky and invariably carried a half-open book in his hand which he consulted carefully.

The Huntsickers began to have strange company. People appeared from everywhere and especially at night. Then it began to be noised about that Huntsicker was a magician and performed strange mysteries of the spirit art. The good church people thereabouts would have none of it, but when they saw the results that sprang from the use of his occult powers they all believed in him, but said in whispers among themselves that it was from the Devil and not from God that such things were done.

Some of the most daring of the country people visited him, when at midnight he conjured up the beautiful and mild human form of a youth who was to bring them whatever they desired (but he said their lives must be entirely blameless; and what wonder if they never got their desires). Many carried or wore the high seals, in hieroglyphics, that, would conjure the realization of these desires or defeat the machinations of their enemies. Some seals were supposed to confer long life, secure the wearer from misery and confer great fortunes. Others conferred the power of conveying to man through dreams what he wanted to know.

The Fourth Table from the Book of Moses was the most important one, and that the settlers openly availed themselves of. It was that governing the Spirits of the Earth and its treasures. If a well was to be dug, Huntsicker came at night, the air was filled with red lights and fantastic shapes, a huge divining rod was thrown by him; the next day they dug at the spot and lo! the best of water and plenty of it appeared.

To wear the seal of the sun was popular, too. That conferred wealth, honor, and power through its strength; and the spirit of the planet Mercury had helped find the ore, in after years burned at the furnace at Hecla, and the potters clay near what is now Ringgold. The charming of snakes was taught from the Talmud and numerous incantations were sought for at Huntsicker's hands; the lovesick swains, disappointed in their hopes, resorted to him for love-powders and lotions; he cured sick headaches, and other diseases, too, with charms and powders. The evil was growing and in vain did the clergy and more cool-headed among the people caution and berate the settlers. Huntsicker was feared, but he was thoroughly believed in by everybody. To doubt him was to doubt the evidence of their own senses; to not credit what they had seen with their own eyes.

One day Frau Huntsicker came over to the Peterpin farmhouse. She was of a very friendly nature and had upon several previous occasions deplored the fact that people dreaded them so, and called then witches. Herr Huntsicker, she said, "had had the whereabouts of the Sixth and Seventh Books of Moses revealed to him in a dream. He had secured them from fire and among scorpions at the bottom of a great mountain and had been commanded to use them to rid the earth of wickedness. He did not like to do it. He was afraid, but it was God's command. They had nothing to do with the Devil except to exorcise him and drive him away." "No one prayed and fasted," she said, "as much as Herr Huntsicker."

On this particular day she said, "the Herr was sick in bed; he took cold the night before while out laying the evil spirits in men and forcing them to return stolen goods," which he frequently did. The negro was away and she could not do the chores herself; would they send some one over from the farm?" "Madam" Peterpin, as the Frau called her, said, "they were all at work at the oats except Peter, who she thought was too small," but the Frau gave him a glance and Peter at once arose from his copybook in which he was making the great round German script letters and said, "he would go," calculating mentally what he would do on Christmas with the coin she was sure to give him. The Frau preceded him and he remained to change into his working smock and shoes that he wore for choring.

There was no one about when Peter arrived at the Huntsickers, but he would not be afraid and boldly he walked up to the door with the kettle of fresh buttermilk in hand that his mother had given him for the sick man. He had never been inside the house, but had heard much about it, and he reconnoitered the inside through the crack in the door. Yes, there was the large black book-case filled with books and yellow manuscripts. The twelve wooden rocking chairs with their gay cushions were gently swaying to and fro, and at the foot of each lay a black cat. A large corner clock ticked solemnly, and in the far corner, on the other side of the hearth, where a bright fire was crackling and over which hung the silver kettle in which the spirit lotions were brewed, stood a large high-posted, silk-curtained bed, and in it Herr Huntsicker with a funny high-peaked night cap on his head, his yellow claw-like hands with the big seal rings clasped in front of him on the heavy skins and silken coverlets, for he was "sweating out" the cold and chills.

Just then, leaning too hard upon the door, it lurched open and Peter, half falling, sprawled into the room and in his confusion he said, as he would at home to old Tom, "Seat." The twelve black cats that had been lying each on their own rugs in front of their rockers flew up. Spitting and with tails in the air, the largest one mounted the top of the corner clock, the others ran up the wall to the beams overhead and glowered down at Peter, snarling, spitting and yelling. Peter recovered himself, however, without spilling the buttermilk and began, hat in hand, in his best German, a little speech to the Herr. They were the witches, he knew, but they were only black cats now, he thought; he would not be afraid of them. Just then the Frau appeared. She, too, had apparently changed her visiting black silk for her more ordinary everyday garb.

The cow was soon milked, the kindling wood split and brought in, the numerous chores about the stableyard performed, hay taken down from the loft, and everything that a little boy could do, was done for the Fran that she might go along until the morrow when, if the negro did not come back or the Herr get well, he would go over again. She would send Nero, the big black dog, to tell him. "The dog would talk in his own way," said the Fran, "and he would know but if he would bring a couple of pails of water from the spring, supper would be ready and he must eat some before he went."

Peter would rather have gone home for his evening meal, but he did not like to offend his kind hostess. His heart, however misgave him when he went into the living room, where the table was already set, and there were the twelve black cats, each in his or her own seat. blue china plate, knife, fork, and spoon and a pewter mug in front of each, all sitting waiting on their hind legs with their front paws crossed on the edge of the table. The Fran took the foot of the table, the head remained vacant for the Herr, and Peter sat at her side where he felt tolerably secure There was a moment's pause and Peter said his little German grace mentally as a means of protection against the witches and then the Fran clapped her hands and the cats all fell to with a gusto and ate the porridge from the china plates and drank the milk from the mugs. Peter was a country boy with a good healthy appetite and there were some delicacies on the Table not always visible on the table at the Peterpin home, where there was a large family and plenty of wholesome food, but not many dainties.

The Frau gave him a cup of coffee, which was a forbidden luxury for the Peterpin children, and he drank it as he had seen his father do, last of all for his dessert. When he finished it he saw a thick sediment of something white in the bottom of the cup. It flashed over him in an instant, it was a witch powder; he would be turned into a black cat, too. In a flash he had left the table, was out of the door, and ran as fast as his short legs would carry him over the meadow, up the hill, until he came to the large pine tree that stood at the head of the lane that led into their own pastures and here he lay down and parted company with every atom of his good supper, leaving it under the tree (with the story of which he had intended to excite the envy of the other children), and oh! how white and sick he was when he entered the home kitchen. By degrees the tale of his undoing was wormed out of him and the mother laughingly told him that, "the white powder at the bottom of the cup was only sugar which he should have stirred up to sweeten the coffee."

About this time Father Peterpin had a brand new black oil-cloth cover, wagon-top and all stolen from the farm wagon in the wagon-shed, attached to the barn. He related the circumstance to Herr Huntsicker, who volunteered to get it returned. The Herr wished no money for it, he said. His clients never paid him outright, but left their scant cash on the gate post. "He dared not ask anything, but they must live, too," said the Herr. "Peterpin had been kind to him and he would like to repay him." Now the farmer had been most pronounced in his protests against the belief in the magic art. But Huntsicker said he should pray for the return of the wagon cover and he would do the same; and that disarmed Peterpin and he consented.

The children were all safely stowed away in bed and the "Mutter" was sitting at the light of a rush tallow-dip candle reading her Bible and prayer-book, for they were staunch church people, when Peterpin betook himself to the upper barn chamber to watch for himself.

The old clock in the kitchen had struck the hour of twelve and he was beginning to feel drowsy, when he felt a slight stir in the air and a mellow yellow light was cast over the surroundings and there was Huntsicker with his head bent forward coming toward the barn, reading from the black book of Moses. Huntsicker made a large circle in front of the wagon shed with the rod he carried in his hand, and within it numerous signs and figures; his incantations grew louder and louder and as he proceeded the air was peopled with mysterious fiery shapes.

All at once flashes of lightning lighted up the scene and a loud report like a cannon, or thunder, filled the air and a huge wagon wheel of red fire rolled down the hill, followed by a motley crew stumbling as they ran and drawn on apparently against their will. Who they were Peterpin could not tell, but he said mentally, again, the "Long Swampers." In the midst of them they carried the wagon-top and cover and others brought pitch-forks, bags of grain, farming implements and other articles that had likewise been stolen from the farm and which Peterpin had either never missed, forgotten or overlooked. They deposited them in the wagon-shed and withdrew muttering and cursing as they went. The big drops of perspiration stood out on the farmer's face and hands, but he kept his post at the barn loft window until they were gone and Huntsicker had obliterated the figures in the strange circle, and he, too, gradually disappeared in the same mellow yellow light he came in, and that finally died out, towards his own home. Then Peterpin retired, too, to tell his good wife. Madam Peterpin hinted that he might have slept and dreamed it all; but acknowledged that she, too, plainly saw the yellow light and flashes of lightning and heard the strange noises but feared to look out further.

At early daylight, after a sleepless night for both, they repaired to the barn, where they discovered that the things enumerated by Peterpin were all there and stowed in the wagon shed.

Old Court House, Orwigsburg

Shortly after the Huntsickers disappeared without any sign of their belongings being left in the cabin. No one had seen them come and no one had seen them go. The belief existed for a long time among the country folks that Huntsicker was in league with the Devil and that he and the Frau had been spirited away by the same spirits that they had conjured with just once too often.

The Orwigsburg Postmaster, however, said that Herr Huntsicker had disappeared just after receiving a large official-looking envelope from Germany. The belief gained credence after a time that he was a political refugee and had been in disfavor with the German government, but was finally pardoned. Huntsicker shunned and feared all strangers and would remain in hiding for days at a time. He was doubtless a learned man and practised the experiments of chemistry and astrology, with magnetism and the use of pyrotechnics, on the honest, but simple country folks to mystify them and to keep them at a distance; and perhaps the results of the use of his occult powers served to while away the time of his enforced exile and contributed to his own personal enjoyment.

Huntsicker and the lame negro were probably one, for neither was ever seen when the other was present. The necromancer possibly thought himself above being seen performing menial labor. It might detract from his prestige as a magician and it might be he had never performed it in the old country. Thus Huntsicker's powers might be explained away in the light of the present day, but he was no mythical personage, and many more stories of what he performed are still related among the descendants of those who lived in West Brunswick township in the early days of Schuylkill County.

UNWRITTEN HISTORY OF ORWIGSBURG

The Court House was erected in 1815, the cost of the building was $5,000; before it was built, a Court of Quarter Sessions was held in the public house of Adam Reiffsnyder (Arcadian Hotel), on the third Monday of December, 1811, before President Judge Robert Porter, when the following attorneys were admitted: George Wolff, Charles Evans, Frederick Smith, Wm. Witman, James B. Hubley, John Spayd, John W. Collins, M. J. Biddle, Samuel Baird. and John Ewing. Courts were authorized to be held in the same place until the building of the Court House was completed.

Wm. Green, Sheriff of Schuylkill County, reported the precept directed to him as duly executed. Township Constables were appointed and a grand inquest of twenty-one citizens were sworn and affirmed. Sheriff Green was the grandfather of the late Judge D. B. Green, of the Schuylkill County Bench and Bar. He removed to Orwigsburg from McKeansburg. He built the old Orwigsburg Hotel, erected about 1815, at the northwest corner of the big square known as the "Rising Sun" Hotel. The Arcadian Hotel on the southeast corner was built prior to this, in 1796, and was known as Orwig's and Reiffsnyder's. In front and on the sides of both of these public houses stood the town pumps. John Kobb owned the hotel directly opposite Reiff Snyder's. The jail was not built until 1814. The house two doors below the Court House, owned by associate Judge Rausch and subsequently occupied as a residence by Dr. Henry Haeseler, was utilized as a lock-up. The cellar was used as a prison cell, the windows being protected with iron gratings. The prisoners were handcuffed and chained to stumps of trees which had been left in the "-round. Among the first Judges of the Schuylkill Courts were: President Judge Kidder, of Wilkes-Barre, who came every three months to attend court, and Associate Judges Yost, Rausch and Jacob Hammer. The latter resigned when the Court House was removed to Pottsville, not desiring to leave Orwigsburg. These Judges were all appointed by the State and were subsequently succeeded by Judge E. O. Parry and Judge Hegins, the latter of whom it will be remembered was afflicted with curvature of the spine.

With the building of the Court House in 1815 came many new citizens, the legal lights of the County; Christopher Loeser, considered one of the best lawyers in Pennsylvania and a soldier of the War of 1812; John Bannan, Wm. B. Potts, E. O. Parrv, Wm. Witman, lawyer and Justice of the Peace. "Squire Witman was married to a sister of Mrs. E. O. Parry. John P. Hobart, James H. Graeff, J. W. Roseberry, these were, with several others, the leading lawyers of that period. Mrs. Roseberry, a widow, and mother of the above, kept a private school for girls in the town. There were no public schools then. There came to Orwigsburg from the South a widow named Bartlett, with two daughters named Louisa and Lavina. The former married Christopher Loeser, Esq., the latter became Mrs. Charlemagne Tower, whose husband, a large owner of coal lands, was one of the only two millionaires Schuylkill County has produced and whose family history is too well known to need recapitulation here. Charlemagne Tower, Ambassador to Germany, is a son of this union.

NOTABLE CITIZENS

Orwigsburg was the pioneer town of the County and had many notable citizens during its early years. Edward B. Hubley represented the district of Berks and Schuylkill County in Congress. He was a Democrat. Francis Hubley sat on the bench as Associate Judge. George Rahn, grandfather of the late C. F. Rahn and father of Charles Rahn, Clerk of the Courts, was Associate Judge, Sheriff and Prothonotary. John M. Bickel was State Treasurer and County Treasurer. Frank Hughes, Attorney General of the State; Jacob Hammer. Associate Judge, member of Legislature, Clerk of Sessions, Register and Recorder and Prothonotary. John W. Roseberry, member of the Legislature. Michael Graeff, hotelkeeper, also a Legislative member. Charles Frailey was a State Senator. Associate Judge and Prothonotary.

Of these, Jacob Hammer and John W. Roseberry were Whigs. John T. Werner, editor of the first Whig paper published in Orwigsburg, which he purchased from a Lebanon County man, who ran it for a short time, was elected Sheriff. The "Freiheitz Press" enjoyed great popularity for its fearless, outspoken opinions. Sheriff Werner was subsequently re-elected to the office of Sheriff and was succeeded by his son, the late J. F. Werner, P. & R. Land Agent. Sheriff Rausch was a native of Ringgold.

The early merchants were, the Schalls, Hammers, Becks and Jacob Huntzinger. Other familiar business people were the Graeffs, Linders, Schafers, Zulichs, Shoeners, Bodeys, Kimmels, Fegleys, Hummels, Hoffmans, Dr. Benjamin Becker, Dr. Douglass, Dr. Medlar and others, whose names have been obliterated from the scrolls of time, but yet live among the memories of their descendants.

The surroundings of Orwigsburg belong to one of the richest agricultural sections of the State. The fertility of these lands has been enriched to a high degree of cultivation by the industry of the farmers, many of whom have become well-to-do, if not wealthy, through the fertility and production of their broad acres. The Kimmels, Hoys, Deiberts, Fegleys, Folmers, Yosts, Albrights, Buehlers, Moyers, Scheips, Kemmerlings, Potts, Zerbes, Wagners, Scbollenbergers, Matzs, Krebs and Haeselers, were among the early tillers of the soil. Some of their descendants of the third generation are living upon the same broad acres tilled by their forefathers.

THE LOCAL MILITARY

There were two military companies in Orwigsburg; the Greys were the oldest in point of service. John M. Bickel was captain. Jacob Hammer, too, served six years; one more year would have freed him from military duty. Fourth of July was a great day and celebrated at least by the military. On one occasion when the Declaration of Independence was read Jacob Hammer made a speech on the sentiment, "The land we live in." Those were great days. Stands were erected in the public square, where gingerbread, small beer and peanuts were sold. The day usually ended with a dance and "frolic" at the hotels. If the farmers were not too busy haying they came as far as from Lewistown ("Tuyfel's Luch"), for the day and those south who did not travel to Hamburg came to Orwigsburg. The girls walked barefoot until near the town, where they might have been seen washing and dressing their pedal extremities at some of the many meadow brooks. Whether this was to save their shoes or because they were accustomed to it is not explained, but perhaps they were actuated by both motives.

BATTALION DAY AT ORWIGSBURG

It was just after the county seat had been removed from Orwigsburg to Pottsville. Naturally the ancient burghers felt hurt over the removal and sought for some means to retrieve their lost prestige. They could not retain their population, but they could still draw crowds on Battalion Day. Pottsville at least should not take from them the Battalion.

What a day that holiday was. Fourth of July was nothing to be compared with it. The rural swains came from far and wide for the great event, some even from Womelsdorf, which was a great concession, for Berks County, too, had its "Battalion," and the rivalry was great between it and Schuylkill. It was then that the busy farmer took his day off and local happenings were counted from before or after Battalion Day.

The country boys and girls who walked about hand in hand, carrying their knotted handkerchiefs in which were tied the precious "lebe kuchen," "grundniss," or other dainties of the day, which in some cases included "knock wurst und kimmel brod" from the beer counter or crackers from the oysterman's stand — all were in their happiest vein. The oysterman was colored and came from Long Swamp. He was considered an important man in those parts and was seldom seen outside of the Swamp only at Battalion and at the vendues. It was rumored that he had once cooked oysters at a stand in Reading, and that prior to these festal days he hitched up and brought the bivalves from that city, from the results of the sale of which and the peddling of herbs and a medicine he concocted he made his slender living. The hot stews were made of the thinnest and bluest skim milk, with a lonesome looking oyster or two floating around in the bowl. But they were a great feature.

Pink lemonade was on sale and beer was plenty. A well-known Courthouse official from Pottsville. who formerly lived in Orwigsburg, was heard to remark that, "you could make money by remaining in Orwigsburg over night, as the beer was two cents cheaper than in Pottsville and the mugs half again as large." The interest, too, in the "Frolic" at the Hotels, which would close the day's festivities, was never greater.

The chief attraction of Battalion Day was the military. The Young America drum corps was only youthful in name and the veteran drummers and lifers strutted about with a martial tread that would have been hard to counterfeit. Banners floated about and the old flags hung high on their flag staffs, manipulated by their sturdy carriers, who would not have flinched had they been twice as heavy or the march a day's length, for had not they or their sires done the same in the days of 1812 or '76 for the liberty of their beloved country?

On this particular Battalion Day everything was being done to outshine all previous ones, for was not the reputation of the oldest town in the County at stake? Should hated Pottsville have everything, even to this great, first and only real gala event of the year, in Schuylkill County! Never!

The "Greys," the crack Orwigsburg military company, strutted about in their well-worn regimentals and every man in the company felt as if the safety of his country and the success of Battalion Day depended upon him alone and did his duty accordingly. The drills began early and all the movements of camp life from sunrise to sunset were carefully carried out by the militia.

A new soldier company, however, had been formed by a younger element and they were alike the pride and despair of their Captain, a veteran of the war of 1812.

Henry Rheinheimer was a "Pruss," who came to America in his young manhood and entered the army for the defense of his adopted country in the war of 1812. He was a good soldier and a brave man, and although there was but little fighting he came out of the contest a corporal, a fact of which he could not have been prouder of had he been made a general. "Henny" had wandered to Orwigsburg after the war and lived in a little two-roomed cottage in the outskirts, where he maintained himself with an occasional day's work on the farms around and about the town and with the manufacture of a home-made brand of coffee essence. If the essence was made of burnt rye and beans and cheap molasses it was purer and better of its kind than any of the concoctions of the present time that masquerade under the high-flown name of superior brands of coffee and often, too, come under the ban of the Health Boards.

He was known everywhere as "Henny wot makes the essence" and was popular all through the country, where he could obtain a night's lodging or a meal anytime among the farmers, in return for which he rewarded his entertainers with stories of the war and his experiences in army life and at the old home across the sea.

When he had a batch of the mixture ready he packed the tin boxes in his old, black oil-cloth knapsack with its crossed straps, donned his battered silk hat and with the few necessaries he needed en route tied in his red bandanna and hung from the end of his staff, which he carried over his shoulder like a musket, he was equipped for his long tramps.

He had drilled the country bumpkins and yokels until flesh and blood could stand no more. His was the inventive genius that placed a straw on one foot of each of the awkward squad and a wisp of hay on the other, and instead of the "right" and "left" which they could not learn had used "hay-foot, straw-foot," over and over again until he was so hoarse he could shout no more. But the thought of Battalion Day and of being sainted as Captain Rheinheimer sustained him.

The sun arose bright on the fateful day and the crowds in wagons, on horseback and on foot began arriving early. The flag was run up the staff in front of the old Court House, guard was mounted, the drums beat, the fifes played, and the usual drills and tactics of a day in camp followed. As the hour of parade drew near, the wind changed and a heavy storm began brooding in the west. The veterans had acquitted themselves nobly and with the same precision that veterans alone acquire and the new company's turn came.

Captain Rheinheimer swelled with pride; now he would be justified and see his reward. Their "left, left, left, right, left," could not have been better, their wheeling was unsurpassed, the manual drill and tactics of the new Company would follow and certainly all would be well. But it was just at this juncture the clouds began to thicken, the sky grew dark, gusts of wind came up, and the big rain drops began to patter among the leaves of the trees and a heavy storm broke over the town. People sought the friendly shelter of the surrounding doorways and over-anxious and solicitous relatives who had scurried home at the first warning of the oncoming downfall had returned laden with umbrellas which some of them pressed upon their offspring in the new soldier company. As the rain fell the awkward squad raised the umbrellas and the confusion was great.

Twice had the gallant captain given the order, but with the crowd pressing down upon the scene, the guards could not keep them back at the point of the bayonet, and the raising of umbrellas by some of the raw recruits the confusion was great and the scene indescribable.

Captain Rheinheimer would make one more effort. Drawing himself up to his utmost height and in his most stentorian tone of voice he shouted:

"Umbrellas oder no umbrellas, I tell you; Shoulder arms!"

REMINISCENCE

Daniel De Frehn, of Pottsville, relates the following: It was during a term of court in the seat of justice at Orwigsburg. 'Squire Witman was approached by a fellow lawyer who asked him the time of day. The 'Squire felt in his waistcoat pocket for his watch when he discovered it missing and said:

"I changed clothes this morning and left my watch in my other vest." After a time he bethought himself again, and being inconvenienced by the want of the chronometer sent a man from court with a message that the bearer should be entrusted with his watch which he had forgotten.

The man returned and said the maid-servant had already given the watch to a man, who said the 'Squire had sent him for it. 'Squire Witman had doubtless been overheard. The thief made good his escape and the watch was never recovered.

THE SOMNAMBULISTS

It was before the 'Squire married Katrina; she was only seventeen and had been an inveterate sleep-walker from her youth. Her brother John was not much better and between the two there was not much peace about the house.! Neither might walk about for months, but sometimes both got up in one night and wandered around and made times very lively for the mother who was alone with them much of the time. That is, if the aged grandsire was not considered or the other children taken into account. The father was pursuing his business in the distant city of Buffalo and only returned home at long intervals, for those were the days of slow and uncertain locomotion.

In vain did the mother caution and admonish. It did little or no good and matters seemed to have reached their climax when Katrina was discovered trying to climb into the smoke house one night, where she might have smothered if the spring lock on the door had closed on her. After that she was locked in her room, which was a low, half-story chamber over the kitchen. Matters had apparently quieted down with Katrina, but not so with John.

He had been engaged in driving a balky young horse to and fro, from the 'Squire's new mill, in West Brunswick. The horse had a freak of standing still; nothing could induce him to move, and then of starting just as abruptly. Threats, blows, coaxing, nothing availed when these tantrums came on, and John was determined to break him. He thought and talked of nothing else by day and on this particular occasion must have dreamed of it.

One night there was a terrible noise and thumpety, thump, in the house. It continued from time to time and the family all turned out of their beds to see what had happened. John slept in the attic and the noise appeared to emanate from the front part of the house. At the head of the stairs in the large old-fashioned hall stood a big wooden chest with drawers and old-fashioned brass handles. John had imagined the chest to be the balky horse. The horse would not go and in his zeal he overturned the chest and pushed it with all his might. It slid face down the entire flight of stairs. He mounted the chest and received a blow from contact with the wall below that knocked him senseless, rendering him ill for several days,

Katrina had not been heard from for some time. Locking her in seemed an effectual preventive. It was during moonlight nights that her sleep-walking was worst and the mother said, "she was affected by the moon." Katrina herself was very much ashamed of her escapades and besought the family not to mention them before the 'Squire or his family. One beautiful moonlight summer night, however, she awoke suddenly to find that she was not cured, and Oh! horrors, that, that worst of dreams that she had always feared had been realized and become only too true.

There she was, clad only in her night dress, barefooted and bareheaded, walking on the main street of the town, south of the big square toward Reading. The stage from Sunbury to Philadelphia passed through Orwigsburg about two o'clock at night. The night was almost as bright as day, the passengers had seen her; it was indeed their hooting and jeering that had awakened her. She had climbed over a low porch roof from her bedroom window, down an arbor and made her way several squares to the spot where she was rudely awakened. Poor Katrina! how many bitter tears she shed over that event, but she never walked any more in her sleep, at least not outside of the house. The 'Squire married her shortly after, and it is to be presumed that he was wakeful enough to prevent it.

COURT HOUSE REMOVED

In 1844 the business of the court had increased to such an extent that an addition was built, in which was located the several county offices. With the discovery of coal in the County, the coal industry eclipsed that of the commercial interests of the agricultural districts. On December 1, 1851, the County seat was removed to Pottsville. With the removal came a large influx of the citizens of Orwigsburg, the lawyers and others connected with the workings of the legal business of the County. This was in accordance with an act of the Legislature which gave a majority vote in favor — 3,551 being for and 3,091 against the movement.

A movement for the removal was started as early as 1831. A meeting was held at the Exchange Hotel, Pottsville, on November 19, at which Benjamin Pott, Burd Patterson, Thomas Sillyman, Jacob Seitzinger and John C. Offerman were appointed a committee to solicit subscriptions to defray the expense of erecting public buildings in Pottsville. The people of Orwigsburg fought the movement. A meeting was held at the Court House, where these men were denounced as "idlers" and "lot holders," and so strenuous was the objection that it was not until 1812 that it took definite shape.

The first bill passed by the Legislature for the removal, was declared unconstitutional and after the election a second bill was passed and Pottsville was declared the County seat. The second Court House was erected on ground purchased from the George Farquhar estate and the building was erected through the contributions of the citizens, and the total cost was $30,000.

Two men were executed for murder during the establishment of the seat of Justice in Orwigsburg. The first white man hung in Schuylkill County expiated his crime for the murder of his grandparents. The other, a colored man named Rigg, was hung for murdering an Irishman. There were extenuating circumstances in the latter case. John Bannan, Esq., the lawyer for the defense, considered the provocation that led up to the killing very great, and frequently was heard to remark that if his client had been a white man he would not have been made to suffer the extreme penalty of the law. So great was Mr. Bannan's sympathy excited for the doomed man, that on the day of Rigg's execution the Bannan mansion, on the opposite corner from the Court House, was closed as if for a death within its precincts.

Henry Hammer, of Minersville, eighty years old, relates that at the time of one of these executions, he was clerking for his uncles, Eli and Elijah Hammer, who kept store in Pottsville in the building now occupied by P. F. Brennan, as the Boston store. The whole county turned out and went to Orwigsburg to witness the hanging, and the proprietors of the store with others drove to the scene. There was nothing doing that afternoon; Pottsville was empty and trade was suspended. There was a Camp Meeting in session at the Lessigs, half-way between Orwigsburg and Schuylkill Haven, and the young clerk and a friend of his had planned to spend the evening there with the young ladies whom they afterward married.

In the middle of the afternoon they took time by the forelock, closed up the store for the nighty hitched up and drove to the Camp Meeting. Just before reaching Lessig's they encountered the crowd returning from the execution; among them were the Hammers. What censure the young employees received from their elders for betraying the trust reposed in them, and how much of it they deserved, may be left to the imagination of the reader.

Frederick Hesser, who served in the Revolutionary War as a drummer boy and suffered with the struggling patriots through the hardships of Valley Forge, was court crier. It was his custom to call the court together with the beating of the drum. He is buried in Orwigsburg.

The people of the early days were very superstitious and after the hangings, believed firmly that Sculp's Hill was haunted. Francis B. Bannan, Esq., relates, that, "near the scene of the execution there was a large board fence. It was said if anyone approached that fence at midnight and touched the middle board with his lips the apparitions of the murderers would appear. Being of an investigating turn of mind he tried it, but saw nothing.

On the Lizard Creek road there was an old German who was desirous of buying a valuable farm. He tried to depreciate its value by gaining for it a reputation of its being haunted. He played ghost himself, and was detected in the act. He had hired a Long Swamp negro, who, with himself, was robed in white; they walked about the farm and woods with head pieces or masks of phosphorescent wood. The eyes were cut out something like the lanterns the boys make nowadays. He did not get the farm.

"Know anything about the first jail?" "Why, of course, I do," said Mr. Bannan (who has the reputation of being something of a wag and an inveterate joker).

"Why, I was a prisoner in it myself once. It was when Sheriff Woolison had charge of it, and who with his wife lived in one side, in the residence part. I was only a little shaver then, and thin and small for my age. I was mischievous and Mr. Woolison loved to tease me. One day, after I had been troublesome around the jail, he took me and locked me up in one of the new cells, and looking at his watch, said, 'You must remain in there one hour, when I will come back and let you out, if you will promise to be a good boy.'

"I grew somewhat sober after he turned the key and time seemed long. The thought occurred that I might wiggle through the hole left to pass food through for the prisoners. It was somewhat larger than those in the jail of today, and the grating was up. I crawled up and came out feet first. The door was open; I fled. After that the jail was not one of my stamping grounds any longer."

A GHOST STORY

Superstition was rife in the region of the Blue Mountain ridge and West Brunswick township was not exempt from it. All sorts of stories circulated among the country people and many declared they had seen ghosts in the vicinity of the old White Church that stood on Sculp's hill above Orwigsburg, which was then the county town of Schuylkill.

A colored man named Rigg had been hung there for murder, one of the first two murderers executed in Schuylkill County. The scaffold had been erected in the jail yard and the settlers from far and wide flocked to the scene of the banging. The culprit prayed and begged for mercy but the Sheriff and his assistants turned a deaf ear to his entreaties. He was buried at midnight outside of the sacred limits of the churchyard and the country people were much exercised over it. Then as now there were those who were opposed to banging and none would venture past the spot, especially after nightfall. It was declared that a clanking of chains could be beard and loud moans; and some even asserted that they had seen the colored man, dressed all in white, approach and with clasped bands petition for "Mercy! Mercy!"

Peter Peterpin had gone to O___ to attend catechetical instructions in the church, for the Mother was "Reformed" and belonged to the old White Church and the Father was a staunch Lutheran and a member of the red brick church which stood below the jail near the Court House and in the heart of the town; and the children were all confirmed when they reached the proper age. Peter was twelve years old. It was on a Saturday afternoon, in the late Fall. The farmers were in the habit, some of them, of getting such small supplies as they needed at either of the three stores in the great open Court House square— which has never since been equalled in dimensions in any town in the county, Pottsville not even excepted.

Peter had a commission for his mother at the store. The "Parrah" was a circuit rider and had been rather late in coming to town. He lived at Hamburg and made the trip, once in two weeks, coming on horseback with his sermons or such books as be used in the ritual and services of the Sabbath, and his black but rather rusty gown, stowed away in the saddle bags that hung over the old gray nag. The boy was pleased that he had been able to answer all the questions that had been given him and if he could only have gone home with the other boys and girls from his part of the country, all would have been well. It was growing dark when he got through and he looked hurriedly among the few yokels left in the store to see if there was anyone from his locality, but there was none.

He kept up his courage, however, and resolved to not think of anything and get past the haunted spot where lay the lonely grave, and perhaps he might avoid that terrible colored ghost he felt sure was lurking about somewhere. He tried to think of other and more pleasing things, as he reached the place, and even longed to whistle to keep up his courage but dared not for fear of attracting the ghost. He had just congratulated himself that he had cleared the spot when he heard a slight noise from the bushes on the road side and the patter of feet. What was it? And oh, how near was it?

Already running, he increased his steps, but still he heard the dull tread, tread, behind him. He dared not look back but ran on at the top of his speed. Once he thought he had outdistanced his pursuer and slowed up to breathe a little, when glancing over his shoulder he saw a white form and two fiery eyeballs gleaming like red hot coals in the darkness and he spurred himself on to renewed effort.

It was a mile or a little more from the church to their own lane. Peter had often counted the steps, and he knew he had gone almost half of the distance and would soon reach their own "veldt," where he could turn in and reduce the distance; he would feel safe on their own land; and surely that dreadful ghost would not follow further. The ghost certainly must go back; others would pass his grave and he would have to attend to them.

Peter could clear the fence at one bound. He had often done it before. But, alas! when he attempted it, hampered by the articles he was carrying which he knew he must bring home with him, his foot caught on the top rail and he fell on his face on the other side and the horrid creature was over, too, and on top of him, pawing him and licking his hands. He did not protest but feebly lay there awaiting his end. Hearing a low playful growl he took courage to peep out of the corner of his eye and there stood "Wasser," the old white farm dog, who had probably gone to meet him, or else was out on one of his nocturnal trips for the carcasses he persisted in dragging to his kennel. The dog stood by wagging his tail and Peter in the excess of his emotion placed his arms around his neck and kissed him; and who can wonder if he cried big tears of gladness and relief.

Peter's ghost story was one long related and enjoyed by the Peterpin family.

DIRT OR SOURCROUT

Sourcrout and panhause, or scrapple, are noted dishes among the people of Pennsylvania. Yankees, East and West, may sneer at the mixture of the latter or the lusciousness of sourcrout, but the famed New England boiled dinner of beef, carrots, cabbage, potatoes, etc., is not to be compared on a cold winter day to the culinary triumph of a well-cooked dish of sourcrout. The piece-de-resistance of side-pork cooked as tender as a chicken and flanked with a side-dish of flaky mashed potatoes and followed with a cup of coffee and a piece of home-made mince pie.

It was just on such a cold wintry day that the usual number of loungers congregated about the huge cannon stove in the barroom of Shoener's hotel at Orwigsburg. It was snowing and blowing hard outside and the tobacco chewers and smokers sat about the huge iron circle around the stove and bespattered the sawdust ring in their aim for the large spittoon within, with more than their usual zest and enjoyment. Their wives and the women folks at home might do the chores, it was too stormy for them to venture out.

A lone traveling man sat at a window apart, looking morosely out at the increasing storm. He had finished his round among the country stores, and was awaiting the arrival of the stage for its second trip to Landingville, three miles away, and from where it had not yet returned. Word had been passed around that the road was blocked, and it was uncertain if the up train on the Philadelphia and Reading Railway, then the only outlet in the region, had gone north to Pottsville, and the "drummer" desired to go south.

Perturbed and anxious, he sat there, when the unmistakable odor of sourcrout permeated the atmosphere. The traveler belonged to the effete civilization of the East and despised the toothsome Pennsylvania dish. Irritated beyond measure by his disappointment, the, to him, hideous smell was the crowning insult to his misfortunes, when the following occurred:

"Sourcrout! Ugh, Sourcrout! How anyone can eat sourcrout, I cawn't see, I'd just As lief eat dirt as eat sourcrout," said the disgusted traveling man.

The venerable founder and landlord of the hotel was enjoying his pipe in silence in a remote corner of the room and awoke up from his half somnolent state to overhear this pettish remark of the storm-stayed salesman, when he replied in the rich Pennsylvania German, than which there is no better medium for a joke; the joke must always suffer by comparison through the translation:

"Well, that is just as you were brought up. If you were brought up to eat sourcrout, you eat sourcrout. If you were brought up to eat dirt, you eat dirt."

("Sis usht wie mier uff-ga-broucht iss. Wann mier uff-gabroucht iss fier Saur Kraut zu esseh, est mier evah Saur Kraut. Wann mier uff-ga-broucht iss treck zu esseh, est mier treck.")

The loungers arose and cast longing eyes at the bar, but the salesman was absorbed in his own reflections and adamant, and they dispersed. But not before every man had confided it to his neighbor that he believed that they were to have sourcrout for dinner at home and the smell just made him that hungry.

THE BLACK MOOLEY COW

The Mooley Cow had been teased by the farm hands and petted in turn by the children of the Peterpin family until like some little people, who receive such unwise training by their elders, she had a very fitful and irritable disposition. Peter had but two pets. One a little white chicken, he called Annie, that perched on his shoulder while he fed the flock, for he had his chores to attend to like the rest; and the black Mooley cow and the chicken he called his own and he loved both.

The Mooley cow knew him and would hang out her great red tongue and look at him sideways out of her big, blinking eyes for the salt he let her lick out of his hand and which he petitioned for from the kitchen.

One day his father sent Peter to the barn for a half bushel measure which he placed over his head like a hat. The Mooley cow stood on a knoll outside the barn door and seeing this queer object coming toward her, did not recognize Peter and made up her mind that it was only another attempt to tease her on the part of the "knechts" and she bore down upon the boy and tossed him down the hill.

It was at a steep point and being only a little boy with the upper part of his body encased in the bushel measure, the force sent him rolling down the hill, spinning round and round like a top, he screamed, of course, and his mother came to his rescue. The Mooley, however, stood quietly on the brow of the slope, lashing her tail and giving vent to an occasional loud "Moo-moo" of victory over the defeat of her small adversary, and seemingly greatly enjoying his discomfiture.

WASSER, THE FARM DOG

Another of the animals on the farm was a real Pennsylvania German dog named "Wasser," a large white bull dog, that lived in a big kennel at the entrance to the farmyard, an excellent watch dog that feared neither man nor ghost, but his especial aversion was the black Mooley cow. To the city Peterpins, who came to visit in the Summer, the antics of "Wasser" were a never failing source of delight. When Peter heard him his German "a, b, c," the dog would bark after each letter, but when the final "z" came he would grunt knowingly, and wag his tail and lie down, refusing to utter another sound. The town visitors would bring with them a hamper of bread and butter and other edibles for the satisfaction of making him scamper over the fields to the call of "Wasser! Wasser! Brod geveh, Brod geveh," which was his call from the German farm kitchen-maid, the only one he knew for his food.

Wasser was fond of Peter and saw his undoing by the Mooley cow. He ran to avenge his little friend, but in his zeal ventured too near the Mooley, who threw him high in the air and over an adjoining fence. The dog was so chagrined at his defeat that he disappeared from the farm, and had long been given up as lost or dead, when one day he reappeared, thin, sad-eyed and dejected, the worse for wear and altogether a wiser dog. In the meantime his adversary had been consigned by the home butcher to the meat barrel to stock the Winter's supply of salt beef.

THE LONG SWAMPERS

Long Swamp, in West Brunswick township, was an underground railway station, and was first used by a few runaway slaves, who succeeded in crossing Mason and Dixon's line in ante-bellum times, as a place of concealment and refuge. As the name indicates, the swamp provided, in its environments, a marshy fastness that few whites cared to penetrate. Its low strata of soil emanated, at certain seasons, gases of a phosphorescent nature. The ignis fatuus (will-o'-the-wisp) was not uncommon. Lights were seen floating about at night in the inky blackness of its depths. The farmers in the vicinity knew little of science, and would have discredited any such an explanation of the Long Swamp Jack-o'-lanterns, and harrowing stories were told about the head of a trunkless man, who had been murdered on the edge of the swamp, was buried in its depths and who could not rest, but floated or wandered about to prevail on some one to listen to his tale, remove his remains and bury them in consecrated ground. Several venturesome young men, the 'Squire's sons and their companions, had attempted to follow it to the scene of the burial. The white light flickered and moved always over the blackest marshes, which they followed in a batteau, but they conjured the spirit in vain to speak or else forever after hold its peace. It always eluded them and disappeared before they reached it or else dissolved, and they passed through it.

The runaway slaves felt secure in the fastnesses of the swamp, and know they could elude their pursuers quite as well in its depths as anywhere this side of Canada, whither they were bound, and they remained. They were soon joined by several Indian half-breed criminals, and some semi-respectable whites, and a mixed colony of a mongrel type was established. They built a series of log cabins from the trees which they felled. They hunted and fished and in Summer lent their services to the farmers roundabout, who, often short of help, were glad to impress them into their employment. They could work when they wanted to, and after the haying and harvest there were always corners left in the fields for the Long Swampers to glean to feed their few lean and sorry-looking cattle and horses with the aftermath. The 'Squire was especially liberal with them. His motto was "Leben und los leben."

There were some very industrious people, too, among the colony, in spite of their miscegenation. Dan Britton, a well-known colored man of Pottsville, came from the Swamp, and who ever knew Dan idle? He traveled the county with horse and wagon as a huckster, and persisted in peddling almost to the day of his death. Dan was a dark man but had a half-brother, a white man, also from the Swamp, who became a prosperous farmer in the southern part of the county. The Kinzelbachs, of Minersville, umbrella fakirs, peddlers and what-not, were of this brood. Lydia, wife of big Jack Martin, a white woman, who married a full blown negro, was raised in Long Swamp. She was an industrious and hard working woman all her life and honest, as Pottsville people who employed her, will testify. The first wife of Wm. Lewis, a yellow man, for many years outside porter at a leading Pottsville hotel, was born in the Long Swamp, her family removing to Deep Creek where they worked among the farmers. She was a beautiful woman of the quadroon type. Tall and erect and of a large, spare frame; pale yellow in color, large, luminous black eyes, brilliant teeth, white and even; she was greatly admired and was honest, industrious and a woman of refined instincts. Her heavy, wavy, purple-black hair reached to her knees when unbound. This feature led to the opinion that her father had been an Indian, or that she had Indian blood in her veins. Two of her daughters were perfectly white. She died, as most of the colored people in the North do, of tuberculosis.

One of the noted characters of the Swamp was "Red Nance." In the early history of the County, from 1824 or thereabouts, to 1850, the Long Swampers held their sway until justice, under its coat of velvet, held them in its hand with a grip of steel, and they disbanded and scattered. Some of these women made good servants and char-women for the housewives of Reading, Orwigsburg and Pottsville. Red Nance hired out among the farmers and lived near the Swamp. She had a daughter, Rebecca, whose worthless husband decamped, leaving her with a small daughter, Amanda.

Rebecca was a housemaid in the John Bannan residence, in Orwigsburg, where she remained for a number of years. When the Bannan family removed to "Cloud Home," their Pottsville residence, they brought with them as a servant, Amanda, then grown to young womanhood, and who had been cared for during the interim of her mother's service by her grandmother, "Red Nance."

Amanda looked askance at the white marble figure of Henry Clay on the monumental pile in front of Cloud Home^ and one day asked her mistress what it was for. Mrs. Bannan gave as lucid an explanation as she was able to, to the questioner, of the life and character of the great protectionist and the principles inculcated through the doctrine and wound up with: "Don't you admire the monument, Amanda?" when the girl with all the superstition of her race answered: "No! I don't like dead men standing up straight in front of people's houses. He ought to be in his grave."

THE SQUIRE AND KATRINA

The Squire had quite a history. He was born in Germany and was the last to come over and join the family, who had all preceded him to the land of the free, and settled at Orwigsburg. The old father and mother, two daughters and three sons. One of the daughters married a German Evangelical minister, the other a farmer, and settled in Illinois. One of the sons was a well-known Orwigsburg doctor, the other a leading Pottsville practitioner. The family seemed to lean toward the practice of medicine and among the descendants of the next generation, four followed in the footsteps of their sires and were doctors. Of the present generation, at least two have flung out their shingles with more yet to be heard from.

Military conscription into the German army was the cause of their immigration to America. The sons had no inclination for military life and they fled the country. The 'Squire, however, was 28 years old when he came. He liked his native country and would not have migrated to America, but for the importunities of his family.

He was educated in Hanover, Prussia, where he went to the common schools, where school opened at seven o'clock in the morning and continued until seven at night, the children taking their luncheons with them. He often related having seen Princess Victoria, niece of William IV, and afterward Queen of Great Britain, going to and fro, from the same school building. Victoria was the daughter of Edward, Duke of Kent, the fourth son of George the Third, and was born in the Kensington palace. Her education was superintended by the Duches of Kent. The Guelphs were of the Hanoverian order of Knighthood, founded in 1815, by George IV, and the orphan princess was very strictly raised. She came in a plain carriage daily to the school house, attended by a servant in plain livery. After entering the building by a private entrance, she remained until her recitations were made and then retired. The 'Squire was wont to say that, the royal scholar was very ordinary looking and very modest and unpretentious in her manner. She wore her thick dark hair in the "Gretchen" plaits common to the school girls of her age, and there was nothing to distinguish her from any other German school girl, except her method of coming to the school.

Mechanism and electricity in telegraphy were experimented upon from the time of the ancient Greeks and Romans, down. One Ersted, in 1819, discovered that a delicately suspended magnetic needle has a tendency to place itself at right angles to a conductor, through which a current of voltaic electricity is passing. Ampere needles, as many as there were letters in the alphabet, came next in 1820. Then Gaus and Weber, at Gottingen perfected the invention. But it remained for Steinhil to make the first perfect instrument, July, 1837. It operated for 12 miles and had three stations.

The 'Squire was a young man, not much more than a boy, and he assisted Steinhil in his experiments, as a helper, and in the outcome of which he was most intensely interested. The 'Squire had been educated by the Government for its clerical service, and had passed the rigorous examination. He had a foothold among the clerical force at the lower round of the ladder, but promotion would follow through civil service rules and a pension would come at the end of a long and faithful service. His life was mapped out for him, and yet the 'Squire abandoned it all, and settled in West Brunswick township, below Orwigsburg.

Homer called beauty a glorious gift of nature, Ovid said it was a favor bestowed by the Gods, but Aristotle affirmed that beauty was better than all the letters of recommendation in the world; and certain it was that Katrina's beauty was her recommendation in the eyes of the 'Squire. He had had no thought of marrying, but here he was in a new world, all his old hopes and ambitions cast aside, and nothing to take their places; he was lonely and needed a tonic to brace him up. He found it. He fell in love with Katrina.

He was twenty-eight and she seventeen, and it was no lukewarm attachment, but a genuine love affair. The Germans as a rule are a sentimental, warm-hearted, romantic race, and the attachment inspired was one that lasted a lifetime, and many are the stories told of it in the family.

The 'Squire tilled his broad acres after a fashion, but he was no farmer, and never could take kindly to tilling the ground. He had a fulling mill, a clover mill, acted as Justice of the Peace for the township, school director, tax collector and was a general factotum for the public business of the vicinity. He was surveyor of the roads, laid out fields, and did much writing of deeds and abstracts, for those were the days when there were no printed legal forms and everything was written.

In everything he undertook, Katrina was his encouragement. She attended to all the business about the homestead and managed the hands about the farm. After twenty-seven years of hard and unrequited labor, the family removed to Pottsville, where a fortunate investment in property gilded the golden years of their old age with the crowning success which the results of their hard and incessant labor had refused to yield.

What a pleasure it was to visit that old farm. Favored nephews and nieces (the former some of the leading professional and business men of Pottsville) recall with pleasure the memory of their experience there. When the Squire met them and after the German fashion kissed them he told them they were welcome, and they were. What fishing and boating on the mill-dam and creeks followed. The haying, cherrying and berrying. The table in harvest, when helpers, children and all sat down, some twenty persons together, and the plenty and home-cooking served on that table. The singing school, the Sunday School entertainment at the Red Church, where the boys went upon one occasion.

It was on the picnic style and served on tables in the church. They called it a "fest," and bread, butter, ham, pickles, cheese, sausage, cakes and lemonade were served as a sort of a reward of merit in attendance. The boys were hungry and ate only as hungry boys can. They were helped and helped, and still they ate, when one of the church wardens took them by the shoulders, and said: "I guess you have eaten enough, boys. Get away now and leave something for some of the rest;" and they obeyed.

There was the red ear at the husking bee, the apple-butter stirrings, the candy pullings, skating and sledding during the winter and the game of "shinny" on skates, on the ice. Is it any wonder that the girls and boys of the olden days say, "there are no times like the old times."

Katrina, too, was an original character, and the best of entertainers. 'No visitor was allowed to go away hungry. Her chicken and waffles, fried oysters and cooking were noted, and nothing delighted her more than when visitors showed their appreciation of them by eating heartily. (The maid of all work was known as "Long Ann." Her name was Ann Long.) When she reached her eightieth milestone, her granddaughters tendered her a birthday reception. Always handsome, she looked regal at that age as she sat in a high-backed chair, clad in a heavy black satin gown and surrounded by palms and growing flowers, the gifts of her children and friends. She received her guests of the various branches of the family, a hundred or more in number (whilst her granddaughters poured tea into the small lacquered china cups, and served tiny wafers) with the same calm dignity that always characterized her actions. Approached by a nephew, a well-known physician, he said:

"Well, Aunt K___, how are you enjoying it all?"

"Not at all," she answered. "I am ashamed of such poor stuff. If they would only have left me, I would gladly have roasted a turkey and fried oysters, so that you would have had something good to eat."

Once upon talking to a favorite niece, whilst they lived in the country, she descanted upon "how much better the 'Squire would have had it had he remained in Germany. He would not have had to work so hard."

"But think of it, Aunt K___" said the niece, "then you would never have seen him."

Nothing non-plussed, she answered: "Well, it would not have mattered, if it would have been for his good. I would have been willing."

All things, even the ideal married life must have an end. One day the 'Squire came home, complained of a cold and not feeling well. Nothing serious was thought of it. After several days about the house, he asked for a dish of oysters. He could not eat more than one or two. He beckoned to his faithful wife to remove the dish. When she drew near he placed his arms about her neck, and whispered:

"Have we not loved each other always and to the end?" She said, "Yes."

Trying to disengage herself from his embrace, he fell back on the pillow, limp and inert. The Darby and Joan attachment was dissolved, the 'Squire was dead.

He was only a little Pennsylvania German boy, a great favorite with the 'Squire's brood. The father and mother spoke English well enough to transact their business, when in town or visitors were present, but on the farm the current vernacular only was used. The children must pick up the English language at school, and as best they could.

"Ho! Boy. Can you tell me where Peter Albright lives, about here?" said the stranger.

The boy shook his head slowly and answered: "No! Aver der Pater Albrecht lifs over dere."

The Episcopal Church at Schuylkill Haven was early established, and one of the outcomes was a Sunday School. The late Charles Hill, a carpenter in his early days, had a class in it for boys and Peter Peterpin walked the distance every Sunday to attend. Mr. Hill afterward removed to Pottsville. On one occasion, John W. Roseberry, Esq., brought with him a lady, who was a visitor at Orwigsburg. She was very handsome and even the boys were not obtuse, but admired her beauty and grace of manner.

On leaving the Sunday School her low Jennie Lind shoe became untied, and Mr. Roseberry gallantly stooped to fasten the latchet. A woman who could not tie her own shoe was an anomaly to the country boys. One of whom remarked: "she might do to marry a lawyer, but such a lazy woman would not make a farmer's wife."

On another occasion the Bishop visited Schuylkill Haven. There was seldom any English service held in Orwigsburg, and the forthcoming service in the little chapel at Schuylkill Haven was much talked about in the county seat. Francis B. Bannan, then only a small boy, secured the required permission to go and see the Bishop. He walked the entire distance to and fro, and on his return was asked about it. when he blurted out somewhat disgustedly:

"Why, Father, the Bishop is only a man."

LAID THE GHOST

Mr. Bannan tells the following story:

"There was considerable talk about ghost in the early days. In the hollow near the Red Church, below Orwigsburg, stood an old stone house known as the "Spook House." It was owned by Abraham Faust, who lived in a new frame house on the same farm, some distance away. President Roosevelt, by the way, would have loved Faust, had he known him. He had twenty-three children and all living, with but the one wife.

"There were mysterious noises about the place. A German refugee had committed suicide by hanging himself to a tree near the house, and it was said that his ghost haunted the spot. Lewis Shoener, Al. Witman (brother of Mrs. Clara Althouse), George Douglas and myself discussed the matter and determined to find out for ourselves if there was any truth in the story.

"Securing lanterns, one dark night we walked to the house. The men who had bantered us said that there was a barrel in the cellar with some peacock feathers in it. If we came back, each boy with one of the feathers in his hat they would believe we had been in the house. We secured the feathers and went upstairs where we discovered that a loose shutter struck the lightning rod, and made that peculiar bang and whir that sounded, clear to the road, like a rattling of chains.

"Mr. Faust had offered a reward for the discovery of the ghost, or its cause, and each of the boys was the richer in a small sum of pocket money, when he next came to town, for having laid the ghost. He was satisfied with the clearing up of the mystery, and shortly after the place was occupied by the family, and he rented the new frame house."

DEATH OF GERMAN PEDDLER AVENGED

In the vicinity of the Old Red Church, there were several settlers that were off-color and ne'er-do-wells, who were looked upon with suspicion and distrust by the thrifty and hard-working German farmers thereabouts. Some of them were suspected of witchcraft, and a witch was a person to be feared and conciliated. Wherever such people lived, the superstitions of the settlers led them to treat them well, as it was not known what spell they might work upon their neighbors, through the machinations of the Devil. If the bread would not rise, the butter would not come, infants withered away, crops were blighted, the cows would give no milk, they were bewitched, and many were the incantations and pow-wows indulged in to remove the malevolent spell. Near Pinedale lived a witch doctor, who was suspected of working these spells of witchcraft, yet no one dared accuse him of it.

A German peddler was murdered. His body was found under a lone pine tree on the edge of the open, his pack filled, all his valuables and some of his clothing removed. The witch doctor was suspected of the crime, yet no one dared openly accuse him of it. The peddler was buried under the tree where he met his untimely end. The grass withered and never grew again, and the snow which fell to a great depth all around the spot, would melt at once, as it fell about the tree. The country people saw strange sights, and one young man, returning home late at night, reported that he had seen the peddler, whom he had known well in life, running around the tree pursued by a man with an axe. So great was the dread of the spot, that no one ventured to pass the grave if they could avoid it, and there were rumors of moans and cries in that vicinity, heard from a distance.

Mrs. Kate E. Bender, wife of the late George Bender, of Pottsville, tells the story most entertainingly, and furnishes the sequel to the old tale.

"My father was Joseph Matz, my grandfather, Christian Boyer. They were farmers and well-to-do. We lived near the Red Church, below Orwigsburg. My ancestors are buried in the cemetery of Zion's or the Red Church. Our family was a large one. We sat down, twenty-two at the table, for the hired people, eat with the family in the country.

"There was lots of work for a young girl in those days, and I had my share to do. Cooking and washing dishes for such a family was more than one pair of hands could accomplish. It took several. I could spin and weave and card wool. We grew the flax, and raised the sheep on our own farm. In my 'housesthire,' some of which I still preserve, there were articles of home-made linen and woven quilts of wool, all of the products of our farm. To spin and card was looked upon as one of the accomplishments of a young woman then, like the outlining and fancy work of the girls of to-day.

"My great-uncles were Gabriel and Daniel Matz. The former was a bachelor, and lived with the latter. Daniel was the father of 'big William' Matz who lives near Rock station, and is well-known in Pottsville. My great-uncles owned several fine farms, but lived then at the tannery, near Pinedale.

"One day our uncle Gabriel made us a visit. He told us that the mystery of who killed the German peddler was at last solved. It happened this way. They were sitting in the big country store of an evening, swapping stories as was the country custom. The talk was mainly on hunting, and the game thereabouts, my uncle having started it by buying some powder. The witch doctor was present, and never much of a talker, he said: "'I heard of a man who was killed, once, with an axe. He ran around and around a tree and begged the man with the axe not to kill him. If you do, he said, you will hang for it. You will be found out. If in no other way, the chickens will dig the news out of the ground. ("Wan die hinkle es ausem treek gratza mus.")'

"Everybody understood it, but no one dared accuse the witch doctor, for everyone feared him. Dwelling on the thought of his crime had doubtless finally unhinged his mind, or, it may be, he thought no one would recognize in the story, that he was the murderer. His moodiness increased, and shortly after this he hung himself to a tree. He was buried near the spot, but the peddler's remains were removed to a corner in the cemetery, that the settlers might have peace, and that he could rest. When they were dug up, a number of chickens were permitted to scratch in the freshly thrown-up earth, that the peddler's saying might be verified; and the green grass grew over the spot and covered his grave undisturbed and unmolested thereafter."

DIEDRICH KNICKERBOCKER OUTDONE

Sleepy Hollow was not the only locality that boasted of a headless horseman. Schuylkill County had one also, but there was no Washington Irving to immortalize him. Of the latter spectre, as the story goes, both the man was headless and the horse. Mrs. Bender, says:

"After the Little Schuylkill Railway to Tamaqua was built, there were many accidents at the crossing near where we lived, and several men were killed. The people were not accustomed to the engines and did not understand the danger. One, a man on horseback, had his head cut off and his horse was frightfully mangled. After that it was said that a man without a head riding a headless horse might be seen on dark nights crossing the railway where the accident occurred.

"There was a man, too, who worked in the Matz store, who hung himself in the loft of the storehouse. There was a great ado about where he should be buried. They at first refused to bury him in the Red Church Cemetery, but finally they allowed the grave to be dug in a corner of it, just inside the fence. There was talk of his haunting the storehouse, but my parents discouraged such foolish talk, and the story died out."

Note: — The Matz families referred to are connections of Thomas Shollenberger, the late Sheriff Matz and Wm. Matz, Sr., who formerly kept the old White Horse tavern, Pottsville, and other families of that name and their descendants in the County.

Part Three - History of Coal and Canal

HISTORY OF COAL

Bituminous coal was discovered in England in eight hundred and fifty-three (853), but it was not mined or used until 1239, when Henry III granted mining privileges to the inhabitants of New Castle. It was soon introduced into London, but encountered opposition from the masses of the people, who imagined it was deleterious to health. They petitioned Parliament to prohibit its consumption in the city, assigning as a reason, that it would endanger the health of the King. Parliament granted the petition of the people, restricting its use.

The use of anthracite or "stone coal," as it was called in Pennsylvania, was communicated to the whites by the Indians. Two Indian chiefs, from the Wyoming Valley, visited England in 1710 and witnessed the use of bituminous coal for smithing and domestic purposes. The ignition of the hard or anthracite coal was known to the Indians. The red men in 1700 had some sort of mines in Wyoming.

When a coterie, six in number, of Mohicans and Nanticokes visited Philadelphia, in a talk with the Colonial Governor they told of white men who came in a canoe and took away with them from their mines the ore. The whites not only robbed them, but came again with their implements and dug a hole forty feet long and five or six feet deep and worked the mine and carried away the product in canoes. They took the coal for blacksmithing purposes.

In 1776 two boats were sent from Wyoming on the Susquehanna river to Harris Ferry (Harrisburg). They carried twenty tons, which were conveyed in wagons to Carlisle, where it was experimented with and used in the U. S. Armory. In the first annual report of the Coal Mining association of Schuylkill Comity, formed in 1833 and dissolved in 1845, reference is made to Scull's map of the Province of Pennsylvania, published in 1770. The extract reads as follows:

"A coal mark north of the Tuscarora Mountain, or northeast of Reed's, not many miles from the Schuylkill Gap, within the then bounds of Berks County, may be found upon examination, on Scull's map of the Province of Pennsylvania, published in 1770."

This was the first coal discovered in Schuylkill County, and is supposed to have been found near the site of New Philadelphia or perhaps a little farther south.

In 1791 Phillip Ginther, while hunting, accidentally discovered that anthracite coal would ignite. He made the discovery at what is now Mauch Chunk. It was a year prior to this, in 1790, that Nicho Allen, a hunter, camped out for the night under a ledge of rocks in Schuylkill County. He had built a fire and laid down to sleep, awaking to find the rocks all aflame. Allen lived at the Big Spring on the summit of Broad Mountain. His home was known as the Black Cabin. He afterward removed with his wife to Mt. Carbon. They had no children. He was an Englishman, and afterward migrated to the Eastern States, where he died.

The buying of coal lands in Carbon and Luzerne Counties, immediately after the discovery of coal, gave Phillip Ginther precedence over Nicho Allen as the finder of the black diamonds, and history usually credits Ginther with that discovery. Some authorities, however, state that the discovery of the two hunters was a coincidence or simultaneous almost in date and Allen's name is mentioned with Ginthers. It was not more than five years after the discovery of coal in Schuylkill County, before it was used for smithing purposes. The first coal discovery in Schuylkill County was made in 1790 and the first coal unearthed within the limits of Pottsville was in 1806.

Col. Jacob Weiss, of Carbon County, carried samples of the black stones in his saddle bags to Philadelphia, after Ginther's discovery, and was credited with being "a fool for his folly." Old John Weiss, a connection of his, who lived near the site of the Odd Fellows' Cemetery, Pottsville, and drove the stage on the old turnpike road from Sunbury to Reading, often told this story and waxed wroth if anyone dared contradict him or assert that Allen had found coal in Schuylkill County prior to that discovered by Ginther. John Weiss afterward drove team for Jack Temple, of Pottsville. The Weiss family lived for a time at Orwigsburg.

Jacob Weiss, with others, formed a company for the mining of coal, called the Lehigh Coal Mining Company, the first coal mining company in the United States. In 1803 they sent two ark-loads of thirty tons to Philadelphia hut found no buyers. The City authorities tried to burn the black stones under the boilers at the water-works but it put the fire out. It was finally used for gravel on the sidewalks.

After the discovery, in 1790, by Nicho Allen of coal, a blacksmith, in Schuylkill County, named Whetstone, brought it into notice, in 1795, by using it in his smithery. His success induced several to dig for coal, but they found difficulty in burning it. About 1800, William Morris, who owned a large tract of land near the site of Port Carbon, took a quantity of coal by wagon to Philadelphia. He made every exertion to bring it, into notice but failed. In 1806, in cutting the tail race for the Valley furnace, a seam of coal was laid bare. David Berlin a blacksmith, made a trial of it. His success was complete and it was used continuously ever after, the grate and damper coining into use about the same period.

It was about this time that Jesse Fell, Associate Judge of Luzerne County, discovered that it was necessary to create a draft in order to burn the black stones successfully, and he invented the grate. This first grate was used subsequently in the Fell House, corner of Washington and North Streets, Wilkes-Barre. When the new hotel was built on the site of the old, the grate was retained and inserted in a fireplace where it may still be seen.

John Abijah Smith, of Luzerne, saw this experiment of the grate and took two ark loads of coal to Columbia, but could not sell them. Not discouraged, he took two more and with them a consignment of grates and a small trade resulted. The grates first used for domestic purposes were too small, the heating properties of coal being over estimated; the stove soon followed and the demand for coal increased.

In 1812 Col. George Shoemaker procured a quantity of coal from a shaft sunk on a tract of his land on the Norwegian Creek, Schuylkill County, afterward known as the North American mine. He loaded nine wagons with it, and took it to Philadelphia. He sold two of the wagons only by dint of the greatest perseverance. He gave the other seven away and those who had promised to try it, after a trial, denounced him as an impostor for attempting to impose black stones on them for coal. He not only lost the coal, but was out of pocket for the transportation.

Jacob Cist, of Wilkes-Barre, leased the Manch Chunk mine in 1813 and sent specimens of the coal to all the principal cities of Europe. A year later he sent an ark down the river, the first to Philadelphia, which it reached in six days. The boat broke a hole, which the boatmen stopped up with their clothes. The coal by this time cost fourteen dollars a ton and nobody wanted it. Journeymen were bribed by Cist to use it in blacksmith shops. Bear trap dams were created on the Lehigh river to overcome the difficulty of navigation. The boats were conveyed to the Delaware and Philadelphia until the canal was constructed. Up to 1820 the whole amount of coal sent from Schuylkill and Luzerne Counties did not exceed 2000 tons. In 1844 the amount from Schuylkill alone aggregated 839,934 tons. In 1906 the Reading Company alone has an output of 35,000,000 tons.

In 1812 an application was made to the Legislature for a law for the improvement of the Schuylkill river. The coal on its headwaters was held up as an inducement to the Legislature to make the grant, when the Senator from Schuylkill County arose and said: "There is no coal in Schuylkill County, only a lot of worthless black stones they call coal, that will not burn."

Coal Breaker

The first machine for breaking coal was erected on Wolf Creek, near Minersville, by Mr. Bast. The first coal lands were located in the Schuylkill Valley. These tracts were operated by Bolton Curry, Barlow and Evans, Burd Patterson, Geissenheimer and others. There were many valuable coal lands opened up. William Lawton, Blight, Wallace & Co., Porter, Emerick and Edwin Swift owned some that were rich in coal. Joseph Lyons and Jacob Alter owned a large operation. Their success and the great flow of money that came with the investment of large combined capital induced others to try their hand, but not always with the same happy return. Among these were John Rickert and George Rickert, father and uncle of the late Col. Thomas Rickert, of Pottsville, who opened up a small operation near Tuscarora. Andrew Schwalm, a prosperous boat builder and contractor, at Buffalo, was a heavy investor in the "Rabbit Hole" and the three sunk their capital with no returns but their experience, which was dearly bought. The vein they were operating was faulty. The Hammers, too, of Orwigsburg, lost heavily.

Doctor McFarland, scientist, opened the first vein, in 1814, at York Farm near Pottsville. In 1818 Jacob Reed opened coal land at Minersville. The Wetherill, Gumming and Spohn tracts were considered valuable; they were located at Flowery Field, Wadesville and North America. Certain sections of Pottsville are undermined. The colliery of Pott & Bannan on Guinea Hill had a slope 400 feet deep. When the Garfield School house was built, an old entrance or manway to this mine was discovered on the ground.

Samuel Lewis opened a mine at the foot of Greenwood Hill, which ran under Centre Street near the corner of Mahantongo Street. At one time the old Christopher Loeser building, which was undermined, was supposed to be sinking into these old subterranean passages. These old mine passages ran northwest to the vicinity of Fifth and West Norwegian Streets.

The Lawton-Ellet operation and the Black Mine (York Farm) also ran under the town from Mt. Laurel Cemetery, south, to Sharp mountain. The railway down Market Street from this operation was built in 1836. The Salem mine at Col. Young's landing also honeycombed portions of Greenwood Hill. A small coal operation stood at the corner of Centre Street opposite the Gas House. On the west side of the pavement the entrance to the slope may still be seen. It is boarded up and so small that it looks like the mouth to a spring. The Lehigh Valley overhead bridge runs over the spot.

After the building of the canal, which ran up to what is now corner of East Norwegian and Coal Streets, the coal from Guinea Hill was run down Second Street in small wooden box cars, and conveyed down to that point, across Centre Street. A blacksmith shop stood near the southeast corner of Second and Market Streets. Andrew Robertson, Esq., remembers when a train of these cars jumped the track and ran into the blacksmith shop. The York Farm, operated by George H. Potts, as late as the later 'Fifties sent its coal down Market Street in cars drawn by mules. The first of these cars were very small, and had wooden wheels and no brakes. They were manipulated by men who ran along the side carrying long poles to drag them with. Later larger cars were used, and Thomas Dornan and Jack Temple, both large owners of horses and mules. were the contractors who furnished the motive power (mules) for conveying the coal through town to the railroad. The first coal from the Delaware was handed over the tracks by cars drawn by mules to Mt. Carbon, or to the boat landing.

Note: — Col. Shoemaker was the father of the late James Shoemaker and Mrs. Charles Clemens and grandfather of George S. Clemens and Frank G. Clemens, of Pottsville. The Shoemaker family lived in the Tumbling Run Valley, subsequently removing to Port Carbon. The Mt. Carbon Hotel, built by Jacob Seitzinger and completed in 1826, a small, two-story stone building, afterward torn down and rebuilt by the Mortimer brothers, and known as the Mortimer house, on the corner of West Norwegian and Centre Streets, was kept by Col. Shoemaker. He afterward kept the Pennsylvania Hall, which was erected by him.

THE FORMATION OF COAL

The geologists would have us believe that coal is wholly derived from vegetation. That wood was but changed from one condition to another but this theory must be sanctioned by the laws of chemistry. The geological epochs show that the temperature of our old planet, the earth, has greatly varied from one period to another. That the primary origin of the elements had much to do with the forces that govern the world at the present time. That the solar atmosphere that surrounds the globe was governed by the refrigeration of the heat, then as now confined to the earth's centre.

Chlorific sublimation followed the tendency around the earth's edges to refrigeration and the evaporation of the steam compelled the gases to form new combinations and crystalline arches resulted with the volcanic period. The solidified watery deposits made the ingredients of the soil of vegetation and with the beginning of organic life came the formation of beds of coal and the carboniferous period. Those deeply interested in the subject will find a scientific treatment of the coal period in Leon Lesquereux's "Geological Survey of Pennsylvania; Coal Flora."

The fossil plants found by botanists in the form of coal flora are a source of endless delight to scientists. But scarcely one-fourth of these fossil species of vegetation are found in the coal measures. Most of these imprints are found upon slates. The resinous pitchy matter that goes toward the make up of pure coal is not found in these fossils.

Sixty-two species of fern and mosses form an interesting class of vegetable fossils. The tree formations, of which the pitch pine is the most important are leading contributions to the coal deposit. During the coal period, marshes supported a rich vegetation that was buried in the bogs, which hardened through the fermentation of the gases and thus through a union of the laws of chemistry and vegetation bituminous coal was formed.

In anthracite coal the woody structures of the trees turned into slate and rocks and through the pressure to which it was subjected, the turpentine, oil. bitumen and resinous tar and juices which it exuded formed the strata of pure coal underneath.

To the veins of the bituminous coal basins this article will not refer. The fat bituminous coal of West Virginia, the coal asphalt of New Brunswick, the cannel coal of Kanawha and Breckinridge, the tar coal of North Carolina, the semi-anthracite of Broad Top and Cumberland, all belong to the great coal combination of fuel and heat and steam power producers. But the pure anthracite coal of Schuylkill and portions of other adjacent coal-producing counties overtops them all.

In the anthracite coal basin there are from forty to fifty different veins of coal from one to fifty feet in. thickness. In the Wilkes-Barre region the mammoth vein lies within forty feet of the surface, in the Schuylkill basin it is much lower and was sought for 1200 feet below ground in the famous Pottsville shaft sunk under the direction of Franklin B. Gowen and engineered by

The anthracite coal regions include three distinct coal fields known as the Northern, the Middle and the Southern coal field or basin. They form part of Carbon, Luzerne, Lehigh and Schuylkill Counties and a minor fraction of a small portion of adjacent territory.

The coal scientists agree that the eastern end of the Northern field is being rapidly exhausted. The Middle field, too, will soon be worn out while the western part of the Northern field from Pittston to the western end and the Southern field from Tamaqua to Tremont will jet yield it richest returns and supply coming generations with its inexhaustible resources.

To the scientist, a visit to the coal fields of Schuylkill County is full of interest. The fossil remains of vegetables and animals have often been found and specimens of a most perfect and interesting character, near Mine Hill Gap the remains of a stone forest have been found. It is supposed that at the time of the deluge the mountain was forced apart by the flood and the fossils taken from that vicinity; and geological formations are like the leaves of an instructive treatise on the formation of the periods, and the extent to which the coal traffic has grown from these humble beginnings is a constant source of wonder and congratulation to even those who have been familiar with its inner workings from its inception.

POINTS ON COAL

In 1887 Charles Miesse, of Pottsville, wrote and compiled a work called "Points On Coal." It contains a full description of how coal was formed and gives the statistics of the anthracite coal business up to that period. Some time since, a French savant wrote a treatise on the same subject, and he copied largely from Mr. Miesse's work. The late P. W. Sheafer, Esq., who had a State reputation as a geologist and was heavily interested in coal operations in the county, said of the book that it would be the authority of the future on the coal in Schuylkill County.

Mr. Miesse had met with reverses in business, and his evil genius seemed to pursue him in the publication of his book. Only a few copies were completed when his firm of publishers was burned out, and the manuscript, plates, type and everything were destroyed.

"Points On Coal" contains a valuable and interesting paper on "The Anthracite Coal Fields of Pennsylvania," by P. W. Sheafer and read by him before the meeting of the American Association for the Advancement of Science, held at Saratoga. The author would delight in reproducing this paper, at this point, but lack of space will not permit.

MICHAEL F. MAIZE

Michael F. Maize was born near New Berlin, Union County. He entered the ministry of the Evangelical Church when only sixteen years of age and was known through Pennsylvania and Virginia as the "Boy Preacher." He was stationed at Orwigsburg and Pottsville about 1840, but was obliged to retire from the industry on account of a bronchial affection.

He entered the coal business soon after, with E. Hammer and Jonathan Schultz. In company with Aug. Miller and Fisher, of Philadelphia, under the firm name of Miller, Maize and Co., they operated collieries near New Philadelphia. With the firm name of A. C. Miller & Co., he built the first houses and opened the first colliery at Shenandoah. Some years afterward and with Levi Miller, of Pine Grove, he managed and built the Stanton colliery at Maizeville, which town was named for him. He also built and operated the West Shenandoah City Colliery, under the firm name of Maize and Lewis, the latter being his son-in-law, W. H. Lewis, subsequently Superintendent of Wm. Penn. At this period came the big strike, the great depression in the coal business and the purchase by the Reading Company of the majority of the best collieries in the region.

Mr. Maize pioneered a new enterprise in Virginia and in company with G. W. Palmer and Ex-Governor Bigler, they opened a gypsum mine and mill near Saltville, and also a soft coal mine in Pulaski County, Va. There he contracted, a severe cold from exposure, the result of the burning of his office and the house in which they were (quartered and from which he barely escaped with his life. He returned to his home (a handsome residence on Coal Street), where, after a continued illness for four years, he died at the age of seventy-three. He was one of the foremost and most highly respected citizens of Pottsville.

Mr. Maize was an optimist by nature. His zeal for his parent church, the Evangelical, and for the cause of religion never abated during his long and active business career. His interest in the church of that name was a direct inspiration to others and the result of his work and influence brought many of the foremost of the early business men of Pottsville into its fold.

Mr. Maize was a good collector and his services were in frequent demand to assist struggling churches to gain a foothold. One story told of him was that he was called upon on one occasion to raise $5,000.

The congregation was large but the people would not give. On ascending the pulpit, Mr. Maize at once requested that the doors be locked.

"You want $5000; I intend to raise it," said Mr. Maize, and the usual methods were resorted to with success. The $5000 was raised. When the amount was announced a voice said, "But you have given nothing, Mr. Maize?"

"Well! what ought I to give?" "Five hundred dollars," was the answer.

"Very good," said Mr. Maize; "I will give $500, but I charge $500 for my three hours work, time and traveling expenses. You do not expect a man to raise $5000 in cash for nothing, do you?"

There was a general laugh all around; the account was square. Such calls were frequent and he was a large giver to his home church and the general cause.

QUEER FREAK OF CHILD

Mr. Maize was a man of fine social instincts, very companionable and with a keen sense of all-around humor. On one occasion he was preaching a very effective sermon and was approaching the climax with all the fervor he was capable of, when a small child that had escaped her parents and was running about the church caught her head between the upright sticks that supported the chancel railings beneath the pulpit.

In vain did she try to extricate herself. Her tongue became swollen and hung out of her mouth, her features were strained, her face purple and the child was in danger of convulsions.

Mr. Maize's nerves were already overwrought with his efforts with the sermon, and when the parents came together, and between them, after some effort, released the child, he collapsed entirely and sat down and buried his face in his big red silk handkerchief, not to weep over the short-comings of his flock — but to laugh. He could not control his feelings and always related the above as one of the funniest circumstances he had ever encountered while in the ministry.

WM. H. LEWIS

William H. Lewis, former Superintendent of Wm. Penn Colliery, a retired prominent coal operator, tells several good stories. The Wm. Penn Colliery was until a recent period owned by a firm of individuals, E. and G. Brooke, of Birdsboro, and others. It was one of the last of a chain of collieries in that basin to go into the hands of the Beading Company. Under the skillful management of Mr. Lewis the Wm. Penn enjoyed a wide reputation as being one of the most productive and skilfully managed collieries in the anthracite coal regions. The coal mined was a white-ash of standard quality. From 1000 to 1200 tons were mined in a day and in its palmiest days 1000 men were employed. Mr. Lewis was one of the best accountants and a skillful manager of men. One of the secrets of his ability to keep his colliery working during strikes and on church and other holidays was that he attempted to mix nationalities and employ men of diversified faiths and different religions. If some were idle for cause, the remainder worked.

After some conversation on the coal business and the coal trade now as compared with former years, Mr. Lewis said:

"One thing that has always surprised me is the ease with which you people write up the coal trade or indeed anything relating to the coal business; and then again how gullible the readers of such articles are and how readily they swallow whole all such information."

The writer intimated that when coal trade news was wrongly given, in nine cases out of ten it was the fault of the person interviewed. Either the facts tendered were too meagre or else the party declined to be quoted or furnish any facts, and the seeker after news was bound and compelled to write something, and the vaporings of his own brain often furnished the substitute. Mr. Lewis said, "I will give you two cases in point."

"'We had at Wm. Penn a man of some character named John Zweizig. He was a German and came there from Reading. He had been a Berks County school teacher, where he got into some difficulty with the school board through punishing a pupil. Pie could not work in the mines, but tried laboring and odd jobs and supported his family mainly through a night school. He was an intelligent man. Two of his sons have since become ministers in the Evangelical and Methodist Episcopal churches, the Revs. John and William Zweizig.

"Zweizig came to my house one day and asked me to help him write a coal article. He would be paid for it and he needed the money. I pitied the man, and after some reluctance (I was generally too busy to be interrupted in those days) I consented to give him a few facts on the mining and cutting of coal, superinduced by a general knowledge of the methods employed in our own workings and a little knowledge on the geological formation of the coal strata.

"I had forgotten all about the matter when one day Mr. Zweizig came to me with a money draft in his hand and in great glee.

"He had written the matter up in his great peaked German script hand and sent it to the German Evangelical "Botschafter" or the "Allgemeine Folks Freund," at Cleveland or Cincinnati, I have forgotten which, and signed it "'Prof." Zweizig. The title was misleading; no doubt they thought he was a German scientist and he received $100 for the article.

"The worst of it was, the Scientific American had it translated, and it made a good article, over the same signature, for its next issue."

"Another instance was that of a Welsh miner who lived on our Patch. He was a singer and interested in the competitions at the Eisteddfods. He came to me one day and said that one of these festivals was to be held in Wales. There was a prize for $150 offered for the best treatise written on the formation and mining of coal, its production and market. He asked if I would assist him write one.

"I told him I had no time, but he, being a careful, studious fellow, I gave him access to my library, and pointed out such geological and other works I thought might be of assistance to him, and being a practical miner, he could supplement the rest from his own knowledge.

"Almost a year after he came to me with a letter. He had not gained the great prize, but his essay had received honorable mention, and he was the richer by a minor prize of ten dollars."

MINERSVILLE AS IT WAS

Minersville, next to Pottsville, lays claim to being the oldest coal town in Schuylkill County. In 1793 Thomas Reed, the first settler, erected a saw mill at the mouth of Wolf Creek and its union with the west branch of the Schuylkill River. A log house nearby furnished the home for his family. A tavern erected by Mr. Reed on the Sunbury turnpike, which ran up the Mahantongo valley to Gordon, was called the Half-way House, being midway between Reading and Sunbury. The tavern stood on the site of the K. C. St. Vincent De Paul church. It was here that a relay of horses was made.

The locality was thickly covered with giant trees, and the business, before the mining of coal, was lumbering. A number of saw mills were at work preparing the rough timber which was floated in rafts down the west branch to Schuylkill Haven. The town was laid out in 1830, and incorporated in 1831; with the advent of the English, Welsh and Irish miner came the individual coal operator. Money was plenty, and the social features and entertainments among the leading professional people and the resident coal barons were second to none in the county.

Tradition tells of the evening "parties" (now termed receptions and social functions) given by this class of residents in the olden times; Joseph Taylor (who built the old white mansion with the huge columns in front, still standing on Quality Hill), his wife was a sister of Decatur Nice; Seth Geer, Esq., whose wife was a sister of Hon. James H. Campbell; Dr. U. B. Howell, and others, entertained lavishly. They were in turn attended by the Burd Patterson, James Patterson and Dr. James Carpenter families, and others from Pottsville. The Strattons, Robins, Lawrences, Burns, William Wells, Esq., who married a Miss Cram, of Minersville; the Schollenbergers and Shellenbergers, Joseph C. Gartley, Jacob Fox, R. F. Potter, Col. George Brown, Capt. Roads, C. N. Brumm and many others came later and gave to Minersville a social prestige not exceeded by any town in the county.

MINERSVILLE STORIES SOME FOLKS WILL NEVER DIE

When Sandy came over from Glasgow, he joined a party of the Forty-niners who went around the Horn in a vessel from New York to the Golden Eldorado of the Great West, to dig the precious metal, gold. He returned without any, like many another, and somehow drifted to Minersville. He was a quaint old character, devil-may-care and addicted to his cups.

He sat about the tap-room of the old stone tavern at the top of the hilly street, night after night and day-times, too, when it was stormy, or he did not feel like working, which was often, for, as he said himself, "He was not 'ower fun' o' sach hard wurk." He had a horse and cart, pick and shovel, and was employed on the Borough with the street hands.

How he struck the fancy of old Charlotte, who owned the tavern and other property, bequeathed her by her father, no one knew. They were never seen or heard talking to each other. Sandy was the broadest of Scotchmen and Charlotte was German and could not talk a word of English and she was at least twenty years Sandy's senior.

After they were married, Charlotte saw that tavern-keeping was not Sandy's forte. He was the best customer they had at the bar, insisted on giving away, free, half of their liquid stock and had frequent quarrels with the farmers and others who were the best patrons of the old stone hostelry.

At the close of the year she leased the hotel and the pair retired to a small house at the rear of the tavern, and here the singular couple lived attended by an old maid, who did the housework and waited upon Charlotte, who was fast becoming very infirm and decrepit with rheumatism and a swelling of her limbs. They had a large, well-kept garden, where she, assisted by the maid, would totter about and work, as long as she was able, among the vegetables and flowers, which were her delight. Sandy, disliking the confined quarters of the little house, had a bed removed to a room in the little, old, tumble-down barn, where he slept near his horse, which was apparently the only living thing he cared for.

Matters went on this way for several years. One morning, the "auld wife," as Sandy called her, was in her garden pottering about as usual. Her neat, black dress had been carefully pinned up by the maid to prevent soiling from the early dew, when her red flannel petticoat attracted a young heifer they were raising on the place, and which had managed to break through the old fence from the barnyard, and the poor old lady was thrown to the ground and badly gored before the maid could come to her rescue and drive away the infuriated beast.

Doctor Oscar Robins, a leading physician of the village, was called in. and he gave it as his opinion, that, owing to her advanced age and other infirmities, Charlotte could not survive.

Sandy housed the horse and cart in the barn, and quit work at once. He went out and bought a full suit of black clothes, including a high hat and flaming red neck-tie, all in preparation for the funeral.

The "auld wife," however, contrary to the expectations of the Doctor, held her own during the night. "Her pulse was feeble, her fever high, but she was living," said the Doctor to Sandy, the next morning, at the front door, where he stood dressed in his new clothes and anxiously awaiting him. This was repeated on each occasion of the Doctor's visits, until the third day, when he broke the news as gently as he could, that "Charlotte was better, and would probably be as well as ever in a short time."

"Be the jumpin' Moses," said old Sandy, "sae folks 'ill ne'er dee."

When Sandy was turned seventy, Charlotte finally succumbed, at the age of ninety-three, and the old maid died a few weeks after her mistress, to whom she was greatly attached. Sandy did not live long to enjoy his liberty. Just what had been predicted by the neighbors for almost a quarter of a century occurred. A drunken man, a lighted coal oil lamp overturned, and a barn full of new-mown hay, fodder and straw.

The barn burned to the ground, as well as the handsome cottage of the village editor of the Weekly "Schulylkill Republican," on an adjoining corner. Sandy and the horse were both rescued by the "Mountaineer" boys, who worked nobly to save the surrounding property, but he had inhaled the smoke and died from the effects of it soon after.

THE JOLLY FOUR

They were four of the jolliest and most jovial men in the town of Minersville — the rotund, rosy-cheeked, happy-looking lawyer; the retired coal operator and Captain in one of the early wars; the successful storekeeper, and the Philadelphia and Reading Company land agent; and all were fond of a friendly game of poker. "Jimmy's" was the rendezvous, and as many nights in the week as they could shape it, the time.

Their wives were opposed to this loss of their company and perhaps their money, and used every means within their power to keep their husbands at home, even to organizing a weekly social game and card party in their own and each other's parlors, as an antidote to prevent the gathering at "Jimmy's." But it was of no avail.

Poker playing among the "Jolly Four" was broken up for a while. But one night it was rumored about town that the Captain had been seen going in to "Jimmy's" as usual, but attired only in his red flannel underwear, feet clad in slippers and this outlandish rig overtopped with an overcoat and his usual headgear, a silk hat. His wife had hidden his trousers to prevent his going out. This announcement proved too much for the gang, and they each broke harness and fled likewise for the rear room behind the bar.

A jolly evening ensued and time fairly flew, until at last "Jimmy" himself interposed; "they must retire, he did not keep an all-night house," The land agent was almost speechless with good-cheer, and past arguing the matter, and the trio with the assistance of the hostler placed him in his conveyance and hung the reins over the dashboard; the old mare knew the way home. The others were dismayed to find it was almost three o'clock, and they discussed what they would offer as an excuse to their irate wives.

The wily lawyer had provided himself with a box of confectionery in advance, and said:

"He would just give her that and say, they had had initiation at the lodge and he was rather late."

The storekeeper followed the lead, and thought he would say:

"He had been watching at the bedside of a sick lodgebrother." But the Captain was obstinate. He drew himself up in his red unmentionables, donned his overcoat and hat, assumed a military air and saluting with his walking stick as if it was a sword, and the two his superior officers, said:

"Gentlemen! I have no reason to give. I will just simply say, 'Good morning, Mrs. Coats!' and she will say the rest."

NOT TO BE OUTDONE

"Daddy" Schu had been unfortunate in his matrimonial adventures. The first two wives, excellent women, both, that they were, had succumbed to the inevitable and died after a happy year, each, of married life. They were sisters and had lived together prior to the marriage of Melinda, the eldest, and they continued this domestic relationship. It was not unnatural, the gossips said, that "Daddy" should marry Lucy after the year of mourning had expired. But that Lucy, too, should die before the next year ended was more than either they or "Daddy" had reckoned upon.

"Daddy" belonged to that class of men that find it hard to endure life without domestic companionship, and twice thereafter he sought consolation with partners, whom, it must be confessed, did not size up at all in comparison with the two sisters; and that after the death of each, even he, drew a breath of relief that all was over and he was again a free man.

The "Widow" Drury kept tavern on the mountain side above the town of M___. Hearing of "Daddy's" bereavement, she donned her brightest green shawl, best grey alpaca gown and bonnet trimmed with flaming red ribbons, and sallied forth to attend the funeral. No one wept more copiously than she, when Parson Frame recited the virtues of the deceased wife, who was a friend of hers, and it was hinted that susceptible "Daddy" succumbed then and there.

The widow, however, raked up an imaginary cow case with a neighbor, and began the siege to the citadel of "Daddy's" heart by visiting his office the next day after the funeral, and every day or two thereafter, for he was a Justice of the Peace, to consult him about the cow and the advisability of bringing a suit.

She was tired of tavern keeping, and allowed that a fine brick house, like "Daddy's," on the main street, opposite and aside of the two hotels and the post office, was not to be overlooked. It was just after the first visit, that she confided to a crony, that she "would never let that fine new rag carpet, with the double red and green stripes lengthwise, remain in his office, when she was mistress there."

Poor "Daddy;" it was only five weeks after he buried his fourth wife, when he led the widow Drury to the altar, and was again a benedict.

Lawyer Dreer passing his office one morning, en route for the People's Railway and the Court House in Pottsville, on legal business, saw "Daddy" in the doorway and said jokingly, for Dreer was something of a wag:

"How is this, 'Daddy,' marrying so soon again? Didn't you tell me the day Magdalena died, that you were resigned. and that the Lord had taken her away; and if I remember rightly, you even said, 'Blessed be the name of the Lord.'" "Yes, yes," said "Daddy," "so I did! so I did! But as long as the Lord takes, I'll take too."

Poor old "Daddy!" The widow Drury, his fifth, was a virago, as everybody knew, and "the Lord," they said, "certainly never wanted her," at least not just then, for she lived to a doubly green old age. "Daddy" died after a few months of wedded experience, and was buried in the old cemetery on the hillside^ and many were the expressions of regret and the tears shed over his departure; for he was an innocent old soul, an Israelite indeed, in whom there was no guile, and genuinely liked by everybody.

THE SCHUYLKILL CANAL

The Schuylkill Navigation Company was incorporated by an Act of Assembly approved by Governor Simon Snyder, March 8, 1815. Work was begun and during the spring of 1817 the canal was made navigable to Schuylkill Haven. The freshet of 1818 carried away the dams and locks and the work of reconstruction followed, but the work was not completed until 1821, and then only to Reading. The waterway was 108 miles in length. It was not until 1827 that the canal was really completed, although boats were run to Philadelphia in 1824. They were small affairs, rafts and scows, and were towed the entire distance by men who walked at the end of a long line. Sticks were fastened to the ends of the lines and these were placed against the breasts or shoulders of the men who thus propelled them. After the completion of the towpath, mules were used as a means of propulsion.

There were many drawbacks to a successful navigation during these years. The waterway was shallow at points had filled up with sand and debris. The sides of the canal fell in and many difficulties were encountered with the locks and dams, all of which were repaired and reconstructed. It was not until 1846, however, that the canal was enlarged by increasing its width to enable boats of a larger tonnage to pass through; and steam power was talked of for propulsion. In 1843, the amount of coal sent through the Schuylkill, Delaware and Raritan canals, from this region for New York and Philadelphia, reached 119,972 tons. This was the banner year for the canal.

The rate of toll on the canal was 36 cents per ton, with 5 per cent, allowed for waste. The whole charge by ton of coal by railroad, at the same time, was $1.10 to $1.25. Transportation was slow but it was very cheap. So cheap that the railroads could not enter into competition with it and the railroads killed the canals. They bought up the canals and hundreds of miles of waterway that were constructed at a heavy cost were destroyed. In 1870 the canal was leased for a term of ninety-nine years to the Philadelphia and Reading Railway Company. In 1878 that portion of the canal between Mt. Carbon and Schuylkill Haven was abandoned, and in 1886 it was further abandoned to Port Clinton. The Reading Railway forced the Schuylkill Canal out of business.

The rehabilitation of the mutilated and dead canals of Pennsylvania would be a great enterprise and yield a most profitable return to the people. But there is no possible hope for competitive waterways to the rival railways in the business situation of to-day. The centralization of capital, the immense railway interests at stake, the power of the railway companies, all prevent the practical carrying out of any sentiment favoring the re-opening of the dead canals of Pennsylvania; the Schuylkill Canal among the number.

THE FIRST BOAT-BUILDERS

William Wildermuth built the first boat launched on the Schuylkill Canal. The boat was a small one with a capacity of 80 tons. It was built in 1830 on a lot adjacent to the Dr. Douglas home, on the lower street of Orwigsburg. Wildermuth was born and raised near Landingville and learned carpentering in West Brunswick township. He was encouraged to undertake the enterprise by Dr. Benjamin Becker, then a leading physician of the county.

When the boat, which was the only one ever built in that town, was completed it was placed on a Conestoga wagon and hauled to the Seven Stars, above Schuylkill Haven, where it was launched on the canal. The completion of the enterprise was made the source of a general jollification. The people of Orwigsburg turned out to see the boat hoisted on the wagon. The mules that drew the wagon had red, white and blue paper rosettes on their heads, and the wagon and harness were trimmed with the tri-colors and gaily decorated. Horns were tooted as the boat passed through the town, the people cheered and many accompanied the procession to the Seven Stars, where a large assemblage of people awaited the event and a general good time ensued.

In the same year, 1830, Mr. Wildermuth opened the first boatyard at Landingville, with a saw-mill attached. In 1832, Andrew Schwalm, who came to Orwigsburg from Tulpehocken, Berks County, opened another boatyard adjoining Mr. Wildermuth's. Mr. Schwalm had been engaged in boat building at Buffalo, N. Y., where he was successful.

About this time, Wm. Wildermuth took into partnership with him, his son-in-law, Samuel Leffler, who continued in the business until 1876, when he died. He was succeeded by his sons, William and Samuel Leffler.

Wm. Wildermuth retired and removed, with his daughter, to Scranton, where he died in 1868, at the ripe old age of 84 years. He was interred at Orwigsburg. He was the grandfather of C. W. Wildermuth, of Pottsville, the Pauls, of Port Carbon, and Lefflers, of Landingville, and has other descendants in this county and various parts of the country.

Andrew Schwalm continued in the business from 1832 until 1845, acquiring what was considered a small fortune for those days. He retired, but later engaged in partnership in another yard for a short time with Samuel Leffler. The latter subsequently entered into a co-partnership with his brother, George Leffler, which arrangement only lasted about a year.

Hundreds of boats were turned out by these pioneer boatbuilders, Wildermuth, Schwalm and the Lefflers, between 1830 and 1846; when the canal was widened and deepened, the boats were enlarged to double their capacity and with this enlargement in construction, the veteran builders retired from active business life. Andrew Schwalm died in 1863. He was the grandfather of the children of the Frederick Haeseler, John and Joseph Schwalm, Wm. E. Boyer and W. M. Zerbey families, of Pottsville, Philadelphia and Mahanoy City, and has numerous other descendants in different parts of the country.

The writer remembers him as a large-framed man, sparse in figure, tall, about six feet in height. His complexion dark, sallow, smooth face and with hair black as a raven's wing up to the time of his death. Andrew Schwalm was a man that inspired the confidence and enjoyed the respect of all who knew him. He was grave and dignified, almost to austerity, and belonged to that class of the early settlers who were impressed with the seriousness of life and had little time or taste for its frivolities. It was Bill Nye who said of his New England progenitors that "they had considered it not only a misdemeanor to laugh but almost a crime."

Clad in russet corduroy velvet trousers, double-breasted blue cloth waistcoat with golden buttons, a swallow-tailed blue broadcloth coat to match, high round linen collar and huge black satin stock, his thick black hair cut round, like the prevailing style of the Oliver Cromwell period, the black silk hat or high beaver, the latter of which he wore on every occasion, Andrew Schwalm was a perfect type of the old-time Puritan Pennsylvania gentleman. He, with his wife, Hannah Miller, had twelve children, eight of whom survived to man and womanhood's estate. Two sons and six daughters.

George Rickert, father of the late Col. Thomas Rickert, with Menton Ludwig, opened a boatyard, in 1853, near the Reading station, at Landingville. They closed it after an experience of two years. Solomon Fidler succeeded them and remained in business until 1884. Wm. Deibert and son, Henry, were among the successful boat-builders of a later period.

George Adams, of Adamsdale, worked at Landingville, but started for himself in 1858 at Adamsdale. Mr. Adams carried on the business on a large scale, sometimes employing as high as forty men, and had six boats on the stocks at one time. The men worked, during these busy times, in day and night shifts.

The boats built at Landingville were not alone for the Schuylkill Canal. They were constructed for New York, Baltimore and New Haven. Scows were built for the D. and H. Canal. The boats that first had a carrying capacity of 80 tons, were afterward constructed with a freight limit of 200 tons.

During the big freshet of 1850, the boatyards were all flooded and the material and buildings were carried away. The boat "Jennie Lind," was on the stocks ready to caulk. The boat was carried to the towpath bridge. Here the boat collided with the bridge, tore out part of it and then swung around, where it remained. The boat was drawn away with a windlass and brought to dry dock at Schuylkill Haven, where it was finished. Stocks were carried away and boats taken from the stocks in the freshet.

Other boatyards were conducted successfully at Schuylkill Haven, the Saylors; and at Pottsville, John Crosland and Samuel Grey, at Mt. Carbon, and Joseph Shelly on the site of the pioneer furnaces.

The Schuylkill Canal was first projected for the transportation of lumber and farm products down the river, but all this was changed with the fruitful mining of coal.

Abraham Pott, of Port Carbon, built the first railroad in the United States. It was successfully operated in 1826, 1827, and was about a half mile in length and extended from the junction of Mill Creek to a point where it connected with the canal. This pioneer railway had wooden rails laid upon more regular log rails, and a train of 13 loaded cars, drawn by one horse, ran over it, drawing a load to each wagon of about 1½ tons of coal.

It is claimed that the first horse railway in the country was one built in Massachusetts. It was three miles in length and led from the granite quarries, at Quincy, to Neponsit Run. It was not completed until 1827, giving precedence to that built in Schuylkill County. The railway, from Summit Hill to the Lehigh River, at Mauch Chunk, was nine miles in length, and was also completed after the Pott railway, in 1827.

To Abram Pott is also given the credit for first having used coal cars that opened at the bottom for unloading, thus doing away with the dumping of the car. He was the first settler, too, to use anthracite coal to generate steam for the steam power engine. Up to 1829, water power alone had been used at the saw-mills.

SCHUYLKILL HAVEN

Martin Dreibelbeis, who came here in 1775, is generally accredited with being the first settler of Schuylkill Haven. That there were others, notably among them being the Finschers, who were massacred by the Indians, there is no doubt. Martin Dreibelbeis was born near Moselem, Berks County, in 1751. He settled on the eastern bank of the Schuylkill River, where he established a saw mill and grist mill. The latter was built of stone, and part of it was used as a dwelling house by the family. It was strongly built, and during the early incursions of the red men the mill afforded a place of refuge for the settlers against the murderous and savage Indians.

Martin Dreibelbeis lived on lower Main Street, on the banks of the river, until 1799, when he built a house in what is known as Spring Garden. He died shortly after, at the age of 48, his son Jacob, by the terms of his will, falling heir to his land, which embraced most of Schuylkill Haven proper, and his son Daniel that part north, including the land on which stood the newly-built homestead. The first marriage was that of Mary M. Dreibelbeis and John Reed in 1795, by the Rev. Henry Decker, of Reading. Of this couple more will be found in the early history of Pottsville.

Jacob Dreibelbeis laid out the town in lots in 1811, which were sold at a nominal price. It was not, however, incorporated until 1841. Martin Dreibelbeis donated a piece of ground for religious, educational and burial purposes. This log schoolhouse was built upon the ground now included in part in the cemetery of the New Jerusalem, or White Church, on the turnpike road.

Jacob Dreibelbeis retained the mills of his father after the latter had retired to the hotel, afterward known as the "Mackey House," in Spring Garden. Daniel Dreibelbeis built a saw mill and grist mill on the rear of the property now occupied by the First National Bank. These mills were removed by the Schuylkill Navigation Company about 1828. The mills were propelled solely by water power.

From the year 1817, when the work of construction began on the Schuylkill Canal, the growth of Schuylkill Haven was gradual and substantial. From 1827 to 1846, from the time the tow-path was completed, up to when the canal was enlarged, the "Haven" was anything but one of "Rest." After 1886, when that portion of the canal between Schuylkill Haven and Port Clinton was abandoned, and boating on the raging canal was relegated to innocuous desuetude, the enterprising residents of that Borough became painfully aware that something must be done if they would maintain their place in the ranks of towns of enterprise in the county and State. They not only met, they resolved and they acted on this resolution, and the result is that the town is enjoying a period of industrial activity, from the number of small manufacturing interests established and maintained, second to none in the county.

The large Reading Company coal schutes and railway interests contribute their part, also, toward employing a large number of men, all of which contributes toward the prosperity enjoyed by the people of the Haven.

Note: — Benjamin Pott, son of John and Maria Lesher Pott, was married to Christiana, daughter of Martin Dreibelbeis and his wife, Catharine Markel. Their children were: Hannah, Mrs. C. F. Whitney; Sarah, Mrs. Lewis Vastine; John L.; Christina, Mrs. D. K. Snyder; Amelia, Mrs. George Schall, and Miss Emma Pott.

PLAYED BETTER THAN OLE BULL

Henry Hesser was not only a good fiddler, but really an artist on the violin. He was in great demand at all of the social occasions in the village of Schuylkill Haven, and the country people for miles around considered him a musical prodigy of great ability and perspicacity; and more than that, he was noted as a master of the violin by everyone. He "understood the notes," they said, but had in addition a "Blind Tom" facility for taking a theme and interweaving and surrounding it with fancies and interpolations that were very pleasing. He brought out, too, on that king of instruments, with great skill and ease, his own dreams and ambitions and there is no doubt but that Mr. Hesser was more than ordinarily musically gifted.

Ole Bull, during his first concert tour, visited Philadelphia and, in the course of time, an early day traveling salesman came to the Haven, and to while away the evening, sat in the barroom of the Washington Hotel, and told stories of the wonders of the metropolis; and among them, related how Ole Bull had captured musical Philadelphia with his wonderful prowess on the violin.

The room was full, the interest great, and all listened in silence, but with a manifest air of disapproval. This disapprobation grew stronger and stronger as the story proceeded, until the suppression of opinion became almost unbearable, and the crowd arose as one man. The rigid tension was relieved by one, Ike Bensinger by name, their spokesman, who piped up in his thin, falsetto voice: "Did you ever? Did you ever hear "Hen" Hesser play?" And the drinks, of course, were on the traveling man.

INDIAN STORIES

One of the Indian legends related by an aged resident of the Panther Valley, was that of an Indian ghost, who wandered around the crags and bluffs through which the Swatara creek runs, near Swatara. His father told him that the Indians who lived there had been out on a marauding trip, and returned with a large amount of loot and some gold. One of the braves concealed the gold under a rock near the creek. He was killed by his companions for the treachery, and ever after his wraith was seen wandering in and out among the rocks to find his ill-gotten treasure. The narrator remembered frequently tracing his steps in and out on the Indian causeway, to find that treasure. His genii was the red man's ghost, whom he hoped to encounter some time unexpectedly, and wrest from him his secret of wealth, that would prove as fabulous as that of the hidden recesses in Monte Christo's Halls, but he never found him nor the treasure.

Gold was said to have been found upon the "Gobbleberg," and the Indian superstition claimed that when it thundered and lightened the rocks were sometimes cleft in twain and the hidden recesses were discovered to be gorged with nuggets of gold. Whoever could claim them before they closed was in favor with the spirits of the air, and the genii of the mountain. Many hunted for this gold, but it was like hunting for the pot of that precious metal that hangs at the horns of the prismatic rainbow.

Many of the flights, by the thoroughly frightened settlers, to the block houses and Indian forts were superinduced by false alarms. "The Indians are coming" ("Die India Kummah"), was sufficient to startle the sparse communities into almost immediate flight. On one occasion an old woman, whose son could carry her no farther, was left in the woods (at her own request) to die. She could not live much longer anyway, she said, while the rest of the family hastened on to a place of safety. When the Indians came up to her place of refuge they proved to be a squad of Captain O'Leary's Colonial Guards, who were protecting the woodsmen out to sight such timber as was needed to cut for the use of the navy yard at Philadelphia, and they carried the old lady to a place of safety between them.

Another legend is told of an Indian maiden, Wanomanie, who sprang from the highest point of the rocky crags on the pinnacle of Sharp mountain (south of Henry Clay's Monument) into the declivity below and was killed. All because her father Sagawatch would not allow her to marry the dusky lover of her choice. It was said that on moonlight nights, in harvest time, she could be seen on a misty evening, through the clouds, taking the spring into the abyss below, her lover a close second, taking the leap after her, and Sagawatch leaning over the crest of the mountain to watch the lovers going to their certain death. Whether these ghostly sights were only apparent to those who had been imbibing too freely of spirits of another brand, or whether they were the innocent victims of hallucinations of the brain, will be left to the vivid imagination of the reader to conjecture.

EARLY HISTORY OF PINEGROVE

There were settlers about this vicinity as early as 1755. but it was not until about 1795, that a small settlement was formed about Jacob's Church, next to Zion's or the Red Church, near Orwigsburg, the oldest church in the county, about two miles below the present town of Pinegrove, then a part of Berks County. It was not until about 1830, that the village had any reputation as a town, when it contained thirty-one houses. The farmers in the three rich valleys centering here brought their grist to Fegley's mill, on the Swatara creek. The blacksmith's shop, three hotels, and three stores with the mill, formed the business nucleus, from which the town subsequently sprang.

The original name of the town was Barrstown. This was changed to Pinegrove in 1829. The name proper is Pine Grove, with the accent on the last half of the word instead of making a compound word and giving it a nasal inflection on the first part. The first church in the town was built in 1817.

The Union Canal, from Lebanon to Pine Grove was completed in 1832. The coal was first hauled down from the mines in wagons. In 1832, the canal company built a railroad, from the junction to the canal, a little over three miles. The first coal operators were Caleb Wheeler, Jas. C. Oliver (who lived in Pottsville), and John Stees (father of Fred. Stees, of Philadelphia, and for so many years National President of the P. O S. A.), who operated the mammoth vein, at the head of Lorberry creek. The coal was brought from the mines in cars containing from 2½ to 2¾ tons. They ran down a plane from Lorberry, and it took one horse or a mule to haul an empty car back again from the junction to the mine.

In 1840, the Swatara Railway was built, from the Junction to Tremont and Donaldson. It was laid with "T" rails instead of the wooden article used heretofore. The town of Tremont was laid out the same year by Messrs. Follweiler, Miller and Hippie. (A son of the latter, Dr. Charles Hippie, married Delia, a daughter of Judge Seitzinger, of Pottsville, and subsequently removed to the West.)

Judge Donaldson, who lived at the corner of Market and Sixth streets, Pottsville, a handsome old mansion and private residence now occupied by T. W. Marquart, grocer, laid out Donaldson. The tonnage of the Donaldson coal operation was shipped over the Union Canal.

In 1852, the Schuylkill and Susquehanna Railroad Company extended its railroad from Rausch Gap to Auburn, connecting there with the Reading Railroad, and thus giving Pinegrove an additional outlet for the shipment of coal.

The Millers, Levi Miller, Sr., and son, Daniel Miller, forming the companies Miller and Miller, in which was also interested Levi Miller, Jr., and the firm Miller, Graeff and Co., were important factors in the coal trade of the West End. The old Lincoln colliery proved a perfect bonanza to its owners. The newer operation, of the same name, was also a profitable investment. The firm also mined, for a time, an operation at the Flour Barrel, under the name of Miller, Maize & Co. The Lincoln Colliery was among the collieries purchased by the P. & R. Company.

On the night of June 2, 1862, a heavy freshet broke the dam at Berger's mill. The water brought ruin and destruction with it. Mills, dams, bridges, canal banks, everything, went down with the flood. The canal was never rebuilt, the ruin was too disastrous.

Pinegrove has suffered heavily under the discriminations against it in the way of railway connections, the abandonment of the canal and the working out of some of the mines. It has progressive citizens who have made, and are still making herculean efforts to retrieve the business fortunes of the town and with partial success. A large steam tannery, a brickyard and several small industrial establishments, are but a modicum of these ventures hazarded at various times. Pinegrove enjoys the distinction of having the largest amount of invested capital of any town in the county in proportion to its population.

A PASTOR'S ADVICE

Everyone for miles around knew "Parrah" Henry, the pastor of the old stone Lutheran Church, in the beautiful town of Pinegrove. He was there for almost a half-century, and baptized, confirmed and buried more people than the half-dozen other clergymen of that faith in the county, or of those that preceded him.

Of the latter there was one who shall be nameless. "Parrah ___" came to Pinegrove on a Saturday from a town farther down the line, making a circuit of perhaps forty miles on horseback to fill his charges. The "Parrah" was a genial and jolly pastor and enjoyed letting himself down to the plane of the people, and even sometimes below that level. He liked a game of cards and a social glass and frequently forgot himself in the indulgences of the flowing bowl, for which act he would afterwards despise himself. But the times were different in those days, and such license on his part was overlooked by the members of his congregation if he was able to appear at church the following morning and preach one of the strong sermons that was sure to follow such an indulgence.

He stopped at the only hotel in the town, and the usual crowd was there on Saturday night, and on one occasion, he was, as often before, somewhat unsteady when he was helped to bed. He arose betimes for church, and as was his wont, his self-abasement and castigation of himself was more than usually rigorous. He preached on the sin of self-indulgence, gross eating, and grosser drinking, and was particularly severe on card playing. The congregation was large and became somewhat overwrought as he proceeded to admonish them on the error of their sinful ways.

Finally he leaned over the high pulpit, and with tears streaming down his face and with outstretched hands, he said: "My dear children, for I love you all like a beloved Father loves his children. Do not do as I do, but do as I say," and then he sank back and sat down in the big pulpit chair and shed tears until every eye in the congregation was moistened.

EARLY EDUCATIONAL FACILITIES

From an old deed is gleaned the fact that John and Sarah Ann Bannan, April 9, 1829, for the consideration of $20, "good and lawful money," conveyed to the Trustees of the Orwigsburg Academy, a lot of ground on Mifflin street. The former owner was Daniel Graeff. The witnesses, Frederick Hesser and G. Rausch. The trustees of the Academy: John Schall, George Hillegas, Edward Canner, John P. Woolison, George Grim, Joseph Morgan, Daniel Medlar and Jacob Hammer. A brick building was erected on the ground by the County. The State appropriated $2,000 for school purposes, and the Orwigsburg Academy was established.

The Academy, a school for boys, had a succession of excellent teachers. Joseph Ottinger, Leyman, Comly, Carter, of Dickinson College, and Penfield, who afterward taught in the Pottsville public schools. James Inness, a well-known citizen of Pottsville, and teacher subsequently in the Pottsville Academy, was a popular teacher. Of the coterie Paul Beck Carter enjoyed an excellent reputation for erudition and fine scholastic attainments. He prepared Thomas Bannan, Andrew J. Douglas, Collins P. Whitfield, John T. Shoener (afterward District Attorney under Howell Fisher) and Henry Hammer for Yale College. The trio left school for Yale, where they subsequently graduated with honors, but Hammer decided upon a business career and did not pursue his studies any further.

They lost sight of their former teacher, but during the Civil War, Henry Hammer, of the 116th Regt. Penna. Vols, while in Philadelphia, in a clerical capacity for the U. S. service, to which he had been detailed, was approached in the office by a dirty, unkempt, ragged and forlorn looking old tramp, who asked for assistance. Daniel Focht, a prominent Philadelphia merchant, formerly of Ringgold, another of the Orwigsburg Academy pupils, was present, and he recognized in the mendicant, Paul Beck Carter, former Yale graduate, fluent scholar, and polished gentleman, their early teacher. The man took what they gave him, but refused further assistance. "He could not reform," he said, and disappeared.

With the establishment of the public school system, the Academy was discontinued. After the removal of the Court House and prison to Pottsville, the old stone jail was refitted on one side for public school purposes, and the bell on the brick Academy, on the opposite side of the street, was used to call the children to school. The ringing of the bell was manipulated by a wire rope that ran across the street, and was rung by the teacher in the old jail building.

After the removal of the County seat from Orwigsburg to Pottsville — which event was celebrated with a great glorification in Pottsville — the Court House was used as a boarding and day school. The Arcadian Institute was opened in it, by one Burnside, and his assistants, in 1852. It was a successful venture for a time. Elias Schneider assumed charge of the school, but closed it to teach in the Pottsville Academy. Prof. Joseph Jackson, afterward principal of the Pottsville High School, was an assistant. Mr. Schneider returned after several years and re-opened the school, but was not successful. The building was subsequently deeded to the town by the County. A shoe factory, in which the leading citizens were interested, was incorporated and it was turned over to the company for shoe manufacturing purposes, for which it is still used.

THE EARLY TEACHERS

Some of the early teachers were men of ability and learning. Others were like Ichabod Crane as described in the "Legend of Sleepy Hollow." The schoolmaster was abroad. "With the early German settlers it was a common custom to employ the same man as preacher and schoolmaster. These teachers were frequently not ordained ministers, but filled the office through preference. In 1751, the churches of Holland started a scheme to establish a course of instruction for the children of the Germans in Pennsylvania. Two thousand gilders per annum for five years, dating from 1751, were collected and applied to this purpose. Certain British noblemen were moved to assist in the cause and the king granted £1,000 toward the project. Trustees were appointed and a visitor and supervisor was found in Rev. Schlater, who was directed to take the establishment of the schools in charge These schools were established at Reading, York, Lancaster and Easton.

The first steps taken to provide for the education of the poor children under the Common School System of Pennsylvania were the laws enacted in 1809 and 1824. Schuylkill County was slow to take advantage of them. It was about 1835 when the first public school was opened in Pottsville, although an ungraded school was held in the log school house on the site of the Centre street Grammar School building. Prior to that time, the former school for boys was held in the Quaker Meeting House. A stone school building was subsequently erected adjoining the log house on Centre street, and another on West Norwegian street, on the site of the Garfield building. With the passage of the law in 1854, creating the office of County Superintendent, came the regular system of grading the schools, the raising of the curriculum and a constant and steady improvement in the facilities, resulting in a public school system which has no superior, if indeed its equal, in any part of the Commonwealth.

Private schools were common. Among the teachers were James P. Hough, Rev. A. Pryor, an Episcopal clergyman and father of Mrs. C. M. Atkins, who conducted a school in the residence, southwest corner of Fifth and Market streets. Mrs. McDonald and the Misses McCamant conducted girls' schools. The Lutheran Church had its school. Daniel Klock, an excellent teacher, met with a misfortune to his limb and lived for a time at Auburn and subsequently with his wife, was compelled to become can inmate of the County Home. Some of the first business men of the town were pupils under him, James Hough kept school in a room built on his lot, corner of Centre and Sanderson streets. He afterward conducted a night school in the first Evangelical Church. Hough was the strictest of disciplinarians, and many were the stories told of his cruelty. He turned out good scholars, nevertheless.

Prof. Getler or Gertler held school in the Panther Valley about 1828. He was of the old type of teacher and often cruel in the extreme. He walked about constantly and thrashed the boys with a bunch of sticks he carried. One of his methods of punishment was to thumb the boys behind the ears. Spelling was his hobby. An early pupil was inclined to learn all he could, and one morning "trapped" to the head of the class. That was not the end. At noon a class bully, who had been head, waylaid him and beat him severely. In the afternoon, he felt sore at the drubbing he had received and was more or less inattentive, when Gertler gave him another thrashing on his already raw legs.

Gertler was subsequently a night-school teacher in one of the Pottsville churches. His scholars were good spellers and adepts with the pen.

One of the greatest wonders in the teaching line was Samuel Gesley, who taught at Orwigsburg and other points in the county. He was an armless man and had deformed feet. His specialty was writing. He turned out some of the most beautiful specimens of penmanship and fancy scrolls. He manipulated the pen with his toes and could punish a boy with the ruler for an irregular scratch or blot as well as if he had two or even four hands. He taught writing in Pottsville. subsequently, and finally, in his old age, traveled with a circus, visiting his home town with Barnum's on its first visit in 1870. He had learned additional feats during the interim and fired off a pistol with his crippled toes. He was a man with a most remarkable ambition for learning and had a fine head. It was said of him, "that in spite of being so severely handicapped by nature, he mastered everything he undertook." To see him turn the leaves of a book with his teeth and a twist of his head was a study in itself.

PETER F. MUDEY

Peter F. Mudey was an old-time public school teacher. A man of fine physique, strict principles and greatly beloved. He was an old-time Democrat but not a strict partisan. It was during the year of the revulsion after the inauguration of Martin Van Buren as president of the United States, when there was so much pecuniary distress. The Whigs believed that the government was bound to attempt something to relieve the situation, and the President and his party maintained that the faults of the people had brought about the crisis and that individual effort alone would restore prosperity. In the meantime. President Van Buren projected a plan for the keeping of the government finances, called the "Sub-treasury" scheme, which was subsequently very unpopular with the people and resulted in the overthrow of the Democratic party at the next presidential election. The question at issue was:

"Shall the public money be kept in a United States Bank or remain in an independent treasury?"

Mr. Mudey was approached for his opinion on the subject, when he related the following: "A fine horse that had followed the chase, borne his master to the wars and held an honored place in the stud of high pedigree in the nobleman's stables, had the misfortune to break his leg, and instead of being shot, as was ordered, to end his misery, was traded off to satisfy the cupidity of a dishonest groom. He fell into bad hands, where he was obliged to follow the plow. Menial labor broke the poor creature's spirit and at last it lay down by the road-side to die."

"A benevolent man, passing that way, took the branch of a tree and attempted to brush off the loathesome, big bottle flies that had settled in and about the wounded leg, gloating in its putrefaction.

"When the old war horse raised his head and spoke, beseeching the man to let the flies alone.

"'These pests, he said, have had their fill. If you drive them away, a new horde will take their place and I will suffer the more.' So it will be with a change of administration," said Mr. Mudey.

General Harrison, a Whig, was, however, elected and died a month later, and Vice-president Tyler false to the trust reposed in him by the Whigs, refused to hold himself amenable to the party that elected him and vetoed two of the bills passed by Congress to re-establish a national bank, and the first set of flies remained in possession of the public moneys.

QUAKER MEETING HOUSE

In 1831, a piece of ground near the corner of Ninth and Howard Avenne was donated to the Society of Friends by Samuel Griscom and Thomas Lightfoot for the building thereon of a meeting house. It was a stone building, with a basement of a dark slate color. Meetings were held there during the 'Thirties, when they were discontinued on account of removal of Friends. The first public school for boys was held in this building. In 1846, Elias Schneider opened, in it, a private school for boys. The quarters were too small and a company was formed and the Academy built adjoining the meeting house. It was completed in 1846. The first teachers were: Prof. Porter, principal; Duncan, assistant; Elias Schneider, Kirkwood, Angel, Chas. Pitman, Christopher Little, Prof. Angela, James Inness, Schmitt, Albion Spinney, a noted astronomer, and Amos Lewis. Among the boys who went to the Academy were: John T. Carpenter, Peal, James Patterson, Francis Bannan, James Campbell, member of Congress and minister to Norway; Robert Palmer, minister to South America; Lin Bartholomew; A. H. Halberstadt, D. W. Bland, J. T. Boyle, O. C. Bosbyshell, L. C. Thompson and others.

The building was subsequently used for hospital purposes during the Civil War, to house the sick soldiers from the encampment of U. S. forces, on Lawton's Hill and West Mahantongo Street. Henry Russel, Esq., remodeled it into a handsome residence and at this writing it is still in possession of the family.

HENRY C. RUSSEL

It was during the lifetime of the former. Mr. Russel was sitting on the broad portico of his home, enjoying the cool breezes from the adjacent mountain top as they wafted through the magnificent big oaks that surround the old mansion, when he was accosted by a middle-aged man whom he did not recollect ever having seen before.

"How do you do, sir," said the stranger. Mr. Russel replied, not without some asperity, "How do you do, what can I do for you, sir?"

"Not much, but will you tell me, sir, where Mrs. McConnicle's candy shop is? It used to stand about here; I am very thirsty and she made such good mead. I would like to get a glass and a gingerbread loaf."

"Oh, John ___, you rascal," said Mr. Russel, springing up and taking the man by the hand, "how dare you try such a gag on me as that?

"Mrs. McConnicle is dead these forty years, and that," pointing to the German Sisters' Home, "is her monument."

Two of the old Academy boys had met again after a long interim of years.

It was about the same period, or early in the 'Forties, when Miss Marcia Allen established her school for young ladies. She was a woman of line intelligence and the strictest probity of character. After more than a quarter of a century's faithful service, her health failed and she left for California, where she resided at Los Angeles until her death.

A pleasant feature was a re-union of her scholars at the Henry Russel residence on the occasion of a visit to Pottsville. Invitations were sent out broadcast and a number responded. It was a unique scene, not unmixed with pathos, when Miss Allen called the roll, after ringing the bell, and the girls, now matrons or spinsters of middle age, responded to their names; and then as was her wont, she arose and offered prayer, not omitting to remember the absent ones, many of whom had gone to the "Great Beyond."

Among other teachers of private schools were: Miss Kate Ermentrout, Miss Annetta Strauch, Miss Emily McCool, Mrs. Laurey, and Miss Lewis.

LETTER FROM MISS ALLEN

The following is a copy of a letter presented to the Schuylkill Historical Society by Mrs. Sarah Bartholemew, who received it from Mrs. Patterson. It was written by Miss Marcia Maria Allen to B. F. Patterson, deceased, late Borough Superintendent of the Public Schools of Pottsville. It is self-explanatory.

"Washington D. C, February 10, 1877.

"Mr. Patterson,

"Dear Sir: — I thank you that you have so kindly proposed to mention ray school in your report. I am really sorry that I have not a better "work of which to speak. What I have written, you can arrange, shorten or reject at your pleasure. If you wish something different, please let me know, and I will follow your suggestion.

"Mr. John Shippen" (President of the Miners' National Bank) "can tell you of this lady, of whom I make mention. I think she was his brother's widow. James A. Inness was her pupil. Mrs. Inness is at Port Clinton or at the Port Carbon Hotel. She can tell you about the schools of that time and Mrs. Hammekin" (mother of Mrs. Dr. F. W. Boyer) "knows of the others.

"Mrs. Hammekin taught a short time in the public schools, in Pottsville, and afterward, for a little time with me." (She also subsequently conducted a private school for a short time.) "Miss Clement, another New England lady, succeeded her in the public schools; Miss Young taught a family in St. Clair." (Afterward conducting a private school in the building, now the residence of F. P. Mortimer, Second Street, near corner of West Norwegian.) "Mrs. Charles Hill, Mrs. Hammekin's sister, first taught in Schuylkill Haven." (Afterward conducting the Hill School on Howard Avenue, now successfully run by Mrs. S. A. Thurlow, wife of the Borough Superintendent of Public Schools.) "All of these taught in Pottsville and we were graduates of the same school" (in New England). "I mention this because it seems to me unusual.

"The public schools were in no way remarkable when I came to Pottsville. I was the first to hear a class in arithmetic, particularly mental arithmetic. A young lady said to me, 'Miss Allen, what do you mean by a recitation in arithmetic?'

"Mr. Charles Pitman had a boys' school at the time and was assisted by Mr. Inness.

"I am sorry I cannot write more to my own satisfaction, in regard to schools; but as I have said before, if you will ask any questions or make any suggestions, I will try to do better.

Very respectfully,
M. M. ALLEN."

"Miss M. M. Allen, a New Englander, and a graduate there, commenced a Select School in Pottsville, in 1843, keeping it up twenty-eight years, with considerable success. Mrs. Shippen, a widow, and her daughter had a private school before that time and conducted it well, if we may judge from the testimony of her pupils. Very many of the women of the present time in the region, were instructed by Miss Allen, in the lower and higher English branches, in Latin and French. The effort was to make them thinkers — discarding the merely ephemeral and choosing that which has true worth."

Note: — B. F. Patterson came to Pottsville about 1865. He served first as the Principal of the High School, and after the retirement of Josiah P. Sherman, he was elected Borough Superintendent of the Public Schools, which position he filled up to his death, July, 1906. Miss Allen speaks thus of her own work in response to the request by Mr. Patterson.

Part Four - History of Pottsville

WHO THE FIRST SETTLERS WERE

When the Neiman family built their little log cabin, in ___ the locality that now forms part of Pottsville, there were none to dispute their claim to the possession of the land. The vast coal wealth of the county was as yet undiscovered and lying inert and uncovered within the bowels of the earth. The country was a howling wilderness, wild beasts roamed through the forests, and savages, merciless and cruel, wore the foes they had to contend with. The Neimans lived on a knoll where the Pottsville Hospital now stands. The family consisted of a husband and wife, and two children. They were massacred by the Indians, September, 1780.

Timber was cut in this locality as early as 1778, and rafts of logs were sent down the Schuylkill river to its month. Captain Leary of the Continental Navy was stationed below where the black railroad bridge, at Mt. Carbon, stands. His company of marines guarding the wood-choppers who were engaged in felling the huge oak trees. This timber was rafted to the navy yard at Philadelphia, where it was used for the masts of vessels.

Balser Gehr, of Reading, owned a saw mill at the mouth of Norwegian creek and the Schuylkill river. This mill was afterwards known as Bosslers, when it was rebuilt, Neiman had charge of the Gehr mill. Doubtless there were other lumbermen who worked hereabouts, but he was the only one who lived here. Conrad Minnich kept a hotel in 1790 where the Seven Stars hotel stands. It was only a humble log cabin for the housing and entertainment of the few hardy woodsmen who journeyed to and fro in their search for work or land to settle upon.

Wm. F. Stimmel, of Kutztown, found on the Balser Gehr farm two iron door plates, cast in 1742, and sent them to Luther R. Kelker, of Harrisburg, September, 1906.

There is no further record of early settlers on the site of Pottsville, until 1796. On April 7, 1795, William Zoll, innkeeper of Reading, purchased a lot in Orwigsburg. It was located at the northwest entrance, and part of the ground was subsequently utilized for a tannery by his descendants.

After tilling the ground for about a year, William Zoll removed in 1796, to what is now Pottsville, and established a small furnace or forge in the orchard on the site of the Greenwood furnace. The country was wild, Indians roamed about and lived in the mountain fastnesses, and malaria lurked in the marshy soil. He built a log cabin near the forge, which was so arranged that the family could retire to the forge, which he fortified, in case of an attack from the Indians. Here was born his son Joseph Zoll. His wife soon after contracted a low fever, from the effects of which she died.

Alone with a small child the first settler became discouraged. During his working hours in the forge he kept the baby in a small wooden box suspended from a beam in the roof, and out of harm's way. In 1799, when the child was two years old, Zoll sold out the forge and cabin to Lewis Reese and Isaac Thomas, who enlarged and rebuilt the forge. Reese and Thomas settled on the Schneid Berg in 1796-99, or the north side of Sharp mountain. They in turn disposed of the property in 1806 to John Pott, who enlarged the plant and created the "Greenwood furnace," which stood on the corner of Coal and Mauch Chunk Streets, and from which "Greenwood Hill," above the site of the furnaces, was named.

View of Pottsville

Wm. Zoll, with his infant son Joseph, removed to his old home near Orwigsburg, where the latter for many years ran a tannery. The third of that name, Joseph Zoll number two, died several years ago, unmarried, thus practically wiping out the direct line of descent. Wm. Zoll was heard frequently to remark that he was the first settler here and that the town should have been called Zollville instead of "Pottsville." William Zoll was a soldier in the War of 1812, and a member of a Masonic lodge at Philadelphia, Joseph left several adult children when he died at the ripe age of eighty. The Orwigsburg tannery was a large and successful business venture for those days.

When Isaac Thomas, Lewis Reese and Lewis Morris, enlarged the Zoll forge and built a furnace, they sent workmen here to dig a race and build a dam. Among them was John Reed, who brought his wife with him, and who built a small log house two stories high for their home. This house stood about sixty feet east of the hospital, on what is now Manch Chunk Street, and here Jeremiah Reed, the first white child born in Pottsville, saw the light of day, December 10th, 1800. John Reed and wife were born about five miles south of this place, toward Orwigsburg.

Reese and Thomas built a small charcoal furnace on the island where afterward were located the Pioneer furnaces of the Atkins brothers. In 1804, John Pott, Sr., bought from Lewis Reese, Isaac Thomas and Sarah Morris, the ground on which the settlement had been made, including the Zoll, Mayfield, Moorfield and Physic tracts of land.

When this purchase was made the only houses hereabouts were: the John Reed dwelling, before referred to; the Cook house, corner of Coal and Washington Streets, where afterward stood the John L. Pott's iron works; the Alspach house, on the site of the Charles Baber residence; the Swoyer house, near the Philadelphia and Reading freight depot, near which also stood the Nathan Taylor house. A family named Schott lived on Lawton's Hill, west of the F. W. Hughes' residence.

After the building of the larger furnace in 1806, by John Pott, the construction of a straggling row of houses was at once begun. They extended through the orchard and eventually over the marsh and creek to the higher ground now Centre Street. This was practically the opening and foundation of the town, men came to work in the furnace and the homes erected for their families were the nucleus and others soon followed.

April 27, 1808, Lewis Reese sold to John Pott 227 acres of land which covers the old site of the town of Pottsville. The town was laid out in 1816, but it was not until 1828 that it was regularly incorporated. John Pott died. His son John Pott built a distillery in 1819. He was the proprietor of a small two story hotel, known as the White Horse tavern, which was a stopping place for the stages on the Sunbury road. In 1824 there were five scattered dwellings in the vicinity of the Pott tavern between what is now Mahantongo and Norwegian on Centre Street. Others had built along the early roads and when the surveys were made, as in the city of Boston, the old cow paths and turnpike, with their irregular twistings and turnings were not disturbed, but only made the pivotal centres for other and more regular thoroughfares.

John Pott, Sr., took possession of the Alspach house. He weather-boarded it and had it painted red and it became the Pott family home. In this house was born Hannah Pott, grand daughter of John Pott, Sr., and daughter of Benjamin Pott. She was the first girl baby born in Pottsville and afterward became the wife of Lawrence F. Whitney.

In 1810, the year in which John Pott removed to the settlement, he built the stone grist mill, known as the Orchard mill and afterward operated by Stein & Trough. In 1815 he built a stone mansion for the occupancy of his family. This house stood on the site of the brick house owned by Thomas Schollenberger and now occupied by his sister, Mrs. Sarah Bartholemew. He also built a barn opposite whore the Puttsville Hospital now stands.

In the early days the old Sunbury road, from Reading to Sunbury, wound around the hill near the point where the Henry Clay monument now stands. From there it ran to York farm. Bulls Head, thence to Minersville. Centre Street was then a dense hemlock swamp thickly covered with bushy undergrowth, the turnpike road was not entirely completed until 1812 and even then there was much complaint about the lack of stones and the plentitude of mud on Centre Street. It was not until 1816 or 1817, that Centre Street from Mahantongo to west Race Street was covered with stones.

The State road was layed out in 1770. It entered Pottsville near Furnace Island, it ran on the right hand side of the creek and marsh, about Coal Street, toward Fishbach, joining the main road again at Bull's Head. There is a difference of opinion as to which was the main branch, this or the road that ran around the hill opposite.

The survey in 1816 to lay out the town in lots began at Church Alley, or Howard Street, and extended to west Race Street. The plot included all the ground from Second on the west to Railroad Street on the east; from Union Street on the south to west Race; Norwegian Street extended west to Fifth Street and east to Railroad Street.

Site of Centre Street Twenty-Five Dollars

Pottsville is beautifully situated above the gorge through which the Schuylkill river breaks through the Sharp mountain. At no point in the town can the dimensions of the town plot be seen. Closely hemmed in by spurs of mountains and wooded hills, to obtain a perfect view of the town and the beauty of its surroundings it is necessary to climb to a point on the steepest declivity and here a scene of unequalled grandeur may be enjoyed. The town as it now exists, extends into live distinct valleys, gravitating at the centre with the old original town plot as layed out in 1816.

When the town was first formed it was made up of small settlements: Morrisville, now Morris Addition; Greenwood, now Greenwood Addition, or more recently the Orchard; and Mt. Carbon. Salem included Young's Landing, Bath and Allenville, with Salem and Buckleysville, arc now obsolete as names. When Pottsville was incorporated in 1828, there was a strong ctfort made to absorb it into Mt. Carbon, then a thriving shipping mart, and name it Mt. Carbon. Hesse-Stettle, a suburb of later growth, now known as Yorkville, was settled in the 'forties although there were a few scattered log houses on the main road toward Sunbury as early as 1812. They were thrifty German settlers from Hesse-Darmstadt who gave the settlement its name Hesse-Stettle.

SITE OF CENTRE STREET TWENTY-FIVE DOLLARS

The descendants of Charles Siegfried, the Hookeys, Eilers and Russels, tell the following story: Charles Siegfried, blacksmith, from near Port Clinton came to Pottsville in 1807, after the opening of the Greenwood furnace, where he worked for several years. On one occasion money was scarce, John Pott owed Siegfried $25, as it was not forthcoming, he offered his employee several acres of ground to cancel the debt. The ground included all of the tract from a point near the corner of Mauch Chunk Street, east side, to a tree on Lawton's Hill opposite the Grammar School building, Siegfried said, "What do I want with that swamp, I'll wait until you get the money," which he did, Mr. Pott paying the claim.

Siegfried was a powerfully built man and fond of displaying his prowess. In after years a son-in-law of his, Daniel Eiler, a quiet and inoffensive man was loading a car of coal on his wagon at the corner of Coal and East Norwegian streets, where a landing was maintained for the loading of boats on the canal, a branch of which ran to that point.

It was first-come first-served and each took their turn. Dan Holland, of Cressona, something of a scrapper and another heavy weight, took advantage of his reputation and would wait for no one. When the little box cars came down the wooden rails he advanced to the head of the line filled his wagon and was off, Siegfried heard of this and came to the landing to enforce fair play. His son-in-law was first on that day, when Holland came and as usual, went to the head of the line. A few well directed sledge hammer blows by Siegfried on Holland's anatomy convinced him that discretion was the better part of valor and he was never known to take other than his rightful place thereafter.

Charles Siegfried was a soldier in the war of 1812. When he died he was given a large military funeral. Apropos of this it must be borne in mind that when the military of this locality enlisted in the War of 1812 they walked from Pottsville to Reading and from thence, where they joined others, that had been drafted or enlisted, they walked to Baltimore and return. Mrs. John

Wagner nee Schwab, of Pottsville, 87 years of age at this writing, remembers of the condition of her father's shoes and clothing on his return to the Lykens Valley where the family lived.

In 1818 all of the houses included within the town plot and not hitherto named were: Henry Donnell's house on the first lot sold where now stands the Pennsylvania Hall; the William Cassley Log house on the site of the Miller Bookstore, opposite; a log house about in the centre of the square, between Mahantongo and Howard street, built by Joseph Bleckley; a house near the site of old Town Hall and the White Horse Tavern, built by George Dengler and afterward kept by John Pott, Jr., Henry Donnell opened the first store in Pottsville, in his new building, except that opened by the Pott family for their workmen. The Buckwalter Hotel afterward the North western, now the Park, was built before 1829. The Mortimer House, where the Mountain City building stands, now owned and occupied by the Mammoth Miehle Dry Goods and Department Store, was known as the Mt. Carbon Hotel and was built by Jacob Seitzinger in 1826. John Pott in 1824, sold the ground, N. E. corner of Centre and Mahantongo streets to T. Ridgeway. The lot changed hands a number of times, until 1830 when the Pottsville House was erected. The hotel also changed hands often, Col. Joseph M. Feger being one of its most popular landlords. In 1863 Daniel Esterly bought it and removed his hardware business to it after improving and remodeling it. Col. Shoemaker built the Penna Hall. On the southwest corner of Centre and Market streets was the Mover Hotel, built by Daniel Moyer about 1826, and the Central or Lindenmuth Hotel, north of Market on the west side of Centre was kept by a man named Geist. In 1830 Jacob Seitzinger erected the Exchange Hotel, corner of Centre and west Arch streets.

BEAR STORY

Mrs. Sarah Gumpert, deceased, wife of the late Samuel Gumpert who was an expert accountant and transcriber, and for eighteen years a clerk in the law offices of the Schuylkill County Court House, related many interesting stories of the early history of the county. Her parents lived in the Tumbling Run Valley. One wintry day in early December her father, Jos. Webb, started to -walk to Orwigsburg over the Tumbling Run Mountain.

The family butchering had just been completed and as the custom was among the early settlers, he intended to give a friend part of his killing, the friend would return the gift later in the season and thus the two families would be kept supplied with fresh meat during the winter. It was late in the afternoon when Mr. Webb started with the quarter of fresh beef hung over his shoulder. He had not reached the summit of the mountain before he discovered that he was being pursued and by a huge black bear. Bruin had scented the odor of the blood and was determined to exact with it not only the red corpuscles but "the pound of flesh," also.

Mr. Webb was a large and powerfully built man and determined not to part with the meat if he could help it. If he could reach the summit of the mountain with it he might make the descent and save the beef. He had no weapon with him but his huge clasp knife which was stuck in the belt at his waist and the mad race began. The bear gained steadily on the man. He could almost feel his hot breath and his heavy panting would have dismayed any but one of the sturdiest of the old-timers.

The four-footed pursuer had almost reached his prey when Mr. Webb bethought himself and took his huge knife and cut off a slice of meat and dropped it for the bear and sped on as rapidly as he could hoping to at least save some of the beef. But the slice merely whetted bruin's appetite and he was up and after the farmer again with full speed. The operation was repeated again and again and still Mr. Webb ran on. The speed down the mountain, of both, became little short of terrific.

At last Orwigsburg came in sight, the bear would turn back he thought, or someone would see him and come to his assistance. No one came and Mr. Webb feeling his load becoming very light discovered that he was carrying a few beef ribs on his shoulder the rest of the meat having been devoured by the bear. He vented his chagrin by tossing the carcass to the brute and had nothing to offer his friend but the story of his adventure when he reached his home. When the latter brought his gift in return some months later to the Webbs, he came by wagon, up the Sunbury turnpike road, not caring to encounter another or even the same hungry bear that Joseph Webb fed, like a dog, with a quarter of beef.

ON THE ROAD TO HEAVEN

"Granny" Lash, as she was familiarly known, was one of the quaint characters of the early days in Pottsville. She lived on the road to Port Carbon, was a strict Methodist and one of the first members of the class established by Jonathan Wynn. She lived to a ripe old age and saw many innovations creep into the church of her choice. Granny was loud in her denunciation of instrumental music in the church and thoroughly disliked the first melodeon and organ introduced.

On one occasion a young musician, a visitor to town from Philadelphia, played a violin solo at the service at the request of a member of the church, whose guest he was. The selection was a simple old-fashioned hymn tune around which the player wove numerous delicate fancies and musical intertwinings and variations. At the close of the service, the old lady said:

"That was beautiful. It made me feel so happy." "Why Granny!" said the member, "I thought you would not like it; that you would think it a sin."

"Oh, a violin is all right," said Granny. "If it had been a fiddle it would have been different. I love a violin; but I just hate a fiddle."

Granny was fond of walking and as she grew more decrepit she sometimes lost her bearings on her road home from church. Passing her home one day she was toiling on toward Port Carbon when she was accosted by a young girl of the neighborhood with:

"Granny where are you going? You are on the wrong road." "I am on the road to Heaven, Miss! and that is enough for you to know," answered the dame. She did not object to being turned around, however, and it was not very long afterward that she started out for that destination afresh.

A NEGRO GRAFTER

One of the sights on a certain day of the week in Pottsville, was the incoming of the farmers from the Mahantongo ("Mockatunkey") Valley. These townships, upper and lower, with Barry were very fertile and productive and the fruits of the fine farms found their market in Pottsville. The farmers and hucksters came in and departed together and formed a regular caravan, with their green Conestoga wagons one after another, high back and front and covered with white canvass hoop-framed top-covers. As many as seventy wagons were counted in the hotel yards on one night. At first some of this produce was shipped down the line by canal but the population of the county increased so rapidly that it was soon all consumed at home.

One, "Old man Rater," was a regular weekly visitor. Hanging about the old White Horse Tavern, kept then by Wm. Matz, was a half grown negro boy, black as the ace of spades, who came from the Long Swamp and could talk Dutch. He ingratiated himself with the farmers and was always the richer by a pocketful of coppers after market day. He would accost Eater with:

"Father, give me a penny, as sure as I live I have not eaten a mouthful this day." The penny forthcoming, he bought a huge gingerbread and munched it in the farmer's presence, seemingly contented.

One morning he came as usual, with a gingerbread in each hand, and apparently forgetful of the fact, whined as usual, between the mouthfuls:

"Daddy gib mir ein bense. Ich hab ga wis ich labe, heit noch nix gessen."

A few well directed kicks from Rater disposed of the youthful manipulator of gingerbread trusts and he was seen no more about old man Rater's Conestoga craft on market day, nor in the tavern yard.

HAD A GIFT OF REPARTEE

One evening during the 'fifties, the old Methodist Episcopal Church, on Second Street, was more than usually crowded. The Rev. Wm. Barnes, familiarly known as "Old Billy Barnes," was the pastor. (He must not be confounded with the Rev. Samuel Barnes who served the congregation later.) He was a most exemplary man and a radical preacher and when thoroughly warmed up handled wicked doers and the unrighteous without gloves.

Mr. Barnes had been very much annoyed by the frivolous conduct of several young people in the church and he publicly reprimanded them from the pulpit. One of the young women became very much incensed at the action of the clergyman and arose to go out but not without first showing her contempt at the reproof by laughing aloud. Mr. Barnes said:

"Good-night, daughter of the Devil!"

"Good-night, Father!" said the girl.

[This story has been claimed in Lancaster, where Mr. Barnes also served as pastor, but there are several members of the M. E. Church of Pottsville still living who were present when the incident occurred, who are willing to vouch for its accuracy.]

ANOTHER CLAIM FOR NAME, THE SAME YET DIFFERENT

The town was named after John Pott, the founder, who came here in 1806. The place was known as Pott's at the coal mine (pronounced "Putts"), and after the incorporation was known by the German settlers in the southern part of the county, as "Buttsville."

The early newspapers and the first settlers took the matter up and it was asserted that Pott (Pot) had been corrupted through the Pennsylvania German to "Put," and the name of the town was "Potsville" (Pottsville).

During the 'seventies, however, Ramsey Potts, Esq., contended that Pottsville was named from the first, "Pottsville," after William B. Pott, an ancestor of his, who was an old-time settler and one of the first lawyers at the old county-seat, Orwigsburg.

This was the same Wm. B. Potts who so vehemently opposed the removal of the Court House from Orwigsburg to Pottsville. When the great parade and glorification took place and the windows of the houses of the new county town were illuminated with rows upon rows of tallow candles, Mr. Potts followed a float representing the Orwigsburg Court House, clinging to a rope hitched to the rear and objecting at every turn of the wheels to the seat of justice being taken away. It was one of the leading features of the event.

Quite a spirited discussion over ,the matter ensued between Mr. Potts and Colonel Robert H. Ramsey and the tilt between them furnished lively reading matter for a time in the "Miners' Journal" of town.

The name, however, according to both parties was Pottsville, and Pottsville it has remained ever since, with John Pott, who did so much for the town, as the acknowledged founder. He died October 23, 1827, before the town was incorporated.

With the building of Greenwood Furnace small houses were erected for the workmen. These were occupied by John Else, Henry Bolton, Thomas Swayer, Anthony Schott, George Frevie, George Reimer and Daniel Focht, Clerk. These men and their families all lived here before Mr. Pott removed his family from Berks County, in 1809. There were other settlers at Mt. Carbon and other points, but it was not until the discovery of coal was put into practical use that the place attracted any considerable number of settlers. In 1828, with the incorporation of the town, a daily stage to Philadelphia was established, making the trip in fourteen hours.

THE FIRST RAILWAYS

Schuylkill County had seen the evolution in travel from the Indian path, common road and bridle path, Durham boat, stage coach and Conestoga wagon, to the Philadelphia and Heading railway, completed in 1842. In the month of May, of that year, a train of 50 cars carrying 150 tons of coal was sent from Schuylkill Haven to the port at Richmond, making the trip in one day.

The first railway was the Mill Creek, begin in 1829, and extended from Port Carbon to the Broad Mountain. The Schuylkill Valley Railway, was commenced in 1829 and finished in 1830. It extended from Port Carbon to Tuscarora. The Norwegian and Mount Carbon Railway, which was designed to meet the Danville railroad to Pottsville, was completed in 1831.

The Mine Hill and Schuylkill Haven railroad extended from Schuylkill Haven to the Broad Mountain, a line of 15 miles. The Little Schuylkill Railway extended from Port Clinton to Tamaqua, a distance of 22 miles.

All of these roads were run by horse power and connected with the Schuylkill canal. The Tamaqua Railway was the first to run a steam engine. It burned pitch pine and was quite a novelty.

The Philadelphia and Reading road was the first to use steam motive power. The engines were wood burners. When the road to Philadelphia was completed a jubilee was given in honor of the event and people came from far and wide to see the novelty. The celebration lasted several days and the people were carried free. The cars were only open platform trucks and rude freight cars with Tough wooden benches, loosely constructed, set on top. Many that accepted the company's invitation felt that they were not only taking their lives in their hands, but placing them at a great risk in the hands of others. General Winfield Scott, afterward a candidate for the presidency, came up, and the occasion was a momentous one for the coal regions.

THE FIRE DEPARTMENT

Before the days when a town water supply existed and the people depended upon the public pumps for their water for domestic purposes, a bucket brigade existed for the extinguishing of fires. In 1830, a fire took place in Clinton Row where Union Hall now stands), on Mahantongo Street, and in 1831 the store of Lewis and Witman, with the goods, was burned out.

Norwegian creek and the bucket system became inadequate, even when a house was burned on the Landing and the canal was resorted to, and a fire company was formed. It was known as the "Rough and Readies." The Hydraulian or "Drollies" organized about the same time and the Humane, Good Intent and Young America followed.

In 1832, a destructive fire occurred at Port Carbon and the Hydraulian Co., of Pottsville, responded. In 1833, the two-story frame brewery of D. G. Yuengling, on Mahantongo Street, took fire and burned to the ground. In 1835, a fire broke out and consumed a double frame building, on west Norwegian street, next the George W. Gumming residence, when the tenants lost everything even their clothing. Their lives barely being saved. In 1849 the stable, horse and carriage of G. W. Cumming were burned. The building was in the same locality.

In 1837 the apothecary store of Wm. T. Epting (uncle of the wife of President Judge of the Schuylkill County Courts, O. P. Bechtel) took fire and was destroyed with all its contents. The fire was caused through the carelessness of a boy who held a lighted candle in his hand while filling a bottle with ether. Morris Brothers lost heavily in this fire.

In 1838 the steam grist mill belonging to Clemens and Parvin was partially destroyed, and in 1846 four wooden dwellings belonging to the same firm, on George Street, were destroyed. They were occupied by Isaac Higley, John L. Mennig, Nicholas Madara and Jacob Olewine. A woman living in one of these houses became so terrified she was temporarily insane and fled from the building without her babe which she left in the burning house. It was found by a neighbor in a room next the roof, laughing and crowing at the sparks that fell from the roof that caved in shortly afterward.

STORY OF CENTRE STREET FIRE

One of the most destructive fires was that in the old Arcade, Centre Street, east side, between Norwegian and Market. Henry Matter, deceased, who was one of the chief sufferers said: "My store was one of the first and best shoe stores in Pottsville. I am a shoe-maker by trade and made fine boots and ladies' shoes. For a custom made ladies' gaiter and shoe in those days we received as high as nine dollars a pair, and fine custom-made boots brought from twelve to eighteen dollars a pair. Of course there were lower grades. Machine made shoes have destroyed this branch of the business.

"I had several hands in my employ and our store was stocked with our own and other manufacturers' goods. We had an excellent trade when the big fire wiped me out entirely, I having had no insurance on my stock.

"There was no system about fighting fires then, and even the members of the fire department lost their heads. A great crowd collected and everybody lent a hand to save our goods. Shoes were carried to places of safety (?) that were never seen afterward. Stoves and feather beds were carefully carried out and looking glasses and wash bowls were thrown out of the windows; what was not destroyed by fire or stolen was so damaged as to be useless. Wm. Leib a well-known politician, uncle of Capt. Frank Leib, of Harrisburg, an officer in the 48th regiment, in the Civil War, lived in this block."

OLD HAND ENGINE

Other disastrous fires were those on east Norwegian, corner of Centre, in the Johns property, occupied chiefly by saloons. The fire N. E. corner of Coal and east Norwegian, and the great fire September 10, 1848, when the block on the east side of Centre, between E. Market and E. Arch was burned out. In which Glenn and Stine, Daniel Aurand, Abraham Miessie, Patrick Curry, Patrick Fogarty, Solomon Shoener, John Kaibach, Joseph Weaver, Oliver Roads, Charles Moll and Charles Kopitzsch, were the principal sufferers, although many other business men were heavy losers.

It was in 1846 that the Good Intent Fire Company was organized. Some of the citizens deemed the means for fighting fire inadequate, and Benjamin Haywood, Esq., drew up a paper to be circulated for the formation of a new and additional fire company, and it found many signers among the young men at the shops and about town. A ball was held in December of that year to raise funds for the purchase of an engine. The first parade given by the company was April 19, 1847, when the company with the National Light Infantry turned out in honor of Generals Taylor, Winfield Scott, and Col. Wynkoop.

That old hand engine! Every middle-aged man and woman in Pottsville remembers it. How the boys and girls and everybody else, congregated around Garfield Square and the old Market House, where exhibitions were given as to the height the streams could be thrown. Eighty feet were claimed. There were eighty members in the company. The engine had four immense handles and was manned by twelve men on each side, six above and six below, twenty-four in all, and how they did pump. When the first relay were tired they were relieved by another set.

It was this muscular exhibition, one side up and the other side down, that led the boys to form the Young America Fire Company, which was taken under the protection and instruction of the Hydraulian Company, John P. Powers, Captain.

DESTRUCTIVE FLOODS

In October, 1831, a disastrous freshet occurred along the Schuylkill. The river arose to a great height. Travel by wagon was impeded and the mail was carried on foot over the mountains and on horseback over the flooded roads. The Schuylkill Navigation dam and coal wharves in this vicinity were badly injured, and boats and dwelling houses were carried away.

In January, 1841, another destructive flood occurred. Coal Street, Pottsville, was entirely cut off from the rest of the town and many properties along the river, canal and Norwegian Creek were rained or badly injured. The houses on Furnace Island were surrounded with water and the families of some were carried to higher ground. Fifty yards of the embankment of the canal was swept away, carrying wharves, chutes, bridges and boat houses with it. The old turnpike bridge was carried away as was also the towpath bridge. Ruin and destruction followed along in the wake of the freshet down the valley. A sick man was rescued with the greatest difficulty from the lockhouse at the first dam.

TUMBLING RUN DAM BREAKS

Tumbling Run Dam was threatened in the freshet of 1841, but it was not until 1851 that it succumbed to the flood, the water making a passage inside the wing wall of the water-way and working larger until the greater part of the embankment gave way, and ruin and destruction followed in the wake of the great flood. An eye-witness of the breaking of Tumbling Kun Dam says: "When word was conveyed to Pottsville, by a man on horseback, that the dam was about to break, many repaired to the spot over the mountain, and I was among the number. The hillside was filled with people. It was a great sight.

Many of the poorer people, and the working-class, built their little homes in this ravine and along the low lands near the Mt. Carbon bridge. Their homes, everything was swept away. Cows, pigs, chickens, the little cabins, stables, pig pens all were swept down stream. The bridge over the Schuylkill and canal went with the flood.

The railroad at Mt. Carbon was filled with people watching the flood. One man was seen swimming with the current with a pig in his arms. A rope was thrown him and he was rescued.

A Pottsville man, whose wife and year-old baby were visiting a sister who lived on the Schuylkill Haven Flats, when he heard of the threatened disaster procured a horse and rode down the pike at break-neck speed. The flood was there before him, however, and he found the house surrounded with water.

He rescued the inmates one by one, baby and all, with the horse and assisted in conveying others to a place of safety. Several narrow escapes were made from drowning all along the pathway of the flood by people who were trying to save their effects. A Mrs. Meek and "Mom" Pilliard, who afterward kept the Seven Stars hotel, were among those who lived on the flats at Schuylkill Haven."

MILITARY HISTORY

In a work of this nature much that is relevant to, and forms part of the history of the region, must necessarily be omitted. The facts narrated and the sketches drawn are nearly all included in the years from the first settlement of the county to a period anterior to the breaking out of the Civil War.

Schuylkill County was highly honored through its illustrious sons and the part they took in the Mexican War. There is a halo of glory surrounding the military history of this County and the part taken in the great struggle for the preservation of our great and glorious Union, that has never been questioned. Its claims for recognition as a County, filled with noble and self-sacrificing men and women, who offered their all in the dark days of the rebellion, are second to no similar district in the State.

Every Schuylkill Countian, at home and abroad, is proud of the military history of this County. The record, however, is one of such magnitude that it would be impossible to introduce even a gist of it in this volume, and beyond a casual reference to it the writer leaves it with the hope that the local historian of the future will do justice to its rich and already ripened field.

FIRST MILITARY COMPANIES

The National Light Infantry, now Company H., Eighth Regiment Pennsylvania Volunteers, is the oldest military organization in Pennsylvania. It was formed March 1st, 1832. The names of Captains Baird, Dean, Schoenfelter, Bland, Hon. James H. Campbell and Captain Frank Pott occur among its list of commanders. The latter took command at the close of the Mexican War. Its list of lieutenants includes the names of James Beatty, E. Joy Ridgway, Wm. Pollock, Hon. Robert M. Palmer, Henry L. Cake, David P. Brown, James Russel, Thomas Wren and Robert Colburn.

The Independent Blues were organized in 1841, and were commanded by Capt. James Nagle, afterward Gen. Nagle. Thomas Johnson was a lieutenant. The great ambition of the young company was to make a showing beside their older rivals, the Light Infantry. They had scanty funds with which to equip themselves and their first uniform consisted of blue Kentucky jean trowsers and coat and a comical looking cap.

On July 4, 1843, the company was reorganized and rechristened the Washington Artillerists. At that time the company was presented with a beautiful silk flag made by the ladies of Pottsville. The Artillerists were equipped with handsome uniforms and had flint lock muskets from the State arsenal. They met in an armory located over Nicholas Kemp and Muth's carpenter shop, N.E. corner of Sixth and Market streets.

The call for troops for the Mexican War was limited. The Washington Artillerists were the first to answer the summons excluding the Light Infantry, but several members of the latter joined the Artillerists and served through that war. When the troops returned, the honor gained by the Artillerists overshadowed that of the Infantry. It took the combined efforts of Col. Henry L. Cake and Capt. Edmund McDonald (uncle of Captain E. D. Smith) to keep the company together to do good work later on.

Eighteen members of the Washington Artillerists voted to go to the Mexican War. Of this number two afterward backed out and two deserted at New Orleans. This left fourteen members, which with four men from the Light Infantry brought up the original number. This small squad was supplemented by others along the route and a good-sized company was raised before they reached Washington. The following was the roster of the Artillerists:

Capt. James Nagle, Lieutenant Simon Nagle, Lieutenant Franklin P. Ivaercher, Sergeants Wm. Nagle, August Boyer, Peter Douty, Edward Kaercher, Corporals Washington Garrett and Edward Masson, and Daniel Nagle, Benjamin Smith, Owen Thomas, Reuben Samm and Nelson Berger. National Light Infantry: Robert Welsh, Jacob Sharp, Valentine K. Mills and Barney Barr.

The Artillerists are now Company F. of the Fourth Regiment, N. G. P. Volunteers.

JUDGE D. C. HENNING

Former Judge D. C. Henning, president of the Schuylkill County Historical Society, says:

"I heard the late Washington Garrett narrate a story on one occasion when I was present at a meeting of Gowen Post, in G. A. E. Hall. 'Wash' Garrett, as everybody called him, was a good soldier in the Mexican War and also in the Civil War, serving, I believe, his full three years' term in the War of the Rebellion.

"Mr. Garrett was asked to tell something about his experience in the Mexican War. He arose and said: 'I am no story teller or speech-maker, but this I can say. There was never any lagging behind in marching in the Mexican War. The Greasers were a treacherous lot. They made war on the sly and any man who fell behind could expect to be "done" by them.

"'In the Civil War a man could fall out, even in the enemy's country, and catch up again with his command. There were not many Johnnie Rebs who hunted the men in blue on the quiet. But in the Mexican War the fighting was not open or governed by tactics.'"

REMINISCENT OF THE WOMEN OF POTTSVILLE

The following reminiscences by the author appeared in the Pottsville "Daily Republican," J. H. Zerbey, publisher, April 18th, 1900, when a special military copy in honor of the First Defenders was brought out.

"Something reminiscent of the departure of the first troops for the seat of war and their return. In vain do I cudgel my brains for a mental picture of the event. What would a mere slip of a girl then recollect through all these years? Brushing aside the cobwebs of time that obstruct the mental vision, a kaleidoscopic picture of a parade on Washington's birthday flashes over the camera of long forgotten memories. A real soldiers' parade, with martial music and Nicholas Rehr's band. The Washington Artillerists in light blue trousers with red stripes with dark blue swallow tail coats and a profusion of gold lace. The Light Infantry in a cadet grey with black and gold facings and black felt hats with large white cocks' plumes. The Artillerists had bear skin hats like those the drum majors today affect. The Washington Yaegers had dark green and brown uniforms and bandmen's hats, with a dark green tuft or pompon in front. A hunter's costume, it was said, as was worn in Germany. The Continentals, the impression they left on the mind is most distinct, with their pale buff knee breeches, leather leggings, buff vests and blue swallow tail coats covered with gold lace and three cornered hats. They were the admiration of all the girls and boys and were looked upon as veritable George Washingtons in re-production. They marched through the town with a grace and precision that would be the envy of the militia boys of to-day, forming at intervals into hollow squares to fire a volley of blank cartridges in celebration of the day to the terror of the small children on the streets. This, possibly, was February 22d, 1861. The next recollection is when our father, who always read aloud evenings from his daily papers, the "Public lodger" and the "Evening Bulletin," (a custom he maintained during the entire war) with great impressiveness delivered, the President's proclamation and the call for 75,000 volunteers to suppress the "insurrectionary combinations." The children were awed by the solemnity of his manner, but did not understand the situation, They tried to supplement their knowledge by studying the pictures of "Harper's Weekly." The illustrations of the firing upon Forts Sumter and Moultrie are still indelibly stamped upon the writer's brain together with others from the same pictorials in the years that followed, that pictured the blood and carnage of the battlefield and the encounters between the "Blue and the Grey." The departure of the first volunteers and their return, all is a blank. Possibly we were not allowed to wander about on the streets in those exciting times and in the crowds that gathered to bid the troops "God speed." Local historians tell of the day being cold, raw, and disagreeable and that the people flocked by the thousands from all parts of the County to witness their departure. The roofs of the houses about the depots were black with people and the ladies lined every available window along the route waving their handkerchiefs to the brave boys. All through the war this deep interest in the soldier boys was maintained by the women and girls of the town. On April 23d, a flag made by the Misses Bannan of Cloud Home, was placed in the hand of the iron statue of Henry Clay on top of the monument of that name. A multitude of people gathered to witness the ceremonies and patriotic resolutions were passed. Twenty-one ladies signed a communication at this time in which they tendered to the Hon. Simon Cameron, Secretary of War, their services as a nurse corps. His response to Miss Amanda Sillyman and Mrs. Jas. H. Campbell was highly complimentary to their loyalty and patriotism. A sewing society was organized, and up to the following June 800 havelocks, 135 bands, 90 towels and 150 needle cases were sent to the troops from Schuylkill County. The ladies in other towns in the County organized for work with good results. In those times no gala day was complete without the erection of stands for the speakers.

WHEN THE TROOPS RETURNED

The ladies' deft fingers made wreaths and garlands to decorate the stand, market house and along the route. Bouquets of flowers were presented as they marched over the short line of parade, halting in front of the stand near the market house where they were welcomed home by John Bannan, Benjamin Haywood and other speakers. Inside of the market house a dinner had been prepared for the troops in which Mrs. Charlemagne Tower was interested and Mrs. Geo. C. Wynkoop had charge assisted by a corps of ladies, old and young, some of them the wives and sweethearts of the boys who came marching home again.

On the return of the Tower guards, Mrs. Tower had prepared for them a collation at the Tower residence. Mrs. Tower all through the rebellion gave largely of her means and time to the soldiers' cause. Many soldiers' families in town received substantial aid from her private purse during the absence of their support in the army. During the encampment of the 96th Regiment on Lawton's Hill the ladies' sewing society presented each man with a needle book and Testament, and before the regiment left, Miss Allen's pupils, a private school for young ladies, sent them a library of 200 volumes. Miss Amanda Sillyman of the post-office, with the co-operation of other ladies, manufactured a large flag which was sent to the 48th Regiment at Fort Hatteras, N. C. Miss Sillyman, who went south to nurse her brother, Thomas Sillyman, was the first woman granted permission at Petersburg to enter the lines after the battle. Gen. McClellan giving her a pass and granting her an escort. It is a matter of regret that there is so little data of the work performed by the noble women of our town. Many of the ladies interested have long since died or removed to other places, and those still living recollect very little that they can impart for publication. Of those that took an active part in the work of patriotism were the Misses Bannan, Silliman, McCool, Carpenter, Sillyman, Hartz, Haywood, Mrs. S. C. Colt, Mrs. C. Tower, Mrs. C. Little, Mrs. G. Wynkoop, Mrs. A. Cochran, Mrs. James Campbell, Mrs. J. P. Bertram, Mrs. Meyer Strouse and many others whose names are not recorded, but the recollection of their deeds still live fresh in the memories of those who remain. Mrs. Emma B. Bohannon and Miss Christie Miessie had charge of the presentation of a stand of colors that were presented to the Forty-Eighth Regiment on their return home. The scrolls contained the names of the battles participated in, Misses Clara E. Lessig, Matilda P. Russel and Maggie Boyle representing the ladies of Pottsville presented a stand of colors to the 96th on their return. On the return of the 129th Regiment the ladies had a collation prepared for them in the Market House. On Thanksgiving Day of 1863 the ladies of Pottsville under Mrs. Martha Shearer served in the same place a Thanksgiving dinner to the troops stationed on Lawton's Hill and in the west end to preserve the peace and prevent a threatened riot during the enforcement of the draft. Soldiers aid societies under the superintendence of patriotic ladies were organized throughout the County and thousands of dollars' worth of goods were sent to their brave compatriots on the field and in the hospitals. After the work of the

SANITARY AND CHRISTIAN COMMISSIONS

was inaugurated they were used as a medium for the distribution of gifts to our soldier boys and others. Mrs. C. Tower was largely interested in the work of the Sanitary Commission and with the assistance of other ladies large supplies were forwarded. The ladies of the First Presbyterian church worked for the cause. The Ladies' Aid of Trinity Episcopal church was organized with Mrs. Andrew Russel, Misses Sarah and Amanda Silliman, Mrs. D. J. Ridgway,

Mrs. A. Henderson, Mrs. J. C Hughes, Mrs. Michael Bright, Miss Amelia Pott and others as members. 68 boxes of goods were sent the commission, the result of the work of the above ladies private contributions. The M. E. Church also organized. Miss Rachel Bartholomew, the Misses Taylor, Evans, Sparks, Amelia Haywood and others were largely interested and seven boxes of stores, the work of one year and valued at $500 were forwarded the commission. In the great Fair of the Sanitary Commission in Philadelphia in June, 1864, practically the same ladies were interested, although the contributions were from all sources and the organization throughout the County was complete and independent of the work accomplished in Pottsville. Miss Amanda Silliman was the chairman of the committee in the ladies department and in addition to those mentioned Mrs. Wallace Wolff, Mrs. John Noble, Miss Parvin and Miss Wolff took an active part, and Mrs. Benjamin Bannan was chairman of the whole. The business men of the County contributed to the Sanitary Commission and Fair, the Christian Commission, for the relief of soldiers' families and miscellaneous contributions to Schuylkill county soldiers and others during the three or more years of the war showed that the enormous sum of $92,138.08 was contributed to the cause from the people of this county merely for philanthropical purposes. This did not include the aid given soldiers' families, many of whom were taken care of privately by the localities in which they lived, nor the money contributed toward filling the quota. But the work of the girls and boys during that time and the 16 boxes of supplies sent to the Commission by the pupils of the Public School deserve some recognition and must not be forgotten. Large quantities of lint were forwarded for the staunching of wounds. The scholars were requested to bring old linen, which was unraveled by the thread or scraped to make the coveted article. Girls and boys left their play to pick lint for the soldiers. Our school, a sub-Grammar in a building of two rooms on the site of the present Centre street Grammar school, had the distinction of filling one of these boxes. The grammar school below of the Misses McCool did likewise. We worked for several weeks for the box at home and between school house hours on hemming towels, making needle books, havelocks and bandages and the lint. On several rare occasions, our teacher, Miss Fanny Couch, a 'Yankee school marm,' from the green hills of Vermont, and one of the strictest disciplinarians Pottsville's public schools ever knew, unbent enough to allow an hour's work for the box before the close of school hours, during which we sang patriotic songs. Then the box, with what interest we surveyed it. It was no 'measly' little box either, but a huge, square solid box. Dried fruits of all kinds were requested to fill it, cornstarch, crackers and farinaceous foods, together with cured meats. Bologna was forbidden, it would spoil, and glasses did not pack well; the solid glass pickle bottles, however, were sent. There was a quantity of dried beef in the whole pieces and tongues and tongues. Well do I remember with what feelings of pride I carried a huge farmer's summer sausage of the thick stove pipe variety and a contribution of money to help defray the freight expenses. Then the conjectures as to the safety of that box. Geographies were taken out and the route studied which it would take till it reached Hatteras, N. C, and no one felt safe until a letter of acknowledgment was received, which was read aloud in the school. Reading matter was contributed for the hospitals in some of the schools, several of them clubbing together to fill boxes at intervals. These are but few of the incidents of those stirring times, many of which must go down in the unwritten history of the annals of time with the unnumbered deeds of valor of the brave defenders of our country of which history has no record. All honor to the memory of the patriotic women of Schuylkill County whose unselfish devotion and generosity saved many precious lives and inspired with courage and zeal the brave soldiers in the field."

NOT A FOOT WASHER

Bob was the despair and delight of little Susan. They were brother and sister, and only two out of the little Peterpin brood of nine, over the youngest of which Susan exercised a housewifely and motherly care; and to whom the mother relegated much of the supervision of the children that she might the better attend to what she considered other and more important duties.

Susan was a real little motherling, and it was amusing to see the care she took of the brood when they went out or were playing about. A watchful and interested neighbor related (Susan was small for her age and delicate) how upon one occasion a runaway horse came down the street full tear. She could not get her charges away, and taking her short skirts in both hands spread them out to their utmost, like a danseuse, and bidding them be quiet and stand close behind her she stood pale and trembling with dilated eyes watching the beast until he galloped harmlessly by and the danger was past.

Susan had her own ideas about cleanliness, and her rules were iron-clad about how the unruly six must appear before they could have their meals, go to school or to bed. There were many incipient rebellions over the enforcement of the laws about clean ears, well brushed teeth, and combed hair, not to mention their baths, but Susan had all the phlegmatic firmness of her Pennsylvania German ancestry to fall back on during such occasions and usually came off conqueror.

The boys ran barefoot during the hot summer months and when they went to bed they must all first wash their feet. Bob hated water and to slop his pedal extremities in the foot bath when he was tired and sleepy was almost more than he could endure. Coming home one night after a busy day playing around the foundry, for he had a taste for mechanics, he was more than usually black. He did penance, however, by washing his face and hands and then carefully washed off the tops of his feet, leaving the soles black and dirty but dry.

Susan detected the imposition at once and the following conversation ensued: "Oil! Bob, why didn't you wash the soles of your feet? You must go back and wash them over again. You will make the bed clothes all dirty."

"Dirty! Huh! How? You don't stand up in bed, do you?" said Bob!

COLORED WOMAN BURIED IN BABER CEMETERY

It is not generally known that a colored woman lies buried in what was, in the 'fifties, called Mt. Laurel Cemetery, but such is the case. Bard Patterson, Esq., early coal operator and capitalist, imported into his family from the State of Virginia a very likely and comely young colored woman to act as upper servant and nurse. She proved a faithful and efficient servitor, trusted and highly respected by her master and mistress, and beloved generally by the family. The cold winters, however, of the North proved too much for her rather frail constitution and tuberculosis set in, from the effects of which she died after about a year's illness, during which she was tenderly cared for by the family. After her death the Rector of the Episcopal Church read the burial service over her at the family residence. The remains were privately buried in the Mt. Laurel Cemetery, at the N.E. end of the enclosure. A plain wooden head-board with the inscription, Phyllis, aged 38, still marked the spot a year or two ago and the record may be seen on the Trinity Parish register.

THE PRESBYTERIAN CHILL

It was one winter when an Evangelist was holding forth in Pottsville, with a series of Union Evangelistic meetings. The attendance nightly was large and the gatherings among the church people very enthusiastic.

At a meeting in the First Presbyterian Church, close on to a thousand persons were present and it became necessary to hold an overflow meeting in the basement of the church.

A prominent business man of town having been engaged at work rather late, entered the overflow meeting, which was filled with members of other denominations, among them the Baptist, of which he was one.

The "P. B. M." had a cold, and the room was cool and draughty; but the gathering bubbled over with religious fervor. On his return home, his bronchial tubes closed up much to his wife's alarm, who, fearing pneumonia, hastily summoned the family physician, a testy old chap and a Presbyterian, too, by the way, and withal something of a wag.

The Doctor sounded the P. B. M.'s lungs, carefully examined him and ordered the usual remedies, which were at once applied.

"No, there is no pneumonia there," said the Doctor.

"But a Baptist has no business in a revival outside of his own church. He just caught the Presbyterian chill. That's all!"

BEFORE THE WAR

It was in the summer of 1856 that the great Union Gospel Tent stretched its flapping sides and peaked dome, surmounted by an U. S. flag, on the site of what is now the depot of one of the main railways entering Pottsville. It held 3000 people and was considered a monster for its size, and was crowded nightly. The evangelists, Long and Schultz, were zealous for the cause, and the old town never experienced such a revival of religion before or since. Members of the different churches rallied to the support of the Tabernacle and there was a regular rattling of the dry bones in Israel everywhere.

The Tent remained six weeks and many were the sinners that forsook the evil of their ways; some of whom remained staunch to the cause espoused for the remainder of their lives, and were as bright and shining lights plucked from the burning. All things, however, must have an end, and the Tabernacle was removed to Norristown to fill a similar engagement.

It was decided by some of the firmest supporters of the movement to continue the Gospel meetings, at least weekly, and a Union prayer meeting was formed among them to meet Sunday afternoons and thus not interfere with any of the regular church services. The gathering met in the little church on Second Street, abandoned by its congregation for a newer and larger one farther northwest; and on the site of which now stands the large Fire Department House of the Good Intent Company. Lawyer Peasely and Mrs. Cuff were among the most regular attendants at the Gospel Tent meetings and were foremost subsequently among those in organizing the Union meetings. The Lawyer was a fine old-Country German gentleman, dignified in bearing, immaculate in dress, and one of the best read men in town.

Mrs. Cuff was an honest woman and very earnest in her religious zeal and convictions. Her husband had been dead for some years and she in common with her daughters eked out a somewhat precarious existence as decayed gentlewomen bereft of their only legitimate support must do. Mrs. Cuff was not an educated woman, but the townspeople said, "she was extraordinarily gifted in prayer" and just to hear her petitions for the uplifting of the good of the town and the overthrow of sin was considered more of an inspiration than the sermons of a preacher; and no one doubted her sincerity, either, for hers was a profession that would wash and remain fast colors.

Lawyer Peasely had lost the companion of his joys and sorrows just prior to the arrival of the Tabernacle. He had been heard to remark at the grave to his little daughter, Mary, who clung to his arm sobbing as if her heart would break: "Take courage, my child, take courage!" and although apparently genuinely overcome, tried hard himself to follow this sage advice. At the devotional meetings he would pour out his soul in prayer and perhaps Mrs. Cuff would follow with one of her fervent petitions, and thus it was not strange that a soul affinity sprang up between the two; and it was not long before it was rumored about that Lawyer Peasely had promised to marry Mrs. Cuff in the Spring, when a year had rolled around.

The news reached his daughters and they summoned home their brothers, who were engaged in business in New York, and together the family tackled the situation. The old blue blood of their ancestors was aroused; it must not, dare not be. It was a delicate matter, but the old gentleman was approached by his sons and the engagement with Mrs. Cuff was broken off. His attention was directed to another source which it was intimated would be more agreeable to the family, if marry he must, and which he subsequently did, and lived happily long past the allotted three score years and ten, with the object of his children's choice, confirming the wisdom of their selection.

The next Sunday came and with it the Union prayer meeting; people had gotten wind of the affair and the attendance was large. Something might happen, they said, and they were not disappointed.

Lawyer Peasely was in his accustomed place. He arose at the proper time with his golden-headed cane clasped between his hands, made a few remarks and offered prayer.

He had scarcely seated himself when Mrs. Cuff jumped up with the evident intention of doing likewise, but her emotions overcame her, and with uplifted hand and head erect, in a voice that reverberated through the little building, she cried out in the shrillest of tones.

"Oh, Lord! Oh, Lord! How I hate a hypocrite, I hate a hypocrite! ugh!"

Poor woman. She sank to her seat with tears and in sobs; unable to utter another word. The feeling was tense and you could have heard a pin drop, but a better sermon was never preached anywhere.

STICKETY JIMMY AND ELLEN

Consternation reigned among the Peterpin nine when it was told them that Ellen was about to marry Stickety Jimmy. Susan cried, and Bob said, "he wished somebody would steal Jimmy's stick-foot, so he could not go to church, hopping up the hill all the way and when the priest was ready 'Old Stick-foot' would not be there;" and here he darkly hinted that he might be that somebody if he could only get hold of it after Jimmy had gone to bed, for Ellen had said when interrogated that, "he always unstrapped the wooden leg at night" ___ "And get taken to jail," said the sobbing Susan.

Ellen was the maid of all work in the home of the nine and they had never had a girl like her before. She was a new importation from the Sunny Green Isle, and coming over the ocean with friends destined for P___, she made her advent in the family soon after her arrival. Ellen was as handsome as the girl that "sat in the low-backed car." Tall with a milk white skin, blue-grey eyes, pearly teeth, rosy cheeks with dimples, and bands upon bands of chestnut hair which she wore coiled round and round on her shapely head.

She was as strong as any man and could lift a full barrel of flour, which two of the noisy clan together could not do, and which fact gave her an authority over the boys, when in her charge, which she otherwise could never have commanded. They told their chums that she could lift the huge iron bucket the crane brought up from the dirt bank at the coal washery and even carry off a whole freight car on her back, and many were the walks in the vicinity of the railways, she was inveigled into, that they might see her perform the feat, which of course she never did.

Story telling was her forte. "Come, Ellen, tell us a story," Bob would say. "One of your fairies." What remarkable stories they were; of the Banshees and little people, the fairy queen the dragons and the monsters of Tipperary Downs. When the boys were particularly bad, she told them of the headless giants that walked about the outside of the house and peered in through the windows. the blind prince who marked down their good deeds and the dragon who could change them into a pig or a goat. If any of the bolder ones ventured to say, "I don't believe that, Ellen, that is a lie." She would defend herself with something like this: "A lie is it? Shure what is a lie? Me lyin' is given me to plaze me. If I lie against me frind, 'tis a mortal sin, but a lie to plaze meself is a gift from God, sint from Heaven for me plasure."

The kitchen clock needed cleaning and ran down every day or two and refused to respond long to Bob's frequent windings. "It's the Divil in it," said Ellen. "I've heard of it before. He sthops the clocks to hinder people from doin' their work on time, and 'yer father bein' that particular wid havin' his dinner right on noon, but I'll get him out."

She took the poker and gave three vigorous raps on the back of the clock saying with each rap: "Come out, ye Divil, come out." Whether or not the dust and grime fell from the wheels with such vigorous treatment is not known, but the clock went steadily after.

"Never pint your gun at me," she said to Bob who had an old disabled musket with which he was allowed to drill, but from which the lock and chambers were gone. "I've knowed guns like that to go off afore whether they're loaded or not. They always do in the old counthry. The Divil is in a gun when you pint it." Wise Ellen; and she was to be married and leave them.

Stickety Jimmy was a morose looking Irishman. Coarse featured, unkempt, with thick black hair and round under-neck chin whiskers and was not liked by any one. His face was red, his temper bad, and he a hard drinker. He had worked in the silver mines near Vera Cruz, where he lost a leg and wore a wooden substitute, from which fact he gained the sobriquet by which he was called. He came East to P___, where some friends he had known, bought a horse and wagon for him and he made a fair living at hauling coal, or at least could have made it had he let "the craythur" alone. But he came from Tipperary and that was his sole recommendation in Ellen's eyes.

The marriage was not a good one, and Ellen was soon installed again at the family home doing day's work at cleaning, washing and general housework. At night it was rumored Jimmy beat her until she gave him her hard earnings to spend for whisky. Ellen said little, but her proud boastfulness was gone and her spirit broken. Little Jamesy came soon after, and he died from suffocation it was said, though it was never proven, the drunken father rolled on him in the bed while he slept and Ellen was at the washtub.

She appeared again at her washtub and a little later was at work with a huge hole in her head. Doctor Berluchy had shaved away the hair around it and dressed the wound with huge strips of court plaster, and the children wondered if the pretty brown locks would ever grow again. When asked what caused it, she said: "I was just sphlittin' a bit av kindlin' wood and a piece av it flew up and sthruck me on the head."

But word went around that Ellen was at last attempting to hold up her end, that Stickety Jimmy was getting as good as he gave. The neighbors, however, objected to these nightly brawls, and fearing Ellen might be injured or killed, when matters appeared to be reaching a climax they interfered. True to her Irish love of fair play and the traditions of the wielders of the shillalahs at Donnybrook Fair, Ellen helped Jimmy, and together they turned on the neighbors and soon routed her well wishers.

It was too bad. Something must be done and they appealed to the Parish Priest, who appeared on the scene the next evening when matters were about at their worst. In thundering tones good Father G__ berated the brutal Jimmy, who with wooden leg in hand as a weapon was thrashing the luckless Ellen with it whenever he could get in a whack, and she in turn defended herself with the poker. Jimmy fled through the back window using the leg as a cane until he got up the adjacent hillside a sufficient distance to readjust it.

Ellen retained her presence of mind and strove to appear as if nothing had occurred. She courtesied up and down, again and again as she did when a girl on the country roadside in "ould" Ireland when the carriage of the curate passed by, wiped off a chair with her apron, asked the reverend to sit down, inquired about his health and deprecated it that he had come out for such a "thrifle," he might take "cowld" again.

The good man could not be severe with her but told her what a disgrace their conduct was, how they annoyed their neighbors, and asked her "if they both wanted to lose their souls?" and finally said: "It is a shame Ellen for you both to behave so, and you, too, that ought to know so much better. Cannot you and Jimmy live together without all this quarreling?"

"Not wid any pleasure or injyment, your honor," said Ellen.

Whether Jimmy was tired of married life or whether he was genuinely scared at the admonitions of Father G__ was never known. He was never seen in town afterward. Ellen told the nine, she guessed, "the Divil had come for him, or else the Bogy-man had taken him down in 'wan of thim' big air-holes (mine cave ins) on Guinea hill to torment the bogies wid him." Some years thereafter, however, a Schuylkill County man returning from Tucson said he saw "Stickety Jim" driving a six mule supply team over the desert, for one of the Arizona silver mines.

Ellen lived until she was well up in the eighties, working as long as she was able, when the charitable people of the town and her old friends relieved her from the necessity of going "over the hills to the poorhouse" of which she had so wholesome a dread. She was buried according to her own instructions. Her funeral was large, and one of which she would have been very proud, could she have seen it, and perhaps she did.

Part Five - History of Early Churches

Their Origin and Whereabouts

Schuylkill County, having been a part of Berks, its early history is, of course, contemporaneous. Locality, however, fixes certain historical events that occurred east or -west of the Blue Mountains, the dividing line, as early as the French and Indian War.

The "Old Red Church," near Orwigsburg, Schuylkill County, was built in 1754. It was burned in the Indian massacre in 1755 and has since been rebuilt four different times. Jacob's Church, two miles west of Pinegrove, was organized in 1780. St. John's Church, near Freidensburg, and Hetzels, on the Summer Berg, followed soon after. The early settlers in the vicinity of Pottsville attended either the Freidensburg Church or the New Jerusalem organization, below the County Home, which was built later.

The first church here was not within the Borough limits, but stood in a field lying north of the road leading to the Joyce nursery, near the home of Col. Hyde (Mill Creek Avenue). It was built as a place of worship for the lumbermen who operated sawmills along the Schuylkill, as far north as New Philadelphia, and for the use of the few settlers in the vicinity of Pottsville. It depended entirely upon the services of such itinerant Lutheran and Reformed preachers as came this way, for the ministration of the Gospel, the baptism of children and the burial services for the dead. Some of these funeral sermons, being preached months

Old Red Church

after their subjects were interred. The rude stones that marked the graves of some of these early pioneers were still to be seen on the spot after the traces of the first log church near Pottsville were altogether obliterated.

Mrs. Amelia P. Schall, daughter of the late Benjamin Pott, and granddaughter of John Pott, the founder of Pottsville, kindly furnished the author with the following information on the subject: "My mother, who was a daughter of Martin Dreibelbeis, who came to where Schuylkill Haven now stands, in 1775, to make a home for himself and family, told me of this first church. It was known as Keim's Kirche. The Rev. George Minnich, who was one of the first pastors of Jacob's Church, near Pinegrove, the second church built in the county — not Wm. Minnich, who afterward officiated in Pottsville — with other ministers that traveled about, sometimes came there to preach.

"On such occasions, her parents and their family, with others of the early settlers, would come up here to attend the meetings. The women, many of them, rode on horseback and whole families came in wagons. The only other church then was the Freidensburg Kirche on the other side of Schuylkill Haven, which the early settlers attended in the same way. Rev. George Minnich at that time also supplying that and the Jacob's charge at Pinegrove.

"My cousin, Miss Tamson Strauch, sister of Henry and Daniel Strauch, the latter the first white boy born on Mahantongo Street, all now deceased, recollected hearing her mother, who was Magdalena Pott, daughter of John Pott, relate the same circumstance. Some years before my mother's death, which occurred in 1875, we drove to the spot in the rear of the Pottsville water basin, where Keim's Kirche stood, but found only the landmarks to indicate the site of the ancient church.

"There is no record of when my grandfather, John Pott, gave the land on the corner of North Centre and Race Streets for the laying out of a cemetery and the building of the log school house in which the first church services in Pottsville were held. At least none that I am aware of."

THE LOG SCHOOL HOUSE

When it is taken into consideration that in 1824 so little progress had been made that there were only five houses on the site of Pottsville, which was known as "John Pott's at the Coal Mine," it will not be a matter of astonishment that the building of the first churches began almost simultaneously, about 1828, with the incorporation of the town and that three of them were completed very nearly at the same period in the town's history.

The great body of the early Methodist preachers were plain, uneducated men, who came direct from the masses of the people. They were in touch not only with their views, ambitions and aspirations but with their inner everyday lives. They were a set of self-sacrificing men, who could consistently preach of that future state of happiness as the only thing worth striving for in this world. The salary consideration did not enter into their life-work, nor was their religion a mere profession of moral ethics or their teachings confined to the theoretical dogmas of church doctrines. They taught the people their need of God to lean upon, during the hardships they were undergoing and His power to sustain them through the privations of their hardy and lean lives.

One of these, Father Boehm, an itinerant preacher at a salary of $64 a year, traveled from Philadelphia to Fort Augusta on horseback to look after the religious interests of the people and he is believed to have held the first religious service here, long before the incorporation of the town. It was held in the forge of the Greenwood furnace, built in 1806. There was no other place to hold it and it was this circumstance that led John Pott to donate the ground, on North Centre Street, for the log school house, to be used for school and church purposes. The few, sparse settlers united, had a log-rolling bee and built the first church which, however, being non-sectarian, was never consecrated, and, as previously stated, was used in turn by the Episcopalians, Methodists and Presbyterians, to hold services in and here these first churches were incorporated.

The first consecrated church in Pottsville, was the St. Patrick's Roman Catholic, a small frame building, hastily thrown together for use in 1827, until the handsome church building then underway was completed.

On September 3d, 1827, a meeting was held in the log school house and an Episcopal congregation was organized. The first vestrymen were: Abraham Pott, Francis B. Nichols, Samuel J. Potts, Joseph White, Mordecai Lewis, E. Chichester, M. D., George Shoemaker, Koseby J. Hann and John Curry. John Pott gave the lot upon which the present church stands. Rev. Norman Xash, a young missionary, officiated at the laying of the corner stone, and the new church was built and completed 1829-30. The St. Patrick's K. C. Church, which was started about the same time was completed a short time after.

At this date, 1827, Pottsville had forged ahead from a village of five houses to one of a hundred and sixty houses and a population of about eight hundred.

John Comly, an old-time Quaker from Philadelphia, held a Friends' meeting in 1828 at the York Farm colliery store, which stood on the site of the C. M. Atkins' mansion, South Centre Street. In 1830 Friend Comly again visited Pottsville, and held services, and the outcome of these meetings resulted in the building of a Friends' meeting house, on Sharp mountain, near the corner of Ninth Street and Howard Avenue. The building was of stone, whitewashed a bluish slate color. The basement story was used for a Friends' school. The building was completed in 1831.

A Methodist Class had in the meantime been started by William Mills and wife, late from England. Andrew Mortimer, and Jonathan Wynn, who was the leader and exhorter. A church organization was effected in the log school house and the Rev. Joseph McCool was the first pastor installed. Mr. McCool disliked the M. E. itinerant system of moving about and subsequently, after a short pastorate at Allentown. accepted a call to the First Presbyterian church of Pottsville, for which he filled a very acceptable and useful pastorate for over thirty years. Simultaneously with the M. E. church organization, a new building, for the worship of Almighty God, was begun on the site of the old building on Second Street and completed early in the '30s.

The Episcopal, Roman Catholic, Methodist, Presbyterian and Friends meeting house, were the first churches of Pottsville and were completed in the order named. The other denominations, comprising fourteen churches, followed in the early subsequent years.

FIRST RELIGIOUS SERVICE

Of the first religious services held in Pottsville, Miss Emma Pott, daughter of Benjamin Pott and granddaughter of John Pott, relates the following: "It was about 1870, I do not recollect the exact date, but it was during the lifetime of the late Benjamin Haywood, that Father Boehm, then over 90 years of age, visited Pottsville and was the guest of Mr. Haywood and his wife, at their home, now the Y. M. C. A. building. Mr. and Mrs. Haywood invited Miss Rebecca Schall, formerly of Orwigsburg, who was a guest of ours at the time, and I, to meet him. We took tea with the family and had a most enjoyable visit.

"Father Boehm spoke of his first trip through this region. He came here with Bishop Asbury, of the Methodist Episcopal Church, to establish a Class. This they did along the route from Philadelphia to Sunbury, as the aged man said, "wherever two or three praying souls could be found to meet together in His name." There was no place to hold this first religious service and my grandfather offered the forge of the old Greenwood furnace. It was swept out and put in order and seats were improvised and such people as were here at the time attended with their families.

"Father Boehm, at this time, did not recollect any one in Pottsville as being here at that date except the Pott and Mortimer families. He was very bright and entertained us with stories of his experiences in the olden times and sang for us several of the old Methodist hymns that were used in the early days and great favorites with the people."

HYMN BOOKS IN CLOTHES BASKET

Miss Clarissa McCool says: "My father, the Rev. Joseph McCool, was in his early days, an itinerant Methodist Episcopal clergyman. His first work was largely of a missionary character. He traveled through parts of the State on horseback preaching to the people and endeavoring to organize, such as desired it, into classes, that were the nucleus from which the organizations of the M. E. Church in these places were afterward formed.

"My father was a circuit rider and the first preacher, after the M. E. Church in Pottsville was organized, to preach for the congregation in the old log school house, corner of Center and Race Streets. He came to Pottsville, with my mother, from Lancaster in 1830. During this year, on his own responsibility, he purchased from Col. George Shoemaker, the lot on Second Street upon which the old Methodist Episcopal Church stands and on it was built and completed, in the same year, the first M. E. Church. My father's and my mother's families were of both the Methodist and Presbyterian faiths.

"I remember to have heard my father say that the hymn books, Bibles and other books used for worship were kept at our home, and prior to worship and after it were carried to and fro by the members of the church in a clothes basket.'"

A WILD TURKEY STORY

In response to an interrogation made by the author to Dr. Edward Heiser, veterinary surgeon, he said: "Do I know any old settlers' stories? Well! if you would have asked me about thirty or thirty-five years ago, I could have related a good many.

"I kept hotel then down the turnpike and drove up to Pottsville, frequently, stopping at the Penna. Hall, kept then by William Peed.

"The office was a great place for the prominent men and old settlers of Pottsville to congregate and there were many good stories swapped by such men as Larry Whitney, Major Wetherill, L. P. Brooks, Judge Walker, Benjamin Pott, Major Huber, Oliver Roads, James Beatty and others.

On one occasion, Charles Cheny told the following story "My father, Charles Cheny, one of the first settlers, was a very religious man. He belonged to the first Class organized by the Methodists, under the leadership of Jonathan Wynn and William Mills. The class met for worship at the houses of the members, and meetings were frequently held at our home.

"I remember one time, it was on a Sunday, and Bishop Asbury, of Philadelphia, was to preach. Our family was up early and everything about the house was placed in readiness and in perfect order for the church service, which was a great event in those days. I was a small boy and rather in the way, and after being dressed in my best clothes slipped off and betook myself to a point on Sharp Mountain overlooking the town where I discovered a wild turkey pen and in it, two large, wild turkeys.

"Delighted with the find and thinking only of what a fine meal they would make for the Bishop and the other company we were entertaining, I secured them and hurried home The services were going on when I returned, but I hid the birds in a small building near the house and waited to tell my father at the close.

"It was some time before I could attract his attention and have him accompany me to the stable where the turkeys were. I related the story in high glee and expected him to commend me for having secured this addition to our larder, when to my astonishment, he said: "My son! Have I raised you only to become a thief and a Sabbath breaker? Have all my religious instructions to you been in vain? I will attend to you first, my son. Then you take those birds to the top of the mountain and free them. They are God's wild creatures and do not deserve to be trapped."

"Then followed the most tremendous whacking I ever got with a convenient barrel stave, for my father was not one who believed in sparing the rod and spoiling the child; and I sorrowfully left for Sharp Mountain, where I did as he bid me, and set the turkeys free."

"Why you infernal, young scoundrel!" said old Jeremiah Reed, the first white child born in Pottsville, (both men were nearing their four-score mark), who was one of the number that listened to the relation of the narrative, "was that you that robbed our turkey pen? Col. Shoemaker and I built that turkey pen. Turkeys were scarce and we saw by the marks that someone had robbed us. Why, your father never gave you half what you deserved.

ST. PATRICK'S R. C. CHURCH

St. Patrick's Roman Catholic Church was the first building in Pottsville erected and consecrated exclusively for religious purposes. It was a small frame structure built at a cost of less than $1,000, on a lot near the corner of Fourth and Mahantongo Streets and the present magnificent structure. The ground was donated by John Pott. Worship was held here 1827-1828, until the first permanent church was completed in 1830.

The first rectors were: Rev. J. Fitzpatrick, Rev. Edw. McCarthy, Rev. Hugh Lane, Rev. Dr. Wainwright, Rev. Edw. Maginnis and Rev. Joseph O'Keefe.

ROMAN CATHOLIC CLERGYMAN GOOD FINANCIER

The Roman Catholic population was constantly increasing and the first St. Patrick's Church completed about 1830, was soon found to be too small to accommodate the members of the growing parish. It was the only Catholic church in the county, and people came from the entire Schuylkill Valley to attend Mass here. The church would be crowded almost to suffocation and large numbers of the faithful, who could not find accommodations inside, knelt on the pavement outside, during the celebration of the Masses.

The church was enlarged several times, but it was not until other churches were built up the Valley, that relief was afforded St. Patrick's.

Abram Miessie, a prominent early resident of town, related the following story. Mr. Miessie was a shoemaker and built and owned the upper two of the block of brick houses, east side of Centre Street, between Market and Callowhill Streets. He was one of a Class that formed for the organization of the first Evangelical Church, of town, in the 'Forties.

"I was an early resident and remember when the Roman Catholic Church, at New Philadelphia, was built. I was interested in an early coal operation and went up there frequently. The priest was a fine man and very energetic. He did all he could to clear off the debt and pay for the building of the church, but the people were poor and the struggle a hard one.

"At last it was all raised except a certain sum for which he plead for in vain. One Sunday he locked the church door and placed the key in his pocket and told the assembled congregation that no one could go out until he had paid the sum of ten cents. Those that had no money could borrow from their friends. Many paid at once but others could not and those that had the cash were finally stripped of all they had by the borrowers. Twenty cents was still lacking when the bank treasuries were exhausted, when there was a tap on the window, and a hand was extended from outside with a silver quarter between the forefingers and the door was unlocked.

"A man outside who had been listening, becoming tired of waiting for his wife to prepare the dinner, furnished the quarter and the debt was cancelled."

OTHER EARLY CHURCHES

Trinity Lutheran Church was organized in 1834. Services by Lutheran pastors, from lower Schuylkill and upper Berks, wore held in Keim's Kirche and in the old lon' schoolhouse on Centre Street, in the earliest era of Pottsville and this locality. The first pastors of Trinity Church were the Rev. Wm. Minnig, who took charge 1834. The first church was dedicated October, 1837. The English Lutheran Church was organized out of this parent church in 1847. In 1850, a split occurred in Trinity Church and a number of members withdrew and organized Zions Church. The latter worshipped in a small frame church on the site of the Good Intent Fire House. The pastors of Zions Church were: Rev. C. F. Nanz. Rev. F. Walz, Rev. Julius Ehrhart. In 1864, under the latter, the two congregations reunited and Mr. Ehrhardt was retained as pastor of the congregation. During the long interim from 1834 to 1859, Rev. Wm. Minnig remained the pastor of Emanuel's Church (Trinity) except for a short period after the trouble, when he retired but was recalled.

Rev. C. F. Lampe succeeded him. He married Miss Sarah Kohler, of Pottsville. Rev. S. A. Holman, of the English Lutheran Church also married one of his congregation. Miss Fanny Hazen. The frame church on Second Street was known as "Billy" Leib's church, he having subsequently purchased it with the adjoining property, now occupied as a residence by the Lee brothers.

The remaining pastors of Trinity Lutheran Church, which was rebuilt in 1868 were: Rev. Wm. Hoppe. Rev. G. A. Hinterleitner and Rev. J. H. Umbenhen.

The First Reformed Church was erected in 1860. Prior to this time, the people of the Reformed faith were supplied with services, according to their creed, by the Rev. John Felix and Rev. H. H. Knobel, who preached occasionally in Keim's Kirche and the old log school house. The Revs. Knoll, David Hassinger, C. T. Hoffman, and J. W. Hoffmeier supplied the Pottsville and other congregations of adjoining towns, from 1836 to 1853. Others who came after were Revs. John Gautenbein, I. E. Graeff, Samuel Miller, J. C. Bucher (father of Mrs. John R. Hoffman) Kurtz, C Baum, A. S. Steckel. Trinity Reformed Church was an offshoot of this church. The latter congregation purchased what was known as "Thompson's" Church, on Market below Fourth. This edifice was called the Associate Reformed and was known as the Scotch Covenanter's Church and was built and owned by Samuel C. Thompson. It was an independent Presbyterian or Congregational church. Its members were subsequently merged into the Second and First Presbyterian Churches. The Second Presbyterian Church, organized in 1857, for a time, under the pastorate of the Rev. Samuel Colt, a chaplain in the U. S. army, in the Civil War, held services in Thompson's Hall, the third story of the building corner of Second and Market Streets, now known as the Archbald building. The congregation also worshipped in Thompson's Church. They purchased their present church building, since handsomely remodelled and enlarged, from the trustees of the Second Methodist Episcopal Church, a congregation that flourished here for a brief period, in the early days. Dr. W. S. Plummer, Dr. G. W. Smiley and Dr. O. W. Lawson were renowned pastors of the Second Presbyterian Church.

The First Presbyterian Church was organized in 1831. The Rev. Sylvanius Haight was the first pastor who served. Rev. J. A. Mines came next. He, in turn, was succeeded by the Rev. Jos. McCool. In 1832 a church was dedicated. It was a small frame structure on the northwest corner of Third and Market Streets, built on ground rent to Jacob Eyre. In 1838, the corner stone was laid for the white frame church, corner of Third and Mahantongo Streets, on the site of the present fine mountain stone structure which was built in 1872-75. The old church was completed in 1842. A delay was caused, owing to the opinion of some of the members that the foundation was insecure. The lot was purchased from John Biddle, the ground at one corner was undermined by the Charles Lawton and Samuel Lewis coal operations.

Some of the first members and attendants of the early church were the most influential and progressive citizens of the town; the Fosters, Solomon and Jesse; Oliver Dobson, David A. Smith, the Wrens, Stevenson, George Bright, Wm. Lerch, Wm. Pollock, the Thompsons and others but the church was not built and paid for without a struggle. Col. Robert H. Ramsey told many interesting stories of the early days of this church.

Col. Ramsey was subsequently a Superintendent of the Sunday School. On one occasion he related that after the building had been completed a bell was considered necessary before the work was done. Everybody had given and given again and again what they thought was their due apportionment toward the church when the women of the church volunteered to raise the money for the bell. His mother was an earnest worker and those were the days of genuine sacrifice. Mrs. Ramsey had contributed and worked for the bell but at last the amount still lacked two dollars and a half of being complete. Mrs. Ramsey made up the sum from money she had laid aside to buy a new winter bonnet and she wore her old bonnet another year. Col. Ramsey always spoke very feelingly of this and other incidents in his mother's history that told of her charitable and generous nature.

The pastors that succeeded Rev. Joseph McCool were, Rev. Isaac Riley, Rev. Prentiss De Veuve, Rev. J. W. Schenck, Rev. Jacob Belville and Rev. John Huse Eastman.

ST. JOHN THE BAPTIST CHURCH

The German Catholic Church, now one of the largest congregations in Pottsville, with one of the handsomest and most imposing buildings, began with a very humble and unpretentious origin. In 1840, Rev. Hirslaus Steinbacher came to Pottsville from Reading, on horseback, once a month to celebrate mass for the German Catholics. In 1841, a lot was purchased, corner of Fourth Street and Howard Avenue, and the stone structure, now the Italian church, was erected.

The Rev. Jos. Burg was the rector of the parish until his death, in 1849. Rev. Peter Carbon, Rev. Daniel Overholtzer, Rev. Phillip Wigmeyer, Rev. Francis Newfeld and Rev. Francis Wachter, succeeded Father Burg in the above order. Rev. Father Wachter built the present imposing structure, corner of Mahantongo and Tenth Streets. Then came Rev. Bernard A. Baumeister, from that date assistant rectors became necessary. In 1878, the present beloved and popular incumbent. Rev. Fr. F. W. Longinus, took charge of the parish, the affairs of which he has so ably administered for twenty-eight years, during which many improvements have been accomplished by him through his energetic endeavors.

The late Francis Alstatt, Adam Keith and others told many interesting stories of how the building of the first church was accomplished. The members met and cleared the lot of its timber and undergrowth. The foundation was dug through their assistance. There were some stone masons among the members and they contributed day's work or overtime toward the quarrying of the stone and the erection of the stone walls. Ferdinand Boedefeld, Francis Ackerman, Peter Well, Peter Ochs, Lawrence Fisher and Anthony Redelberger, wore among the first members.

OLD RECORDS DIFFICULT TO TRANSLATE

In searching for the past history of the County, the records of the old churches are invaluable. Most of these records are in the possession of the churches of which they form part. Some, however, were retained by the early itinerant ministers who had charge of a number of churches and traveled from place to place. If the descendants of any such still have these records in their keeping, if they will— no matter how meagre the facts— restore them to the churches they represent or to the Schuylkill County Historical Society, they will assist materially in completing or adding to their histories and in furnishing; the historical link.

The State of Pennsylvania, at present, has experts at work translating these old church records, and it is expected that several years, at least, will see the publication, in the "Archives" of these records. The new set of Pennsylvania Archives, now in the hands of the State publisher and printers, and which will be out soon, contain much that will be valuable to those searching for their ancestral line, Revolutionary War heroes, etc.

W. W. Brown, of Rock, a member of the numerous family of that name, who hold their annual reunions on the Brown ancestral acres near that place, and who is the caretaker of the records of the Summer-Berg church, the second oldest in this part of the country, says: "These old church records are very hard to read. Most of them are written half in English the other half in German. The paper is colored with age and the ink is so faded that it is almost impossible to make out the names.

"I have gone through our book many times and always find names I have not found before. It may be that in time to come I may find the names you have inquired about?"

PREACHED AGAINST VANITIES OF DRESS

Parson M___ was one of the early and ablest ministers of Pottsville. He was a God-fearing man, an earnest and zealous preacher and endeavored to carry into practice precepts upon which he dwelt in the pulpit.

His wife was a fine-looking woman and one of the most stylishly dressed of that period, in town. She wore her silks and laces with a grace peculiarly her own, and it must be admitted they were becoming to her.

She had been heard to say that she thought that, next to the consolations of religion, the satisfaction of being well-dressed came first; and that, indeed, if she had to choose between the two, she would prefer dress even before the former.

The parson argued and expostulated against this love of dress, in private, but Madame M___, otherwise an exemplary wife and obedient to his wishes in other respects, pursued the calm and even tenor of her own way in this.

One Sunday the Parson preached a sermon on humility and bore down hard upon the vanities of dress.

He was very much moved, and at the conclusion he leaned over the high board of the pulpit, and, with streaming eyes, said to his congregation:

"My dear children! You may think when I preach thus against the love of dress and the sin of it, that I ought to look at home. I want to tell you, dear friends, that I do look; and I look until my heart aches."

THE OLD TOWN HALL

The old Town Hall, on North Centre Street, was built in 1839 by the Town Hall Association. Charles Gillingham was the contractor. It was sold under a mortgage in 1840 to Messrs. Bray and Bancroft, who engaged Adam Eiler to complete it. It cost $34,000. In 1865 it was purchased by George Slater and is now owned by his son, Harry P. Slater. This building was burnt by fire, March 10, 1876, the fire originating in Mahlon Nichol's store room. It was rebuilt at once and has since been known as the Centennial Hall.

Prior to the Civil War and until the building of Union Hall, it was the rendezvous for all the balls, fairs, assemblies, theatricals and other entertainments in Pottsville, and there were many of them, for this was always a good show town. Prof. Kemmerer and Prof. Alexander, singing masters from abroad, held singing schools here for the school children and at the close of the terms gave concerts by their pupils that were largely attended by the public. The original Signer Blitz came here periodically, and Prof. Stouch taught the boys and girls how to dance in old Town Hall. Prof. Alexander was the father of Prof. James Alexander, band-leader and all-around musician, of Wilkes-Barre. He boarded with the family of 'Squire Lewis Reeser, but subsequently brought his family here.

It was here that ye olden time Old Folks' Concert was held. The singers dressed like the dames and 'squires of colonial times. It was in old Town Hall that Artemus Ward (Charles F. Browne), who came here almost unannounced, delivered his lecture to one man, John T. Shoener, District Attorney under Howell Fisher, and "Tom" sat it out and said he never enjoyed anything more. Plere Francis B. Bannan, dressed as a clown at a masquerade ball, made his famous hand-spring and jumped over the head of dignified John P. Hobart, six feet tall, and then with another jump, leaped up and turned out the gas of the chandelier.

Several resurrected invitations to these assemblies have the names of Francis B. Gowen, Matt Richards, Willis Hartz, Lewis C. Thompson, William Thompson, F. B. Bannan, Francis Parvin and William Clemens engraved on them. Another, of the Celo Patrol social club, a hop, has the names, John Clayton, Benjamin Whitney. Frank Hazzard, Charles Vandusen, of Pottsville, C. D. Elliott and James Trexler, of Reading, and Ben Snyder.

CHARLEMAGNE TOWER

"Did I know Charlemagne Tower? Why, yes!" said veterinary surgeon Dr. Heiser, "everybody about Pottsville knew him. He came here from Waterford, N. Y., where the family still maintains a country home, and was the largest owner of coal lands in the county, except P. W. Sheafer.

"Tower City was named after him. Ambassador Tower is his son, he was named Charlemagne for his father. Mr. Tower was Provost Marshal for Schuylkill County, when the U. S. troops were stationed in Pottsville, during the Civil War, to enforce the draft.

"The Tower children were raised very sensibly. Great attention was paid to their education. They had a private tutor, Prof. H. A. Becker, who came here expressly from Germany for the purpose of instructing them.

"Young Charlemagne went to military school afterward, then to college, and finally finished his education abroad at one of the German Universities.

"One of the daughters married Richard Lee, dead now, another, Thomas Alexander Reilley, son of Judge Bernard P. Reilly, of town. The family live in Philadelphia.

"Everybody in Pottsville liked the Tower family, and young 'Charlie' was generally beloved. He loves Pottsville, his birthplace, too.

"An instance of his feeling for the old home-town occurred a short time ago, when Alex. Faust and party called upon him in Berlin. He came forward at once and called 'Alec' by name, shook hands with him warmly, bade him sit beside him and then he inquired about everybody — the odd characters about town as he remembered them thirty years ago, not forgetting to ask if 'Ed. Saylor' and 'Wm. Tarr' were still living.

"No wonder Emperor William likes a man like that. A millionaire and the son of a millionaire and one of the greatest official dignitaries representing the Hnited States in a foreign country and yet not above remembering the humblest in the town of his birth.

"Oh! yes, I knew Charlemagne Tower and his son 'Charlie,' everybody in Pottsville in the 'Sixties' and the earlier part of the 'Seventies' knew them."

Note. — Charlemagne Tower was one of the most notable of Pottsville citizens. He made his fortune in Schuylkill County through the ownership and sale of coal lands, and retired a millionaire, removing to Philadelphia after his retirement, where he died.

SOCIAL AND LITERARY ADVANTAGES

The social and literary advantages of Pottsville have ever "been of the highest order. Dr. J. F. Powers, rector of Trinity Episcopal Church, strongly endorsed this statement in a clause of his sermon on "Old Home Week," Sunday, September, 1906, when he said: "Clergymen, called as they are from time to time to minister to churches in widely separated localities, have an unusual opportunity for comparing and discriminating between the people of these various communities — the tone of society — local peculiarities— social refinement and general culture. This is the expression of one in regard to Pottsville (doubtless himself) having served for three years a parish in Cambridge under the shadow of Harvard University; another for nine years in Maiden, dominated by the influence of Boston culture; still another for twelve years in the city of Philadelphia, a city never slow to assert its own superiority, he came finally as rector to Trinity Church, Pottsville, to find a congregation in every way equal and in many ways superior in education, in refinement, in social culture and religious earnestness to any congregation he had ever served. And what he found true of the congregation, he found in a large degree true of the community of which it formed a part.

"In an eminent degree the people of Pottsville are cosmopolitan. They are of the world. They know what they owe to it and what is due to them from it; with dignity they demand the one, and with promptness pay the other."

Col. O. C. Bosbyshell, former superintendent of the U. S. Mint at Philadelphia, says, "The social life during the 'Fifties was of the very best. I never knew of a town where the society was better.' The people were hospitable, intellectual, generous and neighborly."

Another in speaking of the early literary treats afforded the people adverted to the lecturers, Wendell Phillips, Henry Ward Beecher, De Witt Talmage, Artemus Ward, Schuyler Colfax, Paul Du Chaillu, Horace Greeley, John G. Saxe, Fred. Douglass, Charles Sumner, James G. Blaine, Petroleum V. Nasby and others who visited Pottsville. Josh Billings was advertised to lecture on milk. He had a huge goblet filled with the lacteal fluid to the brim on the stand in front of him, but he never said a word about it.

Then there was the first debating society that met in Thompson's Hall, where Thomas K. Bannan, Francis B. Gowen, John T. Shoener, Howell Fisher, Mat Richards, James Ellis and others met and argued on the leading questions of the day. Private theatricals and Shakespearian readings were popular. Mrs. G. W. Farquhar, mother of Guy and Fergus Farquhar, Esqs., was a great assistance in such matters. The family lived in a house on the site of the present Court House. It was erected by Archibald Ronaldson, a Scotchman and coal operator. Queer noises were heard in the night time and it was reported to be haunted. Mrs. Farquhar, who was a Von Schrader from Germany, said: "I do not mind the noises in the least. I do not believe in ghosts" and Mr. Farquhar purchased the house. It was afterwards discovered that the sounds came from the underground workings of the miners of the Pott & Bannan mine.

They afterwards sold the house to the promoters of removing the Court House from Orwigsburg to Pottsville, and the family removed to the Orchard, corner of Washington and Baber Streets, the residence now owned and occupied by Mrs. Sarah Loeser Briscoe. The John Bannan family removed to their newly built mansion, Cloud Home, in 1853 and also proved invaluable coadjutors to Pottsville society and were liberal entertainers.

FORTISSIMO VS. PIANISSIMO

Every lover of music has felt its soft and entrancing influence when from some grand organ, perhaps, the tender and soothing strains awaken the intellect to the subtle and inspiring influence of a vague harmony, that breathes to the soul a memory of some undefined aspiration or ambition that has never been fulfilled. The thought grows through the skillful manipulations of the organist, as he presents his theme from pianissimo to fortissimo and then when the emotion is at its height and mental musical pyrotechnics fill the brain and swell the soul, the imagination descends from its empyrean heights and runs the gamut of descent to the normal again as the music subsides and finally dies out.

The "Passing Regiment," too, illustrates the difference between the contending forces of sound. The band with its muffled drum beats in the distance. As it draws nearer, the music becomes plainer, until at last the sound swells to the volume of a tornado as the imaginary organization arrives in front of the house and with flying colors passes along down the street and is lost in the distance.

More than one person has suffered embarrassment at an entertainment, or perhaps in church, by trusting too much to the "ff" (double forty or fortissimo) of the music; by talking aloud when suddenly the strains ceased or became just as soft as they were loud a moment ago.

At one of the early County Public School Institutes held in Pottsville, a young man accompanied by a lady attended one of the evening entertainments.

The Pottsville Academy was crowded to overflowing and on the stage were seated the prominent instructors of the institute, with the lecturer of the evening, the School Directors and others.

Among the former was Deputy State Public School Superintendent Henry Houck, at this writing a candidate on the Republican State ticket, for the coming election, November, 1906, to the office of Secretary of Internal Affairs,

There was a loud buzz of small talk among the teachers and the orchestra was sawing away like mad, in a fortissimo passage, when the following occurred: The young woman who had been chatting to her escort, indicating Mr. Houck, said, "Who is that black-whiskered man with the skull cap on?"

"Deputy State Superintendent Houck!" yelled the Y. M.

"Deputy State Superintendent Houck!" said a soft voice in response. But alas! there was a crash, the music had ceased and quiet deep enough reigned to hear a pin drop. The audience was breathless. The Deputy State Superintendent had been called and in response he came forward to the edge of the platform and bowed his acknowledgments, awaiting the pleasure of the audience. There was no response but two very red-faced young people (the man is now a prominent Government office-holder) shrunk into the corner of their seats and subsided for the evening. Both had learned a lesson on musical acoustics that lasted them a lifetime.

* * * * * *

On a later occasion Henry Ward Beecher had been engaged to lecture before the County Institute. It was a cold evening, the train was late and Mr. Beecher just arrived and proceeded directly to the Academy. Tired out and not very enthusiastic over his subject he proceeded in a somewhat desultory fashion to demonstrate to young people, men and women, "the importance of saving the half of their earnings, no matter how small, for a start in life," when Michael Ryan, a one-armed schoolteacher, of Shenandoah, in a loud voice, interrupted him with,

"And live on bread and water?"

The effect was electrical, Mr. Beecher brightened and answered at once,

"Yes, Sir, and less if necessary." Then followed one of the most brilliant lectures of which Mr. Beecher was capable. The silvery tongued orator had been awakened and a flood-tide of glittering generalities, specialties and facts were presented in a manner that was irrefutable and permitted of no contradiction.

Mr. Ryan died a short time ago. That he had crossed swords with Henry Ward Beecher was his obituary.

SUPERSTITIONS OF SCHUYLKILL COUNTY

All peoples, lettered and unlettered, have their superstitions. The heterogeneous mass of inhabitants gathered into the two hundred thousand and over, population of Schuylkill County, seems to have centered and inculcated in its make-up the combined beliefs of the folk lore of all nations.

It is not strange that the early stories which the writer has attempted to reproduce in these pages should have been believed in the early days, but that people should still exist in the county who believe in witches and witchcraft, seems almost incredible, and yet we read in this enlightened age, September, 1906, of one, a farmer in the Mahanoy Valley, who accused a woman of bewitching his live stock. He paid her a liberal sum of money to withdraw her diabolical influence.

For thirteen months horses, cows and swine perished on his land and he was unable to fathom the cause. He had pure water on the farms, clean stables and good fodder. Veterinary surgeons could not stop the spread of death.

Whenever a witch died it was believed that her mantle descended to her daughter and she, it was believed, could cause her neighbor's baby convulsions, his cow to give bloody milk, or his horse to balk or die. Women witches had the power to turn themselves into the form of a sow, cat or rat at their pleasure. Infants who died in a slow decline were supposed to be the peculiar objects of the vengeance of witches, and many were the queer remedies resorted to effect a cure. The "Lost Books of Moses," before referred to, and a book known as "The Long Hidden Friend" (Der Lang Verborgne Freund), by John George Holman, of Berks County, contain many curious remedies for the relief of all the ills that flesh is heir to, in man and beast. Strange to say, these books are still in great demand.

POW-OW-ING

Pow-ow-ing is still largely practiced about the mines. But when it is remembered that these healers of burns are practical nurses and experienced in the treatment and bandaging of the injured parts before they recite the charm or incantation the cures they effect are not so remarkable. In the 'Seventies a woman lived at Millersville, named Mrs. Reed. Dr. Wm. Beach said of her that "She was one of the most skillful dressers of wounds." When a man was burned at the mines she could attend his case as well as any physician. It was this ability that cured or helped the man and not her pow-owing to "draw out the fire." But you could not convince believers in the occult of this.

Erysipelas, a febrile or scorbutic disease, was very much more common in the early days than now and came, perhaps, from eating too much salt meat. Everybody had the erysipelas then, like the appendicitis now, diseases, like the fashions, having their day. An old residenter, John Kimmel, who lived in a log house on the east side of the Presbyterian cemetery, of which he and his sons were in after years the sextons, was very successful in pow-ow-ing erysipelas. The writer recollects having seen him treat an obstinate case that had defied the best efforts of a leading physician and he cured it (or it went away of itself) with a lighted stick which he held over the flaming parts until it went out, pronouncing certain words and making signs. Jacob Hoffman, of

Orwigsburg, was also a noted powow-er. Both claimed their work was done through prayer, and both effected many cures.

L. C. THOMPSON

L. C. Thompson, Esq., the popular hardware dealer, contributes the following reminiscence: "My father, Samuel Thompson, was one of the first settlers of Pottsville. He came here in 1828 from Juniata County. At about the same time Burd and George Patterson also came. They were two of the most noted of the early pioneers of town and established coal and iron industries here of which you are, of course, familiar.

"My father built the brick building, corner of Market and Centre Streets, since occupied by my hardware business, where he established a general store, for the stores then kept everything. He was of Scotch-Irish parentage and was born in 1792. He was thirty-six years of age when he came to Pottsville, and was then already married. He died in 1852, at the age of sixty years. The children were: the late Colonel William Thompson; myself, Lewis C; Emily, wife of Major E. C. Baird, deceased; and Major Heber S. Thompson, Superintendent of the Girard Estate interests in Schuylkill County. We lived in the house, connected with and over the store, until after my father's death, in 1852. I was born there in 1835, when the family home on Market Street, above Third, was built, and occupied by my mother and sister until their deaths. (The house is now owned by Dr. Gillars.)

"My father owned live or six boats on the Schuylkill Canal for the shipment of coal. On the return trip they brought the goods for our store and carried other freight. One was known as the 'Old Post Boy,' another, 'The Rattle Snake,' the names of the others I do not recollect. The farmers then bought rock plaster in large quantities for the fertilization of their lands. They ground it themselves. This practice has been done away with. Phosphate and other fertilizers have taken its place and rock plaster comes already ground. All this was during the stage coach days.

"At that time John Morris, who was married to a sister of my mother, kept store on Railroad Street, between Race and Arch Streets. Their family home was on the comer of Race and Coal Streets, opposite. He removed the store subsequently to Centre Street, near the corner of Market, now occupied and owned by Mr. Rubinski. There were three Morris brothers in the mercantile business, Samuel, on North Centre, in the building now occupied by green grocer Ginther, and Richard Morris built the building known by his name, now occupied by the Dives, Pomroy and Stewart firm.

"My father was a Presbyterian. Juniata and Mifflin Counties were peopled with those of that faith. There were several others here of that church and they organized the Associate Reformed Presbyterian Church. My father gave the ground on the site of which Trinity Reformed Church now stands, and a church was built. That branch did not believe in instrumental music in churches and they sang the psalms of David as hymns. After my father's death the congregation was merged into the other Presbyterian churches.

"There were some fine people here, but it was not until about 1850 that the best social features were developed. The early days were largely occupied in the struggles incident to establishing new business ventures. The Patterson families did much toward promoting the social features. George Patterson lived on the corner of Seventh and Mahantongo, now Supt John Wood's, of the Reading shops, home; James Patterson, on the corner of Eighth, and Burd Patterson's home occupied the entire square where I now live, on the opposite side of the street, between Eighth and Ninth. Miss Mary Patterson owned and lived in the handsome home now owned and occupied bv Andrew Robertson, corner of Market and Sixth Streets. She was a maiden lady and sister of Burd and George Patterson. George H. Potts, who married a daughter of George Gumming, Esq., and sister of Mrs. George W. Snyder, afterward lived here. Mrs. Potts was in delicate health, when a severe thunder storm broke over the town. She died from the bursting of a blood vessel, superinduced by the shock of a flash of lightning which struck nearby and during which storm the thunder and lightning were terrific.

"George Gumming, Esq., father of the late Benjamin W. Gumming, and grandfather of Attorney B. W. Gumming built a fine home on West Norwegian Street, between Third and Fourth Streets, on the site of the present family home. He built here with the firm conviction that, owing to its being more level than Mahantongo, Norwegian would be the fine residence street of the town.

"The fanners would come in to town in great numbers from Fishing Creek and the Mahantongo Valley prior to the holidays. They brought large quantities of beef and pork here, for most people did their own butchering then. It was a busy sight to see the long string of wagons on Centre Street. We had a long porch, from the second story of our home on the Market Street side. On Saturdays and holidays, the town would get very rough. As children we would sometimes sit on this porch and watch the fighting going on below.

"Geist's Hotel, above, next to Hoover's store, was known as 'The Lamb.' On the S. W. corner of Second and west on Race Street stood the tavern of Natty Mills, it was called 'The Trappe.' He was a great politician and during election times the place was crowded. Natty Mills was a great character. He turned out a fine family, however. His son, Samuel, was educated at West Point. Samuel's son, Samuel, was an instructor at the same Government Institution. Another son, Paul Dencia Mills, married Miss Willing, of Philadelphia, one of the old historic families. Mrs. Lefevre Womelsdorf, mother of Aquilla and Oscar Womelsdorf, was a daughter of Natty Mills."

Part Six - Interesting Local Stories

THE UNDERGROUND RAILWAY STATION IN POTTSVILLE

In 1787 when the town of Columbia was layed out a majority of the settlers, Quakers from Bucks, Montgomery and Chester Counties settled there. The Quakers bore a decided testimony against the holding of human beings in slavery.

Lots were given free to all the colored people in the vicinity. They formed a community of their own and it was to be expected that the colored people going that way should be harbored by them.

In 1804 General Thomas Boude, of Columbia, a revolutionary officer of renown, a member of the Legislature and who had represented Lancaster and Chester Counties in Congress two terms, purchased a young slave named Stephen Smith from a man named Cochrane, near Harrisburg. The slave's mother came to live at Gen. Boude's, when her former owner attempted to kidnap her. Gen. Boude liberated mother and son shortly afterward.

Soon after a wealthy planter in Virginia liberated his slaves. There were 56 of them. They were brought to Columbia in wagons. The heirs endeavored to retain them, but after years of litigation the Virginia Legislature decreed them free. Sallie Bell, a Quaker of Virginia, emancipated about 100 slaves. They also went to Columbia.

After this period slaves began escaping in large numbers and most of them sought refuge in Columbia. William Wright, (father of Benjamin Haywood's son-in-law, Wright) was an uncompromising hater of slavery. He had a thorough knowledge of the law and a strong nerve power. He assisted all fugitives who applied to him and, after disguising them, passed them on to another Friend six miles east of Lancaster, and thus the Underground Railway began.

As the number of fugitive slaves increased pursuit was more frequent and the kidnapping of the human chattels by the owners and their agents made it imperative that a direct line to the Eastern States and Canada be layed out; and it was but natural that the slaves should be conducted from bondage to freedom by those who believed in their emancipation, the Quakers.

These earnest sympathizers were found in York, Lancaster, Chester and Montgomery counties. Phoenixville, Philadelphia, Norristown, Reading and last but not least in Pottsville. While some of these stations were not the principal or dividing depots; when the slaves arrived in great numbers they were divided and sent out in bunches or alone to the branch stations, of which Pottsville was the first north of Reading;.

There were two routes through Gettysburg and the stations close to Mason and Dixon's line were only ten miles apart. The benevolent abolitionists divided the slaves; half went to Columbia the other half to Harrisburg. The majority however came through the southern route of Lancaster and Chester Counties. When they were in danger of apprehension by pursuers they were at once distributed to more remote points, from Norristown, Phoenixville, Heading to Pottsville and on toward the east or Canada.

The slaves, many of them came direct from the more southern slave States. They traveled by night alone and were guided solely by the North Star. Some of the women had no covering except a single garment made of sacking, many of the men were without shoes or hats. They had to be secreted until they could be fed, washed and clothed and then were moved to the next Station. The great number of sick and injured were mainly cared for in Chester County. It is a notable fact that all or nearly all who assisted the slaves to freedom were members of the Society of Friends. The slaves were usually tracked to the dividing point and here all trace was lost. Some of the first pursuers stated in their bewilderment that there must be a *railroad underground* from there. This remark led to the naming of the secret system.

THE UNDERGROUND RAILWAY

If the slave hunters were not in immediate pursuit the runaways would remain for a while and work on the farms. The riot at Christiana occurred in this way. Three non-resisting Quakers who were harboring 38 of these miserable refugees were pursued by one Gorsuch, a slave holder from Maryland who with a posse of constables and about 20 whites attempted to capture them. Two men fired upon a colored woman, which was the signal for all the colored people in the neighborhood to assemble to defend those of their race. Firing began and the slave holder was killed. The three slaves who caused the trouble were raided to Canada that night.

Four lawsuits followed out of this affray. To refuse to assist in the arrest of fugitive slaves was considered under the act as "Treason" which means, in the language of the Constitution "levying war against the United States or in adhering to their enemies to give them aid and comfort."

Theodore Cuyler in his famous speech for the defense said that this force, it was claimed, levied war against the United States," and another legal authority stated that, "in this riot at Christiana and in the death of Gorsuch and the wounding of others occurred the first blood shed in the great contest of the Civil War."

Immediately after the riot the U. S. Government ordered a portion of the Marine Corps to be stationed at Christiana. The police scoured the county and arrested every person white or black who was suspected of being in the fight. Hanway and Lewis, the Quakers, who refused to assist the slaveholders in capturing their slaves were arrested for treason. They were confined in Moyamensing Prison 97 days and were then tried in the U. S. Court of the Eastern District of Pennsylvania and found "Not Guilty."

Norristown became a station in 1839 and it was after that, that refugees were sent to Reading and Pottsville.

On the 18th of September, 1850, Congress passed the law known as the Fugitive Slave Law of 1850. Zachary Taylor, then President, would not have signed it. After his death, Millard Fillmore appended his signature and it became a law.

One of its provisions was that any person harboring a negro slave on his premises as a fugitive, was liable to a fine of $1,000 for each such negro.

Under this iniquitous law Thomas Garrett in a trial before Chief Justice Taney, U. S. Court sitting in New Castle, Delaware, lost $8,000. all he had in the world. It is not to be wondered at that

FRIEND GILLINGHAM OF POTTSVILLE

preserved a discreet silence in regard to the aid he was giving the runaways and that but few except those of the Society of Friends knew of his assistance and that his home was a station on the road to freedom. Friend Gillingham was not a rich man and the tax for even one of the slaves, $1,000, was more than he could have afforded.

Friend Samuel Gillingham lived in the brick residence northeast corner of Seventh and Mahantongo Streets which he built and owned, his son Charles built the brick house northwest corner of Eighth and Mahantougo Streets, afterwards bought and occupied by Frederick Patterson now the home of Mrs. C. K. Wingert. Wm. Mardis, of town, says: "I owned a farm at Germantown but lived at Indian Run where friend Samuel Gillingham was interested in a saw mill. He had three sons, Charles, Samuel and William; and two daughters, Phoebe and Ann.

"Friend Samuel Gillingham went to Virginia where he engaged in the lumber and store business and where he died.

"His son Charles, who was also known as Friend Gillingham, and the daughters never either of them married but lived in the home property until his death and the death of the last one of the aged ladies about 1865. They were tenderly cared for by two nephews, Samuel and Charles and a niece Sallie who afterward married Edward Paxson."

Friend Samuel Gillingham is believed to have been a secret emissary of the Underground Railway System and that during his residence in Virginia he was active at the other end of the line in sending fugitive slaves North, and that through his direction they found their way to the old home, where his son Charles cared for them.

On one occasion a party of six colored persons were sent to Pottsville from Reading. Dr. Smedley, of Lancaster, is the authority for the statement, that it became imperative that they be sent at once by rail to the farthest station. They came here disguised as Quakers, their black faces covered with veils their hands with gloves. In his description of them he narrates that the youngest of the runaways, a little girl had a scoop bonnet on and as a concession to her youth there was a bunch of bright red roses pinned on it. They were harbored by Friend Gillingham.

John R. Hoffman, P. &, R. Coal and Iron Company Engineer, who bought the Gillingham property and has handsomely improved it, invited the writer to inspect the original part of the dwelling and described how it looked before being occupied by his family.

The house was a plain two-story brick, with two rooms on the parlor floor, two large and one small bedroom on the second floor and an attic. In the basement there was a kitchen and dining room. In the front the space was divided into two parts, one for a cellar, the other presumably for a pantry. The latter is a good-sized room and was undoubtedly fitted up for the refugees, as it was known by the neighbors to contain a bed, chair, table and washstand, when women were of the party it is thought they slept in the attic.

AGED RESIDENT PRESERVES SECRET

Miss Elizabeth Whitney says: "I lived with my brother, Wm. Whitney (former President of the Miners Bank) in the house next the Gillinghams, on Mahantongo Street. Colored people were frequently seen about the Gillingham house. Sometimes they did chores for the family, emptying ashes, chopping wood, sweeping the yard as if they were hired for the day; but the most of them remained pretty close in hiding or within the yard which had a high board fence. Friend Charles Gillingham was then a gray-haired man.

"Those of the neighbors who were aware of their presence preserved a discreet silence, knowing well what it might mean to the Gillinghams if the matter was made public, for there were Southern slave-holding sympathizers even in Pottsville as well as elsewhere.

"One morning I was at the window of our home and from the second story watched a large, black negro man in the adjoining yard. He saw me and seemed to become very much frightened and repaired at once to the inside of the house.

"In a few moments Phoebe Gillingham came over, her usual calm manner somewhat ruffled and she said to me: "Friend Elizabeth! Thee saw something a few moments ago in our yard. Thee knows what it means. Thee will keep silent about it for our sakes, will thee not? The man is being pursued and dreads capture."

"I assured her it should be the same as if I had not seen anything and we never spoke of what transpired around their dwelling, either before or afterward. The black people came and went through the gate on Seventh Street or the rear gate at the foot of the yard.

"I kept my promise, but Abraham Lincoln emancipated the slaves almost a half century ago and the principal actors in the Underground Railway Station in Pottsville and those that knew of it have long ago gone to their reward. I tell it now believing that it should form part of the history on record of Pottsville in its early days."

THE EARLY STAGE COACHES

There is no definite record of the year the first stage ran over the State road from Philadelphia to Sunbury. The Lightfoot survey was made in 1759.

It was the forerunner of the "Great Road" from the Falls of the Schuylkill to Fort Augusta, which was constructed in 1770. The road was built to command the Indian trade of the district included, which was already recognized as one of great wealth. It was not entirely completed until 1785, although opened in 1777, and was made to connect the Schuylkill with the Susquehanna river. Ellis Hughes, who lived at Catawissa and owned a saw mill at Schuylkill Haven, where the local branch started from, was one of the promoters, if not the instigator, of this part of the highway. Construction was commenced on the Centre turnpike in 1808; it was completed in 1812 and with it doubtless came the first stage.

It was not until 1828 that a daily mail began running between Philadelphia and Pottsville. In 1830 three lines of stages between this place and the Quaker city were competing for the patronage. The passage took 18 hours. The lines were called the "Coleman," "Reside" and the "Clover" lines. One of these was owned and run by Michael Mortimer.

William W. Mortimer, Custodian of Union Hall, says: "Of the original Mortimer family there were three brothers; William, Andrew and John Mortimer. Andrew Mortimer, who was the father of Borough Treasurer Samuel Mortimer and Nelson A. Mortimer, was postmaster in 1849. The post-office was held in the building on Centre Street, afterward occupied as a store room by James Focht and now owned by Lieberman, the dry goods merchant.

"William Mortimer, father of William Mortimer, whose sons are W. Horace, G. Wesley, Frank P. and Charles W., was my grandfather. His sons were William, G. Washington, Morgan, and Michael, my father.

William Mortimer, Sr. kept the old hotel known as the Mt. Carbon Hotel and afterwards, when it was rebuilt and owned by my father, Michael Mortimer, it was called the Mortimer House. My Uncle Washington was a partner with my father for a time. The Feathers, of Reading, were proprietors of the hotel after we went out.

"My father ran a stage line to Philadelphia and made money with it and the hotel. I was born in 1840. When I was a young man he was determined to give me a good education. Disliking the association of the hotel for a growing boy of my age he sent me to Prof. Elias Schneider's Arcadian Institute, at Orwigsburg, where I remained four years as a boarding-school pupil.

"Of the early local stages, there was one running to St. Clair, one to Minersville and Tremont, another ran from Tuscarora to Tamaqua. The Philadelphia lines stopped at our house, too, but these were discontinued with the advent of the Reading Railroad in 1849. The others ran until 1872, when the People's Railway was built to Minersville and the Schuylkill Valley branch of the Pennsylvania Railway was opened to St. Clair. Michael Weaver, hotel keeper, of Minersville was an early stage driver as was also his brother, Jos. Weaver, of Pottsville.

"A singular coincidence connected with the three drivers of these stages was that they were all lame men and cripples. The first, whose name was

John Kronse, was the worst afflicted. John Gagor was the most accommodating of men. He would take care of his drunken charges as if they were children, nurse the babies of his women patrons until they attended to business about town and would stop anywhere on his route to Minersville for passengers or bundles.

"Andy Irwin was a natural born poet or rhymster. He rhymed on everything he said and was a most comical character.

"'Here comes Andy, he loves his brandy,' (he was a sober man) or when upon taking up his lines, he shouted, 'St. Clair, we'll soon be there,' are well remembered by the patrons of the line to that village."

REMINISCENCES OF OLD SETTLERS

Daniel De Frehn, aged 80 years says: "I was born in Orwigsburg in 1825 and came to Pottsville in 1846, bought a lot, the site of my present residence, next the corner of Fourth and West Arch Streets. Col. James Nagle, afterward commander of the 48th Regt. in the Civil War, owned the corner lot and together we erected our dwellings which have both been occupied by our families, continuously, for almost a half century. I had previously built and lived in the house now occupied by Water Company Supt. Wm. Pollard, on Mahantongo "Street above Eighth.

"There was nothing but a dreary waste and a marsh on West Arch Street then; and trouble constantly arose over the course of the creek which ran along there and turned the corner toward the tannery. After every heavy rain our cellars were flooded and the Borough would do nothing to relieve the situation.

"The miners who worked at the Pott and Bannan mines all lived on Guinea IHU, in little mining cabins like those built at North America, where I worked at the erection of the houses for the 'Patch' belonging to the Centreville collieries, on the Lewis and Spohn veins. The timber was not cut off Bare Field and wild beasts roved around on the hill above Brown's Hollow.

"There were lively times in those days on Fourth of July. Daniel Klapp, a butcher who kept a stand in the old market house, in later days, was appointed a special police officer to keep order. He was a man six feet in height and weighed about 300 pounds. His appearance alone impressed evil doers with the power and majesty of the law, as he walked about in his best black suit, huge star on the lapel of his coat and heavy club in his baud, the silk hat on his head adding to his height and importance.

"On one occasion the He's, the O's and the Dutch were more than usually obstreperous and one after another were run into the town lock-up through his exertions. The Borough "jug" was in the rear part of the fire house, corner of Centre and West Race. where the Grammar school now stands. The lock-up had been filled full with a struggling mass of men fighting and cursing, all the worse for liquor, when Officer Klapp arrived with another customer. On opening the door he found the coop empty, the birds had flown. The rear wall was not very strong. The prisoners had united their strength and burst out the back wall of the structure. There were no more incarcerations on that day; there was no place to confine the prisoners.

"Those were the days when snow in winter was often two feet deep on our streets. On one particular St. Patrick's Day men went out on horseback to break the roads in order that the Ancient Order of Hibernians could parade.

"There were Indians about Pottsville as late as 1830 but they were of the harmless sort. The corner stone of the Henry Clay monument was laid July 26, 1852. There was a great parade. The firemen turned out. There were speeches and music and great crowds."

THE NORWEGIAN CREEK

The west branch of the creek which ran over parts of the upper end of West Market Street and along the base of Guinea Hill, proved very troublesome to the early settlers, who desired to build along the streets then laved out as far as Sixth Street. John Wagner, the oldest resident now living and aged 95 years, has this to say:

"I was born in the Lykens Valley, near Fredericksburg, Lebanon County, in 1811, and came to Pottsville 62 years ago. James Lick, the great California millionaire and capitalist worked at learning his trade of cabinet making in the same place, then called Stumpstown. I knew him well as a boy. In after years he had the cemetery laid out there and made other improvements. The late Peter W. Sheafer, of Pottsville, the second wealthiest man in Schuylkill County, was born and raised near that place. I learned the trade of tanning and worked at it for Wm. Wolff and his son Wallace as long as the tannery was in operation. The plant was an extensive one and occupied the present site of the new Methodist Episcopal Church, corner of Market and Fourth Streets.

"Irving Gallagher, tanner, came here at the same time. We built homes in the woods at Yorkville. I sold my house, now occupied by J. H. Williams, to the late Thomas Bannan, Esq., and removed nearer to my work. A man named Kline operated the tannery afterward owned by D. B. Seidle, at the corner of Eighth and Market Streets. These tanneries used the water of the creek which ran along there to fill their vats. We used the black oak bark which came principally to us in wagons from the vicinity of Freidensburg and Pinegrove. Wm. Wolff erected a large new dry house and increased and improved the plant at different times. He was very successful in his business and died leaving an estate worth several hundred thousand dollars, all of which was lost or swallowed up in a short time by his heirs and the business was closed.

"The west branch of the creek which ran through the tan yard and across Market Street, through a culvert, frequently overflowed and made no end of trouble. At such times Gallagher and I took torches and entered it and cleaned out the bed.

"We entered the culvert at the tan yard and went under where now stands A. W. Schalck's residence, down to the Trinity Reformed Church, where it turned over and ran under Dr. A. H. Halberstadt's house.

"There was always trouble at the archway at that turn of the creek, the dirt and offal collecting there and stopping it up. Gallagher and I came out near the Rosengarten property, corner of Third and Market Streets. We wore gum boots, trousers tucked in, but were always wet through. There was little said in those days about sewer gas, but it was a dangerous thing to do.

"There was a brick yard on the site of G. W. Mortimer's house, corner of Third and West Norwegian Streets. Fisher and Depley made bricks where the silk mill now stands. The old blacksmith shops were the great news centres of town in the early days. Men congregated around them and in the shoe shops as they do now about the cigar stores, to gossip and learn what was going on among their neighbors.

"There was a blacksmith shop at the corner of Second and Market Streets, near the Archbald building site. One near the Post Office building, another on the northeast corner of Sixth and Market Streets and one next to the English Lutheran Church. Gabe Fisher, who was a noted town character, removed to different places as the lots were bought up and finally died at his shop in the rear of the P. & R. Coal and Iron Shops, W. Norwegian Street.

"No! There were no ghosts or witches about Pottsville that I ever heard of. In the Lykens Valley, when I was a young man, there were great disputes over fences. Wherever these feuds existed the witches were said to come together at night and dance on the disputed lines and at the nearest cross roads. I went to a party one night and had to pass Koppenhaver's where the witches were said to be. It was very dark and late when I came home. As I neared the place I saw something white coming toward me. I did not run, I could not. "When it came close I found it was a white calf."

FOUGHT THE READING COMPANY

"To keep the telephone people from planting their poles on your property by sitting on the spot is nothing new. When the Schuylkill and Susquehanna branch of the Reading Railroad was first surveyed and laid out from Reading to Harrisburg, a woman did something greater. She prevented a great railway company from building their new line over a point on their farm, where her father lay buried. She was a widow with two children. The farm from which we had considerable black oak bark for the tannery, lay beyond the Summit near Auchey's.

"The engineers surveyed directly over her father's grave and told her to remove the remains, the company would pay the damages and the route of way over the farm would be assessed and she would be awarded its market value. The woman refused. The grave should not be disturbed, the road could not pass over that spot. For two weeks, night and day, she camped beside it, the children bringing her such necessaries as she needed from the house and attending to her wants. At her side was a heavily loaded rifle and she threatened to shoot the first man that attempted to come near the enclosure.

"In vain the surveyors and officials tried to parley with her. The gun was loaded for bear and no man's life was safe. At the end of that time the route was changed and the road ran farther down, the declivity. The lonely grave on the knoll may still be seen from the car window as the train passes by the spot.

"Fourth of July was a great holiday in the early days. The main streets were trimmed with spruce and evergreens and the houses were decorated with red, white and blue bunting. There was a parade of the military in the morning. The fire department turned out. A hay wagon trimmed and filled with little girls and a goddess of liberty in the centre represented the States. Stands selling root beer, cakes and mead, peanuts and candy, were strung along the curbstones. The Declaration of Independence was usually read. In the afternoon, when many had taken something stronger, free fights were frequent and a fire at night often finished the day."

STAGE COACH DAYS

Mrs. Annetta Brobst, wife of Daniel Yeager and daughter of Christian Brobst, who died several years ago, at the age of 83 years, had a remarkable memory. She related many interesting incidents of the early days:

"My father. Christian Brobst, of Orwigsburg, built the stone house corner of Centre and West Norwegian Streets, afterward owned by Wm. Mortimer, who kept a general store there, and now occupied by his sons F. P. and Horace Mortimer as dry goods and jewelry stores. My father was a harness maker and did a large business employing one man alone to work on ladies' saddles. He had as high as fourteen men at work in his shop at one time.

"He invested in coal lands and owned tracts afterward deeded to the Ridgways, Samuel Sillyman and John Bannan. There was trouble after his death, I never knew or understood exactly what it was but the lawyers came again and again to examine the papers we held and to investigate what claims we had to the titles. There was treachery somewhere among the Brobst heirs, some of whom must have sold their birthright for a mess of pottage. The Brobst lawsuits have proven at least that much. My grandfather was William Zoll, the first settler of Pottsville after the Neimans.

"I remember coming to Pottsville in the stage before we moved here and also taking the trip to Philadelphia from Orwigsburg in the stage; which was a great thing for a young girl. My father took me to Philadelphia. We were two days going and the same time returning. Part of Centre Street was a corduroy road over the swampy and marshy ground. The stage stopped at a small stone tavern, afterward bought and enlarged by Wm. Mortimer, Sr., and known as the Mortimer House. There was a plank on stilts from the block where the stage stopped to walk across to the tavern, the gutter and street being nothing but a pond or mud hole in wet weather.

"I recollect when my father, at one time, had a sick spell and I waited upon him. He was feverish and asked at night very frequently for cold water. There was a town pump at Hannah Gough's, near the site of the Reading Railway depot, and another on the corner of Centre and Market Streets, where the L. C. Thompson hardware store now is. I went out at night to the latter to get him a pitcher of fresh water but he insisted that the water at Hannah Gough's was so much fresher. I went down there but was very much afraid, owing to the roughness of the locality, most of the places from Centre to the Railroad being saloons. No one harmed me and father recovered again. There was much malaria owing to the swamps. Centre Street was raised a number of times and the early settlers built as high as they could.

"My father, Christian Brobst, built the three first houses on that corner, the two adjoining our own and afterward owned by the Jeannes heirs and subsequently by Jacob Miehle. My brother, Perry Brobst, and husband, Daniel Yeager, were both saddlers and followed the business in Pottsville. There was a brick yard on the site of the Pennsylvania depot and afterward a carriage factory. The road about the Beading depot at Hannah Gough's was corduroy to the canal and mill. The creek from Market Street ran over from Third Street and under the White Horse tavern, corner Centre and Mahantongo Streets. Its course was changed where the Borough built the culverts and it ran under Centre Street. The Philadelphia and Beading Bailway Company also changed the course of the main branch of the creek when they built the branch road on Railroad Street. The coal on this road from the Delaware and other mines was run down by gravity and mules took back the empty cars."

THE MORTIMERS AMONG EARLIEST SETTLERS

Borough Treasurer Samuel M. Mortimer has many recollections of the early days and remembers much that was handed down to the present generation, from hearsay. He says: "My father, Andrew Mortimer, brother of William Mortimer, Sr., built this house (near corner of Twelfth and Market Streets), in what was then a dense woods. I was born here and have lived in the same house almost continuously for seventy odd years. John Wesley Mortimer, Jack Temple, Pott & Bannan and a man named Miller operated the coal mines on Guinea Hill. I remember often to have walked into the old drift from West Arch Street, a gang-way having been left open in the vicinity of Seventh Street, as late as in the 'Sixties. A manway, too, existed in the rear of the old brick school house, corner of Fifth and West Norwegian Streets, where I went to school. The boys often crawled down it to recover their balls and in the earlier days the miners entered the mine from that point if they were working at this end. I remember to have seen them with their lamps on their heads.

"George H. Potts and Job Rich worked the York farm veins. The Minersville Street School House was built on the site of an old colliery and the veins worked by Charles Lawton, undermined the very heart of Pottsville. The gangways coming from the Salem colliery at Young's Landing were still exposed in the rear of the P. and R. Coal and Iron Shops; when improvements were made to extend the shops, they ran under Greenwood Hill; the Potts, McKechner and others worked these veins. A coal breaker stood in North Centre Street, at the corner near the gas house.

"The school referred to was only for boys. Christopher Little taught there and had as an assistant a man named Kutchin. The boys called him 'Little Billy.' Joseph Bowen, in after years Borough assessor, was a teacher. Small boys wore gingham aprons in those days and would sit for hours in school passing a slate pencil through the hems.

"How I hated those aprons, but my mother insisted upon my wearing one. There was a large flat stone in the vicinity of the old water basin, now Yuengling's Park, and under it I hid my apron, returning for it after school. I carried on this deception for a long time but was finally exposed after returning home several times without it.

"I learned my trade of hatter with Oliver Dobson and Nicholas Fox. We made fine wool hats and afterward nothing but silk hats, all hand made and for which there was a great demand. John G. Hewes also learned the trade but never worked at it. I was in the hat business for years until I disposed of the stand and good will to my nephew, C. W. Mortimer.

"Those were lively days in politics. When Henry Clay, the great Whig leader who opposed the annexation of Texas, was defeated and James K. Polk, of Tennessee, the Democratic candidate who favored it was elected, the Whigs were opposed to adding any more slave States to the Union. A barbecue was given by the Democrats on the vacant lot at the corner of Eleventh and Market Streets. A whole ox was roasted. That was in 1844.

"In 1848 when Taylor and Fillmore were inaugurated and in 1856 when Jimmy Buchanan went in there were ox roasts in Garfield square. I was a Democrat then. There were live political clubs formed that marched about during the presidential campaigns shouting and singing for

"'Tippecanoe and Tyler, too.'

"Nathaniel Mills, was a great local politician. He was a rabid Democrat. He went west for a time when gold was discovered in California and returned a Black Whig. The Democratic clubs had it in for him and marched around singing:

"'Oh! Poor Natty Mills,
"Oh! Poor Natty Mills,
Give him a dose of castor oil.
And then a dose of pills.'

"Harry K. Nichols, late chief engineer of the P. & R. R. W. Co., was born in Pottsville the same year I was. His father, Lieut. F. B. Nichols, of the United States Navy, who was active during the war of 1812, built the house on Market Street now occupied by the Y. M. C. A. It was subsequently owned and occupied by the late Benjamin Haywood, who with Lee and Harris formed the firm that operated the Palo Alto Rolling Mills and were with George W.

Snyder and Wm. Milnes, iron founders and coal operators, some of our leading capitalists and most enterprising business men and foremost citizens.

"Those were the days before the Government exacted a tax on spirituous liquors. The farmers, many of them, had their own stills and were moonshiners. What they could not sell of their grain and corn they turned into whiskey and brought it to town to the stores to trade for or sell as part of the results of their agricultural pursuits. Some of the leading families of Pottsville, today, owe their present prosperity and share in large estates to this early traffic in whiskey. The first brewery I knew of was one on the river road to Port Carbon rim by A. Y. Moore. The founder of the Yuengling plant began in a very humble way on Schuylkill Avenue, in the rear and above the present brewery. He manufactured and retailed his first stock. The Lauers' opposite the Hospital came afterward and the Market Street, Mt. Carbon and another brewery near Mechanicsville, still later.

"Circuses often visited Pottsville. They held forth in the vacant block in Garfield Square opposite the English Lutheran Church. The crowds were large and there was no trouble reaching the shows."

OLD TIME SCRAPPERS

George W. Eiler, former foreman at the P. R. C. & I. Shops, now retired, tells the following story: "My father, Daniel Eiler, came to Pottsville in 1846. He built the brick residence next to the corner of Eighth and Mahantongo Streets where our family lived for more than a quarter of a century. Among the many stories he told me of the early days, was one about the old time scrappers.

"There was a great rivalry between Berks and Schuylkill Counties as to which could claim the strongest man, the best fighter in a pugilistic encounter, the best pedestrian and the most powerful man in a hand to hand fist fight.

"Pottsville put up Jonathan Wynn, a blacksmith for Potts' and a well known Methodist class leader, for Wynn could both, fight and pray, and Berks County backed as their man (his name I have forgotten) a regular bully with a big reputation.

"A day was set for the fight. At a given hour the two men set out from Reading and Pottsville and walked toward each other, each man was accompanied by his backers and friends. They met at a point near Hamburg. Wynn not only walked the greatest distance in the given time, but he did up the Reading bully in such a shape that he was never heard of in Pottsville again, and Jonathan Wynn was for a long time known as the champion all-around fighter of Schuylkill County.

"Those were the days when the early constables of the county would walk thirty or forty miles to serve a writ and think nothing of it. If they could get a friendly lift from the driver of a farmer's wagon they accepted, but seldom depended upon it. They had their own routes over the mountains and by circuitous paths, and covered great distances. Among these were Christian

Kaup, of the Brunswicks; William Boyer, of Orwigsburg; Peramus Brobst, a mail carrier; Stephen Rogers, constable, of Pottsville, and others.

"A branch of the Schuylkill Canal, which ended at Port Carbon, ran along Coal Street to a point opposite the coal and iron shops. There was a landing there for the loading of the boats with the coal that came down from the Delaware. There was a mill race near this point to the old grist mill.

"In 1813, several small openings were made around Pottsville for the digging of coal. The article, taken out, was sold to the blacksmiths and others in the neighborhood for 25 cents a bushel at the pit's mouth. The shafts were sunk only a few feet into the crop of the vein and the coal was raised by means of the common windlass and buckets.

"It was not until 1823 that coal was found on Guinea Hill, where horse power was first used as an improvement on the windlass. The railroad was not built nor the canal completed and the common method of transportation was by horse and wagon. Later years brought with them the newer improvements in mining and increased facilities for transportation.

"In 1842, the Pott and Bannan mine on Guinea Hill was considered one of the best in the region. It was known as the "Black Mine." Its veins in the upper lifts were soon exhausted, and not desiring to dig deeper, the working was abandoned. People were curious to see the operation of mining and visitors were frequent. It was here that the Rev. A. Pryor, a retired Episcopal clergyman, who lived at the comer of Fifth and Market Streets, met with an accident through which he was lamed. He had been visiting the operation when the accident occurred.

"There were many of the first business men who came here penniless that left their families well-to-do and even wealthy, some of the present estates held by their descendants having had very humble beginnings. These men were of the sturdy sort, and like all self-made men, were more or less proud of their own work — the carving out of their own fortunes. Many good stories could be related of their thrift, economy and foresight and the sagacity shown in their investments. Among them were: Samuel Thompson, merchant; Wm. E. Boyer, J. D. Woolison, Nathan Wetzel, tobacconists; the Fosters and Daniel Schertle, shoe dealers; David Yuengling, brewer; Joseph Shelly, boat yard; Clemens, Parvin and L. F. Whitney, steam mills; Joseph Stichter, tinsmith; and Daniel Esterly, hardware. The Morris', merchants; John Crosland, who took the first boat load of coal to New York and others. Some of these met with heavy reverses in after life."

THIRTY THOUSAND COPPER PENNIES

Squire J. W. Conrad relates the following: "My grandfather, J. W. Conrad, who came here from Germany, was a Justice of the Peace for many years. He spoke French fluently and was acquainted with some of the dialects of the Gennan confederation and those of Southern Europe, although German was his mother tongue. He was called on frequently to write or translate letters from one language into another and to straighten out matters, legally, for the early foreigners. He conducted a foreign steamship agency at his office next to the corner of Third and Market Streets. Owing to his knowledge of the European ports and his acquaintance with different languages this branch of his business proved a very lucrative one. Those were the days when abstracts of lands were written out and there were no printed forms of deeds. A Justice worked hard, there was so much transcribing.

"'Jimmie' Sorrocco, an Italian, was an early organ grinder. He delighted the children of those times with his barrel organ, which he carried about on his back and rested on a stout oaken stick while he ground out the few tunes in its scant repertoire.

But it was not 'Pop Goes the Weasel,' nor 'Home, Sweet Home,' that the youngsters cared particularly about; but the pet monkey that amused them with its antics, capering up the sides of houses and porches to gather up the pennies given it.

"Sorrocco lived on Guinea Hill, in the locality known as Italy, where he and his wife kept a boarding house for their countrymen. They were very frugal, particularly Catalina, who kept cows and sold milk to add to the family revenue. Catalina was a great beauty, with olive-brown skin, big black eyes and heavy coal-black hair. At times 'Jimmie' became very much incensed at the admiration she excited and the attention she received from his visitors.

"This seemed only to amuse Catalina and she would laugh, showing her great white teeth and shaking the long gold earrings in her ears as she measured out the milk from her bright cans, for she was a clean and industrious woman. Then she would tell her patrons in the soft tongue, she knew very little English, 'Jimmie so jelly, so jelly,' meaning jealous.

"When the couple purchased the property at Eighth and Laurel Streets, known as Tittle Italy,' my grandfather conducted the transfer and made out the deed. The price was three hundred dollars and it was paid for with thirty thousand pennies, the large copper pennies, bigger than a twenty-five cent piece, then in circulation. They had all been gathered together by Sorocco and his barrel organ and the monkey, and were saved by Catalina.

"The pennies were weighed, but as some were worn more than others the result did not even up and they were subsequently re-counted. It took a half day with several at work to figure out the amount.

QUEER CHARACTERS

"There were many queer characters about town. One of these, 'Jake' Danes, a harmless, half-witted man, who acted as 'boots' about the old Mortimer House, was the terror of the children. The mere mention that 'Jake' Danes was coming that way would scatter a whole neighborhood at play in a few minutes. 'Jimmy the fiddler,' was another. He was addicted to his cups, but as his name indicated, sometimes played for dances. Doctor Bobbs (not Boggs) was another. He was a lame negro paralytic and shook all over when he shambled about. He sold corn salve and was the sandwich-board man of his time. No parade was complete without Doctor Bobbs bringing up the rear covered with advertisements.

"'Jimmy Donnegan,' a good workman and a member of the old 'Hydraulian' fire company, was a terror to everybody when under the influence of liquor. He was a strong, broad-shouldered, well-built young man and rather good looking, and few cared to tackle him when he was in his fury. He was incarcerated one night in the old stone lock-up in the rear of the 'Drollies' fire house, next to the old stone school house for girls, corner of Centre and West Race Streets, for safe-keeping.

"Neglected the next day, his thirst after his spree became almost intolerable and he made the neighborhood hideous with his yells and curses but no one relieved him. Recess came and the girls filed out and gathered below the grated window above, where Donnegan appeared and plead:

"For the love of God, give me a drink of water, I am dying of thirst!'

"The girls were afraid and the window was high when one of the most venturesome — now a well-known and sturdy matron of North Second Street, with several grown up sons — matured a plan. The girls stood together, 'London Bridge,' she mounted on their shoulders and others filled the pint tin-cup which 'Jimmie' took from her hand and drank through the iron bars. When the bell rang he was still pleading for 'more, more,' like Oliver Twist."

CURFEW SHALL NOT RING TO-NIGHT

"A curfew ordinance would be nothing new for Pottsville. When the Borough streets were lighted with small oil lamps inserted in the old glass enclosed lamp posts, it was customary to outen these lamps at ten o'clock. At each corner as the watchman, who carried a small ladder to ascend the lamp-posts, outened the lamp, he cried in a loud voice: 'Past ten o'clock,' and the people were expected to be in their houses and ready to retire. Those abroad after that hour were looked upon with suspicion and few cared to brave the darkness of the streets. Corporation moonlight meant something then.

"Opposite our home, on West Norwegian above Eighth Street, the greater part of the square was enclosed with a high paling fence which extended from Norwegian to Mahantongo Street. It was known as 'Russel's Field' and was at first enclosed and cultivated. Crops of corn and potatoes were raised in it by the owners. The huge driving gate had accidentally been left open one night and an individual, rather the worse for John Barleycorn, had lost his bearings and wandered into the field.

"It was a dark night after twelve o'clock when the neighborhood was aroused with the loud yells of one in distress and the oft-repeated cry:

"H___ where am I? H___ where am?"

"The neighbors arose and some procured lanterns and proceeded to the source of the alarm, when a man was found halfway between the square on Ninth Street, inside the field. He had wandered in the gate and was clinging to the palings of the fence, which he had followed around to that point. He was piloted to the street by my father, who took him part way toward his home.

"The early watchmen in those days were brave men. They encountered many toughs in their rounding up of the town but there was little burglary that I remember. The watchman were, Elijah Quinn, a powerfully built man, Wm. Stout, Daddy Meyers, Jacob Mervine and Wm. Beidleman. Chief of Police George Smith came afterward."

ORIGIN OF GHOST STORY

A Pottsville lady, who desires to be nameless, relates the following:

"My father and mother, came here in the early days from Chester County. We lived first at Mt. Carbon, soon after the opening of the Schuylkill Canal. My father was an old-time printer, although he subsequently engaged in the confectionery business and other branches before his death which occurred while he was still in the prime of life.

"Near our home stood a large stone house that had a bad reputation. It had been used as a company boarding house during the building of the Mt. Carbon Railway. After the boarders left, the family contracted small-pox and several members died of the disease. The father and owner becoming discouraged left and went to New York where he worked on the Erie Canal.

"Houses were scarce but no one would rent the big stone house. Strange noises were heard there and it had the reputation of being haunted.

"Once a week, on publication night, for the newspapers of town were all weeklies then, my father was at work all night. Before going to the office he would fill the pail with water from the neighborhood pump for use until morning.

"One evening he left without having performed this little office, forgetting it probably and my mother discovered late at night that there was no water for the children, who were certain to ask for a drink.

"Passing the stone house on her return she heard the strange noise that had so often been described. She set the pail down and softly crept into the house through an open window.

"Here she saw — not a ghost but a frugal German who was building a house for himself nearby, hard at work with an axe cutting out the joists for his own use. The house on examination, afterward, was found to have been dismantled, too, of its doors and other appurtenances.

"My mother left as quietly as she came but the agent of the property was notified and the stone house, though ruined, was no longer haunted."

INDIAN STORY

The early settlers related that an Indian village stood in the locality lying between what is now Centre Street and the railroad, between East Market and East Arch Streets, another stood on the site of the Charles Baber cemetery. Indian arrows and cooking utensils were found at these points. At Indian Run there was a large settlement and wigwams were pitched along the Swatara creek. On Fourth Street there were stones placed around Sharp Mountain by the Indians. They were called Indian steps. They may still be seen. There were not many Indians in this locality, yet the life of the early settlers was one of constant struggle with the roving bands of red marauders. As late as 1825 there were still a few red men in this vicinity, but they were harmless. Of one of these Mrs. B. W. Cumming, Sr., says her father-in-law, George H. Cumming, a member of the Society of Friends and an early settler, related the following:

"The Indian was known as Tecumseh and was an idle and dissolute fellow who lived on the hill above the Odd Fellows' Cemetery. He was detected in stealing from a neighbor, and with his wife was brought before a Justice of the Peace to answer the charge of theft. The poor squaw broke down and sobbed and cried like her white sisters might have done under a similar circumstance. This disgusted the red man who said to the 'Squire:

"'Squaw no good. She cry. Me no squaw, me Injun brave, me not cry. Ugh!'

"Tecumseh was let go, a bystander paying the costs and fine imposed."

THE FIRST PHYSICIANS

Dr. A. H. Halberstadt, who is the last of his generation of leading Pottsville physicians, which included such practitioners as Doctors J. C. Swaving, J. T. Carpenter, D. W. Bland, C. H. Haeseler and Samuel Berluchy, had just returned from the Pottsville Hospital, where he had performed a delicate operation upon a prominent Tremont resident, when the writer ventured to call upon him.

The doctor has long passed his —th birthday but his tenacious grip on youth still enables him to do a tremendous sight of work and he is still as busy and active as he was at any time in his long and useful medical career.

"I would rather wear out than rust out," is one of his mottoes for the promotion of good health and a well-rounded-out longevity.

Knowing from previous experience that he had an appreciative listener, which is far better than being a good conversationalist on such occasions, he at once launched on a technical description of the surgical case in hand and the complications encountered. The operation was a success. (The man is alive and well to-day.)

From that story he gradually drifted into a history of hydropathy, osteopathy, the origin of homeopathy. Christian Science and almost every other known form of pathology, all of which, it is a matter of regret, cannot be reproduced here, for Doctor Halberstadt is a most interesting conversationalist and fluent talker when he warms up to the subject.

During this time he waited upon several office patients that had been awaiting his arrival, attended to a business caller and dismissed another social visitor; between whiles answering several calls on the two phones in his private offices, and keeping up a running but by no means a desultory conversation in the interim.

"You want to know about the early physicians of Pottsville? Why, of course; why didn't you tell me at once?

"Too much interested in what I was saying? Oh! well, I must think about them first.

"My father, Dr. George Halberstadt, came to Pottsville in 1830. His colleagues in the first years were: Doctors McCullough, Sorber, William Tweed and Zaccur Praull. Col. Zaccur P. Boyer, born in Port Carbon, was named after the latter.

"The Pennsylvania State Medical Association was formed in the early 'Forties. It was the parent of the Schuylkill County Medical Society, of which my father was the president for five years. It was formed in 1846.

"In 1832 the cholera was raging in Philadelphia. It broke out in Pottsville with several virulent cases. On the northwest corner of Twelfth and Mahantongo Streets stood a block of working-men's houses. They were built of stone, whitewashed white and were two and a half stories in height, with dormer windows in the upper story, which was unfinished. Here the first Pottsville Hospital was established by my father for the care of cholera patients who were isolated in the upper story of that building. The name, the Pottsville Hospital, clung to the block until it was demolished, after its last owner, Oliver Dobson, had disposed of it.

"Dr. George Halberstadt built our present family home and the adjoining houses about 1838. After my marriage I opened practice and lived in a building on the site of the house occupied by my son, Dr. G. H. Halberstadt.

"Dr. Cecil Berryman was an early physician. He lived on Centre Street, where the Green jewelry store is, or adjoining, and also at the corner of Third and Mahantongo Streets. He was injured in an accident by a runaway horse, from the effects of which he subsequently died. His wife maintained herself with a fancy dress goods and trimming store on the northwest corner of Third and Market Streets. Another early doctor was Dr. Brady, who lived in and built the Charlemagne Tower house now occupied by Baird Snyder.

"Col. Anthony Hagar and John T. Nichols, (the latter lived in the brick house next door to Captain D. H. Seibert) were both surgeons in the Civil War and good doctors.

"Dr. James S. Carpenter. Sr., came to Pottsville about the same time my father did. There were, of course, many others and if I should include the county physicians they would fill a volume.

"Drs. D. J. McKibben, Henry C. Parry, Henry Pv. Sillyman, Thomas Turner, J. B. Brandt, J. D. Brantner, C. P. Herrington, J. F. Kern, Douglas R. Bannan, a young man of great promise, were among the early doctors.

"There were a number of druggists, too, who acted as physicians, some were intelligent men and others were quacks. There was a Doctor Spear here who for a time cut a broad swath. He was smart, too smart, and landed in jail branded as a forger and counterfeiter and subsequently was convicted and served a term of imprisonment in the Eastern Penitentiary. During his trial in the Schuylkill County Courts his counsel set up a plea of insanity.

"In presenting the proofs of his client's condition his lawyer entered the plea that Spear was demented because he asked for a turkey and plum pudding dinner in jail on Thanksgiving Day.

"I will tell you of Dr. G. W. Brown, of Port Carbon, who was one of the best physicians the county ever had. He did not like Dr. Samuel Berluchy, who was an especial friend of mine.

"What was that? You remember how Dr. Berluchy looked? Oh! Yes! I believe the ladies of those days all thought him handsome.

"He was a tall, large, well-made man. Stout, but with not an ounce too much flesh for his height. Smooth face and with skin as fair as a babe's and heavy, wavy, jet black hair. He was cultured and refined, had genial manners and was very companionable; everybody liked him except Brown, whose reasons were solely professional.

"Dr. Berluchy came here from. Gettysburg. His father had been a surgeon in the army of Napoleon and the son studied privately under Harmer, the great anatomist at the U. P., Philadelphia. Berluchy was a widower, he had been married to a member of the Flood family, a wealthy and cultured Roman Catholic family of Philadelphia.

"His last illness came in the prime of life. I attended him and knew he would die. I effected a reconciliation between my patient and Dr. Brown and two better pleased men you never saw.

"After Dr. Berluchy's death. Dr. Brown was taken ill. Knowing more of the former's good qualities and capability than any man in Pottsville, I considered it a duty to write his obituary.

"Shortly after, I met Dr. Brown, who had recovered, and said, 'Well! Brown, I am glad to see you out again.'

"'Yes,' said the testy old chap, 'I fooled you, didn't I? You thought you would have a chance to write an obituary for me and cover me over with beautiful flowers like you did Berluchy, but I was too smart for you.'

"The obituary had gone in the 'Miners' Journal' as the newspaperman's work (C. D. Elliott's) but Dr. Brown understood the technical language and recognized my hand."

LET THERE BE LIGHT

The advance from the primitive stages of artificial light all came within the scope of the early settlement of Pottsville up to the present time. The "Schmutzomsel," an iron receptacle with chain attached to suspend it to the wall or ceiling, with the rush tallow dips, were the first lights used. The former was filled with any fat or grease in which was inserted a wick or rag to burn. Then came the crude oil and camphene or fluid lamps. Many burned the common tallow candle solely owing to the danger connected with the use of fluid.

In 185 — a beautiful young lady, one of the belles of Pottsville, was burned to death through the use of camphene. She was filling the lamp whilst holding it in her lap and it in some way ignited and exploded, scattering the fluid over her clothing, which took fire and parts of her body were burned almost to a crisp. She was engaged to be married and her untimely death created great consternation among the users of that death-dealing source of illumination and many householders banished the fluid lamp and camphene canteen at once and forever from their premises.

* * * * * * *

The thriftiness of the early settler was something not to be sneezed at and would be little understood in these days of easy access to the stores and plentitude of supplies for the family cooking. When Peter Peterpin first came to Pottsville he boarded with a family of whom he was very fond. The wife, a hardworking and industrious woman in addition to cooking for her own family kept several boarders.

One day Peter chanced home early to dinner. The main dish was a generous part of a boiled ham to which were cooked dried string beans and potatoes, a toothsome dish in winter for a hungry man, when well cooked.

Just as the boarding mistress was dishing up the dinner, she discovered that a little mouse, that had in some way gotten into the bean bag, was cooked along with the mess. It was the work of an instant to take the rodent by the tail and throw it into the swill pail.

Peter was enjoined to silence, there was nothing else in the house to cook and the meal was served and as usual enjoyed by the men. The cook and the former, however, confining themselves to bread and butter and coffee. Peter had lost his confidence in his boarding mistress and whether this was an added incentive for his marrying soon after is not related.

* * * * * * *

The road from Pottsville to Sunbury was traveled extensively by the drovers and the dealers in cattle, in the early days, made the trip frequently on horseback with their outrunners of boys and men to corral the steers and hogs. One of these, the founder of a leading wholesale establishment in Pottsville and who retired from the business a wealthy man, said, "there is no animal in the brute kingdom as stubborn as a hog.

"When I was a young man in Germany, where I learned the trade of butchering, I could do any hard work but when it came to killing I always sickened and was compelled to leave the job to others. My employer said nothing but after a time turned me out alone with a large drove of hogs to take them to a dealer forty miles away. I could never relate all the trouble I had with those hogs. They strayed everywhere and would not keep the road but I finally delivered all but two that were drowned. Although I never cared to do it, ever after that I could kill a hog as easily as I could look at one."

OLD HISTORIC MANSION

Home of Burd Patterson, Esq.

No description of the early history of Pottsville is complete without a reference to Burd Patterson, Esq., and the fine old mansion he occupied over a half century ago.

Mr. Patterson came here from the vicinity of Royers Ford and was a large owner of tracts of coal land in the Schuylkill and Heckscherville Valleys. He was also interested in the Pioneer furnace and other business enterprises. He was one of the most enterprising of Pottsville's foremost citizens and did much to further the advancement of its business interests. He had two sons, James and Joseph, who were engaged in the coal business with their father. His brother George, who came to Pottsville with him, had been married twice and had a large family of sons, the adults of which were also engaged in the coal and iron business. Edward, Frederick, Stewart, William, Theodore, James, Duncan and the scions of the younger branch of the family and the descendants of the first named, made an important clan in the old coal town.

Burd Patterson was a direct descendant of James Patterson, who came to America in 1714 from Salisbury, England, and settled in Lancaster County. He was a grandson of Edward Shippen, the first Mayor of Philadelphia, and of Col. James Burd, of the Colonial War, for whom he was named. With such distinguished parentage and with large means at his command, together with his business prestige — he was a fine old-school gentleman, dignified, yet affable and easy of approach — Burd Patterson was a power in the community and "The Pattersons" cut a prominent figure in the social circles of town.

The Burd Patterson mansion, now occupied by Wm. Lewis, Esq., former Superintendent of William Penn Colliery, stood alone in the square, south side of Mahantongo, between Eighth and Ninth Streets and occupied the entire block. That and Cloud Home were considered the handsomest mansions in town. The latter was built later. It was built on a knoll (the street has since twice been raised) terraced in front and with handsome flower gardens. On the east side, on Eighth Street, on the site of the residence of L. C. Thompson, stood a white frame structure used as an office building for the Patterson's coal and other business interests. This was for many years in charge of Owen Keenan, clerk.

On the west side, on the site of the Riollay Lee mansion, was a large enclosure with a high board fence, the vegetable garden of the estate. In the rear was a fine grove of tall pine trees, some of them are still standing, that made a beautiful background to the imposing picture. A natural spring of water from Sharp Mountain furnished the supply for the house to which it was conveyed in pipes from a small covered reservoir on the grounds. So great was the source that a pipe from it to the front pavement ran almost constantly and provided drinking water for not only the surrounding neighborhood but water was carried in pails from the spring by people to West Race Street, where the poorer population and colored people lived in the early days, their houses having no water facilities. The water was cold and was in great demand in the days when ice was not in general use. Patterson's spring had a great reputation, too, as a trysting place for lovers. A fine avenue of trees lined the curbstone and the square was a rendezvous for walks in summer time.

AN EARLY ROMANCE

If Plato had seen Rose Sheelej he would have been more than ever convinced that, "beauty was a delightful privilege of nature," as he is quoted to have said, when he taught the boys and girls of Athens. Rose was tall and symmetrical in figure, and graceful in movement. Her skin was of a milky-whiteness, her hair brown, her teeth white and even, her eyes a deep blue-gray. She was of a quiet, retiring nature, almost a recluse at times and yet had many admirers.

The family lived in the old stone house, on the brow of "Guinea Hill" at the head of Twelfth Street, opposite Samuel Heffner's. The father, a German, was the gardener at the Burd Patterson mansion.

Rose Sheeley, like every other pretty girl, had a lover, whom, as the sequel shows, she adored. Her father objected to this lover and provided another suitor for her hand in marriage, whose claims he strenuously pressed and whom he attempted to compel her to marry.

Poor Rose grew very morbid over the situation and one day after a stormy interview with her father repaired to Tumbling Run dam and drowned herself. She jumped into the water from a small pier jutting into the dam from the centre of the breastwork of the first dam. When her body was found, which was not without great effort, she was discovered to have tied a shawl about her waist and filled it with heavy stones that her body might sink the more quickly.

Her lover, a sturdy citizen, who married afterward and raised a large family, now grown-up men and women, was most beside himself with grief at Rose's sad ending but the suitor provided by her father quietly disappeared from town. The excitement over the suicide was very great. Hundreds visited the scene of the drowning and an immense crowd inspected the remains and attended the funeral which took place on a Sunday afternoon and attracted the curious from far and wide.

A short time afterward, Sheeley, the stem parent, was found dead in the garden of Burd Patterson where he had been at work the night before, according to his usual custom, weeding in the cool of the evening.

Sheeley was discovered by two small boys, Edward Patterson and a companion, in the morning, lying on his face, a tuft of grass in his hand. It was first thought he had suicided but the inquest returned a verdict of heart disease.

He was not an unkind man and it was known that he was deeply worried over the untimely end of his daughter Rose and the part he had taken toward bringing it about. For a long time it was rumored that Sheeley's ghost could be seen walking about in the vicinity of his home, on the hill, and also in the Patterson garden. Two gray-haired citizens, of town, relate that they sat up several nights in the rear of Baber cemetery to lay the ghost but he did not walk on those nights.

DINAH AND VILKINS

Prior to the suicide of poor Rose Sheeley, a circus came to town, old Dan Rice's, the clown of which sang the song, the first verse of which ran:

"As Dinah was walking in the garden, one day,
Her papa came to her and thus he did say,
Go dress yon r self, Dinah, in gorgeous array,
And I'll have you a husband both gallant and gay."
   Chorus.
"Tu-ral, li-ural. liu-ral, li-ay, etc."

The ballad went on to relate that Dinah had a lover and objected to the suitor, provided and cared nothing for the silken gowns and gold jewelry; and on the wedding day set, was found dead with a cup of "cold pizen" in her hand of which she had partaken for Vilkin's sake.

The song took like wild fire. Francis Alstadt, bookseller, who kept store in Mutton Row where Union Hall now stands, or next to it in the wooden building, disposed of hundreds of copies of it (at one cent each) and everybody around town, as was the custom with the catchy songs those days, sang it.

Pretty Rose Sheeley was of a very romantic disposition and it was supposed that this song, which she with everybody else sang and re-sang, influenced her to do likewise and end her young life, like Dinah, for her "Vilkin's" sake.

RECORD OF POTTSVILLE POSTMASTERS

The following is a list of Pottsville Postmasters from the establishment of the office up to the present time. G. C. Schrink, the present incumbent, in kindly furnishing the list to the writer, jocosely says, in appending his own name: "And G. C. Shrink, from March 8, 1899, to as long as the public and the administration will permit him to remain."

Thomas Silliman.....January 11, 1821
George Taylor.....June 4, 1825
Chas. Boyter.....Sept. 20, 1828
Joseph Weaver.....Febr'y 21, 1839
John T. Werner.....Sept. 8, 1841
Michael Cochran.....Aug. 16, 1844
Daniel Krebs, Sr. .....Febr'y 15, 1847
Andrew Mortimore.....May 2, 1849
John Clayton.....April 18, 1853

Henry T. Acker.....June 14, 1858
Margaret Sillyman.....April 20, 1861
Amanda Sillyman.....April 16, 1882
Elizabeth Sillyman.....June 21, 1882
James H. Mudey.....July 27, 1886
Wm. E. Cole, no date on record or file.
Louis Stoffregen.....Febr'y 9 1895
G. C. Schrink.....March 8, 1899

EARLY IRON WORKS - THEIR ESTABLISHMENT

The Pioneer Furnace was started in 1837. Here Burd Patterson, Mr. Lyman and Nichols Biddle, of the United States Bank, Wm. Marshal and Dr. Geisenheimer, of the Valley Furnace, experimented to smelt iron with anthracite coal. They were successful in 1839. The Orchard Iron Works were founded by John L. Pott in 1846, and were operated subsequently by Lewis Vastine.

The Pioneer Furnace passed through different hands and finally was purchased by Charles M. and Hanson Atkins, in 1853. In 1866 the old plant was torn down and a new one erected. Two more furnaces were built. The old furnaces, after being idle for a number of years, were torn down in 1905. The Washington Iron Works, The Wren Brothers, E. W. McGinnes, John T. Noble and Pomeroy and Sons, on the site of the lower P. & P. C. & I. Company shops, or near that point on Coal Street. Jabez Sparks was also in the business. The stove works of Simon, John and Joseph Derr; the nut and bolt works, and the Stephen Roger, Roseberry and other small castings foundries on Railroad Street, gave employment to a large number of men. In 1835 Haywood and Snyder erected the Colliery Iron Works on the site of the upper shops. A foundry was built in 1836. Benjamin Haywood withdrew in 1850. The business was continued by George W. Snyder until purchased by the Reading Company.

The Pottsville or Fishbach Rolling Mill was built in 1852 by John Burnish. In 1864 this mill was purchased by the Atkins brothers who rebuilt it. After a period of idleness it was almost entirely rebuilt and enlarged by the Eastern Steel Company and at this writing, 1906, is one of the mammoth and leading establishments of its kind in the United States.

The Palo Alto Iron Works were established by Richard Lee, George Bright and William Harris. In 1855 they became the property of Benjamin Haywood and Co., and subsequently in '56 Mr. Haywood became the sole proprietor. The Reading Car Shops now cover this site.

The Pottsville Water Company was organized April 11, 1834. The Pottsville Gas Company came into existence in 1849.

The first newspapers were the "Freiheitz Presse," Miners Journal," "Pottsville Advocate," "Gazette and Emporium," "Jefferson Democrat," "Americanisher Republikaner" and "Pottsville Standard," all weeklies.

The editors were John T. Werner, Benjamin Bannan, E. O. Jackson, G. L. Vliet, Henry Hendler, Phillip Hoffa, J. P. Bertram, Henry L. Acker. The Weekly "Schuylkill Republican" was founded in 1872 by C. D. Elliott. Elliott and Beck opened a partnership for several years, when the former assumed charge. The "Daily Republican" was founded in 1884 by J. H. Zerbey who has been the editor and proprietor up to the present time, 1906, Charles G. Meyer is the owner of the "Evening Chronicle," which was established in 1872 and existed until a year ago, under various ownerships.

The early builders, contractors and dealers in mountain stone, and carpenters were: Charles Gillingham, Adam and Daniel Eiler, Jeremiah, Charles, Isaac and Henry Lord, Capt. Isaac Lykens, Isaac Severn, John McBarron and Hugh Dolan and Daniel Old.

Among the lawyers not heretofore mentioned were E. P. Dewees, Hon. Linn Bartholomew, Howell Fisher, G. W. Earquhar, Hon. E. B. Gowen, B. W. Gumming, Hon. John W. and Judge James T. Ryon.

Early coal operators: Wm. Milnes, Wm. H. Johns, Judge Wm. Donaldson, Samuel Sillyman, Andrew Oliphant, John "White, Col. G. C. Wynkoop.

The Hon. James Cooper, a United States Senator, had his residence here for several years. He lived in Morris Addition. He had an interest in the coal business of the county. John Shippen, President of the Miners Bank, was one of the historic family of Philadelphia of that name.

The Hon. Robert Palmer, State Senator, son of Judge Strange Palmer, who had also a son, Strange Palmer, was appointed ambassador to Ecuador and died of a fever while en route to South America. Deputy Controller Frank Palmer was a son of the former.

The life of Francis B. Gowen, President of the Reading Company and for years a resident of Pottsville, is like an open book to residents of the coal region and the State of Pennsylvania. These are but a few of the notable residents of Pottsville.

RECAPITULATORY AND RETROSPECTIVE

It is with sincere regret that the author lays down the pen at this point of the history of the early days in Schuylkill County and the Borough of Pottsville. Much that might prove entertaining must necessarily be omitted. AYc beg the indulgence of any who may feel overlooked by this omission. The share their ancestors had in the formation of the local history of this locality is a matter of local pride to all connected with the best interests of the county in which we have cast our lot. The mere knowledge of such facts is in itself a reward commensurate with the general results involved in the summing up of the whole. To still further carry on the details in story would involve a new era that would include a voluminous recount of the several hundred thousand inhabitants that now people the area of Schuylkill County and the vast industries and business resources that arc productive of its present great wealth and enlarged interests in the business world. Charles Dickens said:

"A troublesome form, and an arbitrary custom, prescribe that a story should have a conclusion in addition to a commencement; we have therefore no alternative."

Part Seven - Other Tales

HILDA, A MORMON BRIDE AND MOTHER

CHAPTER I

Hilda Brunhilde stood at the doorway of the little "brown adobe shack on the great Mojave Desert. Not a living creature was in sight as with hand shading her eyes she scanned the glittering white sand of the broad expanse, in the bright rays of the scorching morning sun. Far away lay the beautiful Wasatch mountains, the Jordan river, Salt Lake and the New Jerusalem.

She remembered when two men in shiny black clothes had visited their little home on the coast of Norway and told them of the beautiful city and the land that was overflowing with milk and honey. The mother died of ship fever on the voyage. Her father, the two boys and she had drifted with others to Utah. Some went farther West but the majority sought work in the silver and ore mines until the missionaries should return and give them each the promised farm.

They had brought their few effects to the deserted hut, once occupied by cattle ranchers. The long pack trains sometimes passed there and the drivers left them supplies, in return for which the girl would cook them a savory stew, coffee or mend and wash their scant clothing until their return. There was little for the cow and burro except the meagre doles of feed left them and the wild cactus seed and sage brush.

Word came that their father was killed. He had been working upon a draft of empty cars and was in the act of applying a brake when he lost his footing on the bumper and was thrown in front and run over, being literally hacked to pieces. His countrymen buried him on the mountain side with no other requiem to sing his praise except the soft soughing of the pine trees, so like the growth in their own dear native land.

Hilda was just sixteen, Hans ten, and Wilhelm seven years old. Slightly above medium height, well developed and plump, with a lithe and active frame, Hilda was the picture of health and rustic beauty. Fair skin, deep blue-gray eyes with blackest eyebrows, rosy-red cheeks, dimples and regular pearly-white teeth. Long thick plaits of yellow-golden hair hung to her shapely waist, which was encased in the low laced bodice with white spencer above. She wore the short skirt common to the Norwegian peasant girls and made a pretty picture.

"Yes, they must go to the city. Hans worked with the charcoal burners. He would return on the morrow and they would go."

A neighbor drove away the cow. They packed the panniers of the burro with their bedding and few belongings and the start was made at dawn.

CHAPTER II

It was after noon when they entered the city. They sat by a stream and ate their frugal meal of black bread and curd cheese, tethering the burro that he might nibble the alfalfa.

The glories of the hills were mirrored in the dense waters of the big lake. The sun shone in sharp relief on the bright silvery gray and blue waters. The far off mountain ranges, snow-capped at their summits, formed a life-like frame encased in battlements of sombre green or smoky blue for the wonderful city that lay at their feet. The caravan soon reached the Temple gates and tieing the burro in an obscure alleyway they went in.

It was Sunday afternoon and they hesitated about entering the great Tabernacle which already contained several thousand people. Inside of the gate was another large building like the old Lutheran Church at home and Hilda said: "Let us go in here. There are Norse people inside from the Skagway; you can tell them by their dress."

A woman spoke to them in the Scandinavian tongue, and after a time and the singing of a familiar hymn, a man arose and preached.

"What mattered it if he talked over two hours on the thirteen Articles of Faith of the Church of Jesus Christ of Latter-Day-Saints and the loyalty of its members to that church?"

They knew nothing of "The Ten Tribes and their restoration, or that Zion will eventually be built on this continent, and Christ upon his second coming will reign personally in paradisical glory in that city." But they knew that at last they were among friends. The boys slept during the long and rambling harangue and Hilda thought she must be brave for their sakes. At the close the woman accompanied by a man approached them and in answer to their queries the pitiful little story was soon unfolded.

Hilda said: "The boys must have schooling; I will work my fingers to the bone, if I can but get the work."

The boys entered school and Hilda was installed in the Bureau of Information, where Hannah Amundsen had charge of the girl clerks. She was assigned the care of the church literature, and all day until three o'clock she dusted and rewiped the shelves and books, then she was free for school where she was fast mastering the language and making rapid progress in the studies prepared at night.

They were cared for under the supervision of the ward visitors and the Mormon Church charity system which has no equal in the world. The Later-Day-Saints fast on the first Sunday of every month and every householder is expected to give the money thus saved to the poor who are helped until they become self-sustaining, then they in turn help others.

CHAPTER III.

Tall and dignified, with long flowing beard and a mustache, hair of light brown mixed with gray, blue-back eyes and of rather delicate physique and gentle manner, if he was a wolf in sheep's clothing, the animal was at least well-disguised. Elder Carter was a handsome man.

After a time Hannah told Hilda: "It had been revealed that she should be sealed to the Elder in marriage."

"But he has a wife," said Hilda.

Hannah explained, "It is one of the rites of our religion. The sealed marriages are sacred and kept private. The Common Law of the Gentiles is against them. You would indeed be an ungrateful girl if after all our kindness you did not obey."

A day came and she entered the Temple accompanied by Hannah. It was early in the morning and they took part in a preparatory service in the Assembly Hall. Removing their shoes they descended to the basement where they bathed in the women's baths. Hilda was given a beautiful robe and they entered the magnificent baptismal font room, where the Elder baptized her. The elegance of the surroundings overwhelmed the girl and she was as if in a trance.

The wall painting, by Armitage, of Christ preaching to the Nephites and the companion to it of Joseph Smith preaching to the Indians seemed to burn the figures of their subjects on her feverish brain. The splendid chandeliers, furnishing and decorations, heavy curtains, beautifully decorated ceilings and cornices of white and gold and artistic paintings, added to her bewilderment.

The series of reception rooms and the private apartments of the President and his Hierarchy all beautifully furnished and adorned with choice paintings and full-length mirrors were passed until the three rooms that open south of the Temple auditorium were reached, each of these exquisite in decoration with large plate glass mirrors, stained glass windows and myriads of electric lights. The middle room was circular in form, with a domed ceiling, completely surrounded by jeweled windows and paneled walls, with red silk-velvet borders, delicate blue, white and gold colors predominating. The floor inlaid with inch blocks of polished hard wood and on the wall the noted work of art of the Father and the Son appearing to the boy Joseph Smith.

Here they stopped. The poor girl frightened beyond speech. Hannah, too, looked pale and could only sign her to keep silence. The curtain of the Temple was pushed aside and a hand motioned them to enter.

Then under the arched roof supported by the Grecian columns with the dim light through the double row of stained glass windows shed upon them and in the shadow of the paintings of Lambourne, the Hill of Cumorah and Adam Ondi — Ahma, the harmonious blending of gorgeous colors, the artistically paneled ceilings, frescoes, borders and clusters of grapes, fruits and flowers, Hilda Brunhilde took the dreadful oath of secrecy and became the sealed wife for "Time and all Eternity," of Elder George Carter, a Priest of the Council and one of the Seventy.

Of what followed she could not afterwards divest it from other dreams. Nature was kind to her; forgetfulness intervened. She found Hannah awaiting her in the Temple corridor, who silently clasped her hand and together in the twilight they went to their humble home.

Hilda lost her brightness. She no longer added her rich contralto voice to the Tabernacle chorus. She was listless, great clouds seem to blur her vision, spells of faintness frequently came and a hacking cough troubled her. Her work was performed painstakingly but mechanically. The girls began to look at her suspiciously.

Or was it her imagination? Her frequent absences under the plea of sickness, when accompanied by Hannah she went into the country and there met the Elder, whom she had respected and loved as a father, and — yes, she must admit it to herself —

"Whom I now hate and loathe like a rattlesnake. Oh I will pray to the God of my mother, perhaps He will let me die young like her," she said. "It is no wonder the girls sneer; I am one of them no longer."

At last the dreadful news was borne upon her; there was another life awakening in her. She had been dull to recognize what others already knew. The Elder chided her for her gloominess and laughed at her fears and Hannah said:

"You will be taken care of in the country miles away when the proper time comes. You must be patient."

A day came when she could no longer endure the thought of her shame. "No wife in the sight of the law. How could she become a mother?"

"I will go to-night to the old home on the desert," she said, "and die there."

She took up her studies that evening with the boys and under one pretext or another remained about the house until they slept.

Filling a leathern bottle with water and placing a little bread and cheese in a 'kerchief, she tied them about her waist and unlatching the door went out quietly.

Her nimble feet soon led her up the Wasatch trail and here she paused to refresh herself from the intolerable thirst that controlled her and refill the bottle from one of the mountain streams.

The moon was low but she ought to reach the shack a few hours after sunup. All night long she walked and when the sun arose paused. Nothing was in sight but the white sand of the desert. A wind gentle at first, now became stronger and blew a perfect gale. The small particles of sand were blinding and the sun's rays burnt her delicate skin as the orb rose higher in the Heavens.

These tracks, Merciful Father! they were her own. She had been walking in a circle all night. Eating the morsel of food she had and wetting the handkerchief with a few drops of water from the bottle from which she drank sparingly, she tied the handkerchief about her eyes and sank under a clump of wild cactus and scooping all the sand she was able to over herself she slept.

The sun was low in the horizon when she awoke. How beautiful it looked as it sank in the West, its brilliant hues enriched with a halo of golden-orange and blood-red flecks in a sea of silver-white sheen and sea blue. But Hilda had no eye for anything but the desert, the sameness of which she felt was fast driving her mad.

All night long she wandered and the next day was but a repetition of the first. Her limbs trembled, her breath came in gasps, her tongue and nostrils were swollen. She had bent her course toward the mountains and, "yes they were nearer," and below that dented ridge was the little hut, the only home she knew.

"I can go no further," she said, "I may as well die here."

She slept and dreamed of the old home. Her parents, that happy childhood; when she was awakened by the cold nose of an animal thrust into her face and the gentle licking of her hand with a rough tongue. What frightful monster was this with his hot breath and great green and fiery red eyes. A gentle whinny awoke her. "It is, yes! it is the burro." The boys had lent him to the charcoal burners and after a few weeks at that work he had disappeared. He, too, sought home at the brown grass-thatched hut of the Mojave.

She clasped her arms about his neck and kissed him, allowing him to lick her hand and touch her cheek with his cold snout; and mounting, bade him go home.

The hut was reached. Some rain water in the little stone cistern quenched her thirst. She bathed herself and stood a stone jar full within reach and then clambered into the bunk and knew no more. Torrid fever and pain racked her and in the delirium she heard a faint wail. Wolves, wolves, or a catamount, perhaps. There was something alive in the bunk. A baby wolf; the fierce old mother would return. She took the creature and laid it high on the stone shelf outside the door. The wolf could get it. Fastening the hasp on the door and wetting her handkerchief in the jug and binding her temples, she rolled into the rude bed. All night and the next day she babbled of water, talked to her father and mother and prayed in her baby-girlhood way.

On the third day old Sam Patch with his pack and team came. His cheerful chirrup and "steady boys" changed into a grim oath as he stopped, as was his custom to cook his coffee and eat his rations at the shack.

"A dead baby by all that's holy," he ejaculated.

The door was soon burst open. "And Hilda too," he said as the fever-stricken girl sat up and gazed at him, but gave no sign of recognition.

"It's them ____ Mormons," he said, bursting into tears.

"Oh! Father, I am so glad you came," said the girl, clinging to his arm.

"Never mind, my dear! Never mind! Old Sam will make them sweat for it. We'll see what the laws of this land are good for."

He bathed her face and hands as tenderly as if she were an infant, cooked some gruel which he fed her, encouraging her to think he was the father she called upon and then watched her until sleep came. Hastily fastening the door, he wrapped the dead babe in a blanket and did not rest until he had deposited it in the office of the District Attorney at Salt Lake and had told the story, not forgetting, however, to send the nearest woman en route to Hilda's relief.

"Take care of her and as soon as she is able she will be tried for infanticide. The post mortem discloses the child was born alive and died of neglect and exposure," said the attorney. "The parentage of the child will appear and the U.S. authorities will make a test case if she confesses to a polygamous marriage and a Mormon as the father."

CHAPTER IV.

The trial came; the court room was crowded. Hilda, pale and wan, sat quietly, apparently oblivious to all about her. Old Sam and the old crone in waiting sat on either side of her.

When the charge was read, her name called, and she was required to enter her plea, she arose and with her slim white hands folded over the bosom of her deep black gown, said:

"I have been very ill. I know nothing."

There was a slight stir and way was made for a delegation of the Mormon Hierarchy, among the foremost of whom was Elder Carter. They entered the court and took their places in the front row of seats among the spectators.

Hilda's passiveness was succeeded by a feverish excitement. She shook as with a chill and drops of perspiration stood out upon her forehead. Look where she would the Elder's penetrating eyes held her spell-bound. "Remember your oath," they seemed to say and she swayed gently in her seat and swooned in old Sam's outstretched arms.

"Clear the room," ordered the Court, "the air is too close for the prisoner." But the order came too late, the mischief was done.

No amount of cross-questioning could elicit more from the horror-stricken prisoner. "She did not know who the father of her child was. He went away. No! she had never been married."

"What mattered one oath more or less to her after the fearful one she took in the Temple?" she reasoned, inwardly.

"It is always so, they will not break their oath," said the District Attorney, and old Sam swore publicly and privately and said, "He believed he could pick out the man from among the long-bearded, gray-haired rascals. He had his eye on him."

The Jury, through their foreman, a blue-eyed, flaxen-haired Norwegian, rendered an acquittal of the charge of infanticide without leaving their seats.

Several years after Sam Patch visited a farm in the Arizona wheat belt and here were Hilda, a happy wife and mother, the Norse juryman and Hans and

"Wilhelm, grown to manhood. They urged him to remain and told him there was a seat for him vacant at their fireside. The old man tossed the flaxen-haired baby in his arms wiped off a tear or two and said: "He was glad he at last had a home, but he must be off to-morrow; the mule-pack would be too lonely without him."

THE HISTORY OF A NEWSPAPER OFFICE CAT

She was a tiny white kitten, a homeless waif that sought refuge in the "Daily Bugle" press rooms from the merciless teasings of the carrier boys and the cold, wintry weather. Her appeal to the fatherly janitor was not without its effect, and he adopted her at once as one of the fledglings of the department, where she bid fair to excel even the "Printer's Devil" in usefulness.

"Betty" could lay no especial claim to cleanliness, although she was a beauty and no mistake, her white coat was often nearer black than its original color, from frequent contact with the coal pits and inky rollers, and her feline whiskers were often smeared with paste from the paste-pot, on which she was supposed to subsist. She had many feline accomplishments, one of which was her penchant for springs on the fly, which excelled even those of the famous Zazel from the catapult in Barnum's, and which were as far-fetching as those of a politician who desires to remain in office under successive administrations. It was nothing uncommon for her to jump from desk to table or rail, a distance of eight to ten feet, and her plunges along the walls were regular sky-scrapers.

Like all of her sex she had a decided predilection for confirmed bachelors. Every evening when the hands departed for home, and the press department was quiet, she solemnly marched up from the lower regions into the counting-room, where she was not allowed during the day, and perched upon the desk or on the back of the chair of the bookkeeper, and gravely watched the posting up of the day's array of figures. Her contempt for the woman hater of the editorial sanctum only equaled his aversion for cats, and she eyed him askance and with tail and fur erect, and this antipathy extended itself to the ladies' man, too, of the force, who offered her the burning end of a cigarette one day, after she had especially distinguished herself — for she was a good mouser — in catching a young rat which she brought upstairs as a trophy for the bookkeeper.

Mice and paste were not her only articles of diet. When any copy was mislaid, proof or manuscript lost, it was all laid to the office cat, who was supposed to have eaten them, and who was put under training for the munching of all original copies on the "Beautiful Snow," or any effusions from the oldest inhabitant on his recollections of a colder winter than that of 1903-4, or any other rejected manuscript; and local authors were warned not to require a return of copy. But Betty became ill after Thanksgiving, when a friendly neighboring meat merchant, who was not in sympathy with the diet the office cat in every well-regulated printing office exists on, surreptitiously overfed her with raw pork scraps, which proved too much for her digestion. The whole staff became alarmed at her condition, and even the disgruntled dyspeptic of the force tried to effect a cure for her with a package of grape-nuts which she kept in her desk for use when she was similarly affected, but the cat "wouldn't eat that stuff," said the janitor, and he didn't blame her; he said "He didn't know how anyone could."

Betty has a great future before her. It is hoped she will not be called to the cat kingdom yet. As a regular member of the newspaper fraternity it is expected that she will develop and eventually show a capability in revising copy and correcting proof, at least so far as puncturing such expressions from correspondents is concerned, as: "In regards to;" "My gentleman friend;" "Quite a few," etc., and that she will teach the reporters to say people died a natural death, instead of "demising," or that she will be able to tell the difference between "classical" music and caterwauling, or the use of any of the thousand and one hyperboles indulged in by overworked writers of newspapers with limited vocabularies of speech and slender repertoires.

When she has accomplished this she will have fulfilled the mission of all good newspaper office cats who have large possibilities in their nine lives mapped out for them to fill, and then Betty may be sure of a flaming obituary, the last that can be done for anyone, much less a cat. Requie "scat!"

TINY TIM AND POLLY

The Welsh of the Valley, and in fact of the entire coal region, had brought with them to Pennsylvania their love of singing, and with this love many of their national customs implanted within them and in the hearts of their forefathers. Among these the Eisteddfod, which is still a prominent feature of entertainment wherever an clement of Welsh exists. Eisteddfod (to sit) was the name applied to the assemblies of the Welsh bards and minstrels, anciently formed by edict of the kings; and the early musicians were of hereditary order. The Eisteddfods were suppressed for a time but revived again during the present century. In both Wales and in this country prizes are awarded for proficiency in the Welsh tongue, for original poems and declamations in that language and largely for chorus singing. At these gatherings some of the best choruses in the State, notably the one from Wilkes Barre that won the prize at the Centennial in Philadelphia for oratorio singing in 1876, and those from Scranton, at St. Louis and Chicago, taking similar prizes; in which choruses were included some of old Schuylkill's best singers, these are examples of the high ideals aimed at and the results attained by these Welsh organizations.

Primrose and the valley northwest of M___, was then heavily wooded. The huge coal operations that have since sprung up in that vicinity had not altogether yet denuded the locality of its primeval beauty and devastated it of its forests. The streams tributary to the West Branch were still silvery in their rippling beauty and uncontaminated by coal washeries. The huge culm banks stood unmolested in their blackness, a monument, with their large proportion of coal in them, to the lavish wastefulness of the early coal miner of the black diamonds — for the proportion in these dirt banks of good coal was large and is a growing temptation to the avarice and commercial enterprise of the present generation, and also the cause of the ruination of valuable farming lands and the contamination of the region's streams with their washings.

Polly Edwards stood at the window of one of the little black company houses. There was nothing to see, if she was oblivious of the beautiful mountain scenery, but the steam ascending from the power house of the collieries and the huge black breakers that were in sight, but she was apparently looking out into space and from the pucker in her freckled but comely face was thinking and the reflections were ever and anon from grave to gay.

A look about the homely little room showed that everything was in apple pie order or as nearly so as she could make it. The step stove had been polished, the floors freshly mopped, the tubs were ready for the huge kettles of hot water, for her father and Tim; the miners wash all over immediately after their return from the shift, they must to dislodge the tiny particles of coal dust or suffer untold torture with their skin and bring on disease.

In the oven was a huge beef heart stuffed and roasting with a dressing of leeks at hand and a pot of vegetables was simmering on the back, while a pot of coffee and a fresh baked pie stood on the neatly spread table, all ready for the toilers.

Polly was just nineteen, blue-eyed and with hair that curled so tight she could scarcely get out the kinkles. Her nose, it was true, was decidedly a pug and her freckles deep-tinted, but she had a milk-white skin and the most good-natured smile. Her mother had died when Tim was a baby, he was thirteen now and she had been her father's housekeeper ever since and a mother to Tim.

Tim was bright and had stood high in the school and ah!' that was just it. Why had her father permitted him to leave and go to work in the breaker? It was not necessary. His tender white skin would become grimy, his bright blue eyes seared, and his curly brown locks entangled with the thick black coal dust. It was all on account of that foolish gibe of the neighbors' boys. "Where do you work, Tim?"

>"I work East, I work West,
>I work over at the Billy Best."

And it was at the "Billy Best" he went that morning for the first time, in spite of her pleadings to the contrary. Her father had said no, at first, but finally said yes, when Dan (he was her sweetheart) had added his "wheedlings" to those of the boy. No good would come of it she felt assured.

It was the miners' Saturday. To-night they would all go to town for the four belonged to the chorus, which met in the Congregational Church in M___ to rehearse for the contest at the Eisteddfod, at Wilkes Barre, on the coming St

David's Day and this was the last rehearsal and St David's Day next Tuesday. Dr. Parry himself would be present that night to arrange about the contest and the prizes, and they would all go over to the other region, nearly fifty miles away, but that was nothing for was not that big man, Dr. Wolsieffer, coming all the way from Philadelphia to be one of the adjudicators?

Their society was small but they could make the welkin ring with the "Hallelujah Chorus" from Handel's Messiah, and was the "Comrades in Arms" ever better sung than at their last meeting? She was among the contraltos, her father a baritone and Dan among the heavy bass; and how Conductor Roberts stamped, fumed, and perspired until he evolved the present orderly harmony out of almost chaos. Evening after evening they had practiced in the basement of the old brick church on S____ street, until the neighbors in that vicinity had declared them the most unmitigated nuisance and said "they would be glad when it was over."

Then there was Tim, how beautiful his boy tenor was. He alone of all the other boys could sing the tenor solos and compete for the prize for Dr. Parry's "Mabz Morwr" (The Sailor Boy) and Ghent's "Yr Haf" (The Summer). Tim could sing them, she knew he could. He would get the five dollar gold piece, and the musings went on. But what was that; the whistle at the "Billy Best?" It was not yet quite time to change shifts and she watched; Yes, there was the mule, boy astride, starting out from the breaker, a sure signal of some one hurt at the mines. Who was it? Surely not her father or Dan, they were too experienced for any of the ordinary accidents that were always happening the raw helpers and the careless laborers. If it had been an explosion the boy would stop at Granny William's, as she was better at dressing burns than any doctor. If not he would come on to the patch and give the alarm and then speed on to M___. for a doctor, for it was before the days of telephone or the organization of the corps of "First Aid to the Injured."

Curiously at first she watched the flying hoofs of the mule and his reckless rider. Yes! he was coming up to the patch. Their's was the last house in the row and still he was coming. The neighbors were all at their doors and windows and some of the fleeter ones ran toward the boy to anticipate his sad tidings, which he scattered right and left.

Polly's heart was in her mouth, a great rushing sound filled her ears, and try as she might she could not understand a word the boy said but he seemed to be waving his hand to her and with dilated eves and trembling form, she watched him, yes, it was their house and an agonizing shriek broke upon the air and with a loud "Oh! Dear, Dear God! It's my Tim!" she sank fainting in the outstretched arms of her neighbors, who had hurriedly come upon the scene.

Soon they brought the inanimate form of little Tim to the house, but Polly could not be aroused and went from one swoon into another, until Dr. B___ arrived to alleviate her misery with an opiate; and kind friends administered to her sufferings through the night and subsequent bitter days of grief that followed.

The same spirit of fun and frolic that led Tim to go to work at the early age of thirteen against the remonstrances of his foster girl mother, caused his death. The head boy who was working at the top rollers communicated that mysterious signal with his fingers down the steplike line of the huge screens to the next and so on down to the bottom, as was their daily custom, that, "It was ten minutes before whistle" when those on the lower level began a species of tag and Tim ran with them. There was a dull thud, a scream, and all was over with tiny Tim. He had fallen between the rollers and his limp body came out with the coal in the chutes. Let us draw a veil over the sorrows of the grief-stricken little family and the recriminations of the self-condemned and heartsick father.

There was no meeting of the chorus in M___ that night. They could not sing at Wilkes Barre now, they said, their chief singers were gone, and there were sad hearts in the little community that mourned with the little family, that like Rachael of old refused to be comforted because their loved one was not.

Tim was buried in the Congregational Cemetery in M___.

There was no hearse but the little body was borne to town on a bier decked with flowers and streamers of ribbons and the same ribbons, the colors of the St Ivor and St. David Societies, with the national rosettes were tied about the right arms of the eight boys who carried the bier. A large concourse of people followed the remains to their last resting place. The Edwards' were well known and many came to the funeral from as far as Lansford, Kingston and Plymouth in the other anthracite coal basin, and delegates were present from the county towns, Mahanoy City, Shenandoah, Tamaqua, etc.

They did not follow in a funeral procession, two and two, as is the American custom, but walked in the broad street and filled it from curb to curb, marching with solemn tread, men, women and children, and singing with a mournful volume of sound, that re-echoed through the village, the familiar funeral hymn:

"Ai marw raid i mi
A rhoi fy nghorph i lawr?
A raid i'm hen aid ofnus ffoi
L'r tragwyddoldeb mawr?"

Which translated into the English is:

"And am I born to die?
To lay this body down?
And must my trembling spirit fly
Into a world unknown?"

Years have passed since then. Polly married Dan and her father sits in the chimney corner and croons over another tiny Tim. And as Polly looks at the constantly increasing number of her little brood, she cannot be too thankful that the State Legislature has fixed the limit that boys may only work in and about the breakers at sixteen years of age, and that the compulsory educational law must be obeyed and they must attend school until that period.

THE DEAD MAN'S FOOT

CHAPTER I.

A great strike in the anthracite coal region of Pennsylvania was on. Word had gone along the line that the miners and railroaders would unite and all transportation of coal cease. The District Superintendents of the great corporation had received private information from the officials of the Philadelphia & Reading Company that the huge plane at Gordon, used for hoisting the cars to the head of the mountain, would be abandoned by the company, in retaliation, and the coal carried around it, thus dispensing with the labor of hundreds of men permanently.

David Davidson was the Superintendent at the plane, over which in prosperous times a gigantic traffic passed. He received a good salary and occupied, with his young wife and sister-in-law, the pretty cottage belonging to the company, on the summit above the village. It was a responsible position, and his prospects for advancement were good, but yet he was not a happy man.

Davidson began active life, as a boy, at the lowest round of the ladder, carrying water, marking "coalies," waking the night crows at their homes, and in the bunk houses, learning telegraphy, tending switches and acting as engine hostler and brakeman in turn; step by step he advanced to his present position. Closely affiliated with the workingman from his youth, it was not surprising that his sympathies were with the men in the impending struggle and against the great corporation.

His wife, Anna, and Kate, her sister, were much alike in appearance. Kate, however, being the taller of the two and fuller in figure. Both were graceful in carriage, with that lithesome, easy stride, common to people who live among the mountains. Anna's hair and eyes were brown, her disposition gentle and retiring, her manner quiet even to that repression of action that denotes a deep and delicate sensibility and the refinement that is part of the natural inheritance of a woman of culture and education.

Kate was a blonde, with masses of light hair, coiled on the top of a shapely head, her forehead was broad, her eyes a deep gray that shifted their color to brown and sometimes, it must be confessed, under deep provocation, to black. She was vivacious, with a vigor of manner that betokened a strong vitality with perhaps a tinge of impetuosity. They were orphans.

They were seated at their noonday meal, which Davidson had left a few minutes before almost untasted. The table daintily laid, with its polished glass, clean linen and bright old-fashioned silver service, figured china, and a carefully-prepared dinner.

"Anna, has David told you he resigned and will leave for the West next week?" said Kate.

"Yes, he spoke of it at noon. If the plane closes permanently, he will be given charge of the lumber yards at R___, which I am afraid he will not accept. He is tired of the struggle, his sympathies are with the men, and he has decided to go West and take up one of Uncle Sam's claims and farm. As if we knew anything about farming." Anna broke down and sobbed. Kate did not reply, and the young wife walked to the window to conceal her emotion.

Gordon is built on the summit of one of the spurs of the Broad Mountains, in the eastern part of the State, in the center of the anthracite coal basin. It was planned for wide, clean streets to intersect at right angles on the broad plateau, which nature had apparently formed for the site of a city of enlarged environments. From any point, on a clear day, seven distinct mountain ranges can be counted without the aid of a glass. It was a familiar scene, but her eyes eagerly followed it.

The spirals of smoke curling into the azure dome of the gold-flecked sky above denoted the location of the different collieries. The "Bald Eagle," "Shoo Fly," "Excelsior," "Coffee Mill," and a dozen others, with the quality and output of coal from each of which she was as well informed as any of the operators. Along the mountain sides ran the branch roads from the breakers, on which could be seen moving the black box cars that at this distance looked like toys with their tiny motors.

Below in the valleys were the lateral roads, that joined the main branch farther on, their rails lay like mere threads aside of the black, sluggish waters of the river. It was early spring, nature wore its wildest dress. The gigantic rocks loomed up bare and uncovered on every side. Soon the mountain laurel would bloom, the wild honeysuckle and mountain lillies burst forth, then the huge pyramids of culm would be hidden from sight in a wilderness of beauty. The monster engines were still throbbing and snorting at the head of the plane, as they drew the loaded cars up the steep incline, the ugly little "barney" in the rear looking as self-conscious as if it alone did all the work. In the cemetery in the valley their parents were buried, how could they leave all they loved for the flat, monotonous prairies of the West?

"We are all alone in the world, Kate," said Anna. "How can I leave you here? I do not like the West, and I always hated farming."

"But stock raising and growing wheat are different from what we know of farming and I will go too," replied Kate.

"What will become of your school? You must not leave it."

"Oh! there are schools everywhere, even in Kamschatka, I will get another."

They cried a little, and after the fashion of their dependent type of glorious womanhood thus accepted the decree of destiny one of the sterner sex had forced upon them against their wills.

The strike followed. The railroad engineers went out first. The collieries suspended, one by one, leaving men for deadwork only. Every effort was made by the Union to make it universal. The company carried its orders into effect at once, and the ponderous machinery of the plane was removed to the city machine shops, making a deserted village in a short time of the pretty little town. The plane had always been a costly plant, and a road was already being built around the mountain to take the place of the abandoned incline.

"I always wanted to follow the course of the star of the empire westward, and the strike makes it easier," said Davidson.

He was a spare built man of middle height with brown curling hair and determined and yet kindly looking blue eyes. His appearance showed strength. His form was wiry, he had great knotty muscles and seemed built for endurance. Self reliance verging on obstinacy was a strong point in his character, this allied to a naturally affectionate nature and good morals made of him a man to be not only respected but beloved by those under him, and trusted by his superiors. The question had come. The company or its employees. He chose the workingmen's issue and went out with the strikers.

Their preparations to leave were soon made. A public sale disposed of their pretty furniture, with the exception of one suite, a few cots, the cabinet organ, the kitchen range, cooking utensils, dishes, linen and bedding. Transportation was too high to take much, besides there would be no room in the Kansas dugout. Davidson left the following week, the girls expecting to spend a month with relatives until their home was in readiness. The month lengthened into two before they received the summons to come. The adieus to friends were sorrowful indeed, on Anna's part, she cried bitterly wherever she went. Kate assumed the philosophic role.

"I do not want to go from the dear old mountains of Pennsylvania; I feel as if I will never see them again."

It was a wail that even Kate's philosophy could not stand proof against, and in spite of her sternest resolution not to give away to her feelings, she, too, succumbed to tears on their departure.

CHAPTER II.

It was early in May when they arrived in southwestern Kansas. The country was at its best. The prairie gently undulating as far as the eye could reach, the broad, flat expanse dotted with here and there a knoll that broke the dead monotone of the vast horizon like a speck against the deep blue sky. The spring rains had been abundant; the heather was in bloom; the prairie covered with a mass of phlox, hyacinths and pinks, and the scrub plums and wild grapes were luxuriantly blossoming and blowing to and fro in the stiff breezes.

Davidson met them with a team of white horses and a high, green "La Belle" wagon, of which he seemed very proud. After fastening and roping their baggage, he told them to "mount the seat and hold fast, or, better still, sit on the floor, the wind would blow them off, anyway," and the ride, Kate said, was "like a sail on an unknown sea."

The country was not yet staked in sections; there was no trail, and the girls suspected David of driving by compass or the sun, one gully being so exactly like another, and no visible landmarks. Twelve miles were slowly and painfully made when a singular figure emerged from a semi-cave in the ground, and was subsequently followed by a group of unkempt, flaxen-headed progeny, of all sizes. A woman appeared with a short woolen skirt encasing her nether limbs, huge brogans on her feet, a knit jacket on her long, lean body, a man's hat on her head, and a short pipe between her teeth at which she was drawing vigorously.

"Good morning, Mother Grimshaw," said Davidson, reining up.

"This is my wife. Mrs. Davidson, and her sister, Miss Harleigh. Mother Grimshaw is our nearest neighbor, and I am indebted to her for many comforts during my bachelorhood."

"Shure they were all paid for," said the woman, coming forward to shake hands with the ladies. Kindliness and consternation spread over her somewhat comely but weather-beaten features.

"The Saints purtect ye!" she said, gazing at them, "and the good Lord forgive ye for ever bringing the loikes of thim to this God-forsaken country," and shaking her fist at Davidson, she disappeared precipitately down the short ladder into the hole in the ground she called home.

"We are almost there," said David. He pointed with pride to the symmetrical stone posts at intervals, which he explained marked his claim.

"Welcome home!" he said, assisting them to alight at the foot of the upland. The girls peered about anxiously, but he was apparently busy adjusting the harness of his horses. A long, low building jutted out from the knoll seemingly a part of the hill that formed its support on one side. It was covered on its irregular sides and roof with the brown prairie turf that surrounded it. The only evidences of its being a dwelling were the windows and a door, and its chimney of brick.

"Is that a sod house?" queried Kate. Anna's eyes filled with tears as she thought of the pretty eastern home with its veranda and climbing vines. Davidson twined his arms about both of them, and said:

"Never mind, it is the best I can do now, with all the stock to buy and seeding to do. Wait until our fall crops are in, we will build a frame house for the winter."

The interior was not as forbidding as the outside and exceeded their expectations. It was floored throughout, had three windows with deep seats in the thick sod walls, and was divided into three rooms. The center was a large living room with two small bedrooms off from it. The rough sides were whitewashed, and the ceiling was made by tacking white cotton cloth to the rafters and frame that formed the foundation. An attempt had been made at rude furniture, a wooden settle and shelves for the housekeeping utensils. The range, organ and rockers they had brought from home were in evidence and great care had evidently been taken to reproduce the home kitchen and pantry.

"How hard you must have worked, David," said Anna.

"Oh, no, the neighbors helped with the house raising, and I installed Mother Grimshaw as factotum to do the unpacking, whitewashing and general fixing."

He neglected, however, to add that he rode for two days to the nearest settlement for the windows and lumber and that he was lost on the prairies for twenty-four hours.

When life is young, everything is beautiful and they began ranching in high spirits. The stock grazing around, flocks of white chickens that settled like a cloud of snow to roost on the housetop, even the black pigs in the corral were their delight. During the early summer it rained, the draws were full of water and they laid out a garden, planting the seeds they brought with them. They would have vines and roses; the" sod house should be covered with them. They also took up an adjacent timber claim, ordering trees from a persuasive tree agent to plant in the fall.

"Ye had best both stay in the house and save yer pretty skins from the wind, nothing will grow anyway," said father Grimshaw.

Davidson was much away from home. Farming implements and high-priced machinery were out of the question with individuals. Land was plenty and the farmers planted, ploughed and seeded together, the owner of the implements taking his pay out of the crops after harvest, and the neighbors united their forces and planted more by working in unison.

"I think it would be best to plant less and hire a hand or two. So many working together do it in such a slipshod way," said Anna, one day.

"You are accustomed to the little patches of the East; hoeing will be hard enough," said her husband, who was not to be argued with.

He had often dilated on "the freedom of living away from the call of the company's whistle to work, where a man was his own master"; but here he rose at four o'clock in the morning without any call but the early breezes shadowing the coming light. Daylight was reckoned by "Mountain Time" and was three-quarters of an hour ahead of the sun dial, making it a quarter after three in the morning.

He milked the cows, Anna attended to the milk, which in the absence of ice they kept in the cyclone cellar under the knoll, while Kate prepared breakfast for David and Tommy Grimshaw, who was now installed as their chore boy, and also put up a substantial luncheon for them to take with them to the field. The butter, eggs and chickens were their stock in trade, and must be attended to every morning. Twice a week the "cheeseman" gathered the milk for the creamery. He came from their nearest market, for their supplies, which he paid in groceries.

How they longed for fresh meat. There was no game but the Jack rabbits, which, though considered a delicacy by Eastern epicures, no settler would shoot except for sport or as a pest to his corn, much less eat.

Salt pork and an occasional chicken was their regular diet. Of the latter and eggs, they dared not use many or they must go without coffee, tea and sugar, if they had none to trade. Their home-made preserves and canned fruit were long ago exhausted, and nothing grew within a couple of hundred miles except the wild plums and grapes. They planted, but the drouth killed everything.

As midsummer came, the hot winds became insufferable. They could not venture out during the day without parched hands and face, from which the skin shriveled. "No one could take care of their complexions in this heat," said Kate.

Then the drouth came. The soil was highly productive, the wheat was thick and certainly looked beautiful, it would yield above the average this year, and their corn crop was immense. Still there was no rain and Davidson looked thoughtful. The work was completed, he was much at home now, but harvesting would soon commence. The heat increased. They had been unable to erect a windmill to draw their water, their pump had but a two-inch bore which was soon exhausted and the cattle were suffering. One lifting yielded but four pails of water and this but once an hour. Davidson pumped when not at work; during his absence the girls took turns. Tommy had all he could do to see that each of the steers got its share in the wild scramble for the meager supply, which did no more than wet their tongues and swollen nostrils.

The draws along the sections were dry and the fissures in them filled with hornless toads, that naturalists say exist without water.

"If we only had those non-drinking cows from France, we, too, might make Roquefort cheese for market," remarked Anna.

Everything that ought not, grew to a phenomenal size. Strange vari-colored bugs flew and crawled into everything. Spiders vied in growth with young sparrows. The cinch bug burrowed in the sod and houses that were guiltless of bedsteads were infested with bedbugs. The grasshoppers, their size a jest in the East, were a serious problem when they alighted in clouds on an object.

The country was infested with rattlesnakes. The settlers held "bees" in the spring, in which days were spent in exterminating them. The drouth brought them out afresh. There were several old wells on the ranch and these were their resort. The girls never went out without a forked stick in hand. Kate could kill a rattler without a tremor, but Anna ran and shivered. Twenty were dispatched about the place in one week and still they came.

The garden was dead. What came up of the seeds, that the hot winds had not blown out of the ground, shrivelled in the heat. Each season the early settlers had planted trees, every year thicker, but only those set in the waterways that were moist, at least in spring, grew at all, and these only attained the height of a scrub bush. The corn still looked lusciously green with its tasselled tops and ripening ears. The early wheat was cut and shocked. But the listless calm that pervaded was ominous.

Then the simoon came. "Could it ever be so hot anywhere?" The cattle hung their heads and stood motionless, wherever there was the least semblance of shelter. The south wind blew with the dawn, at first gently, and then, as the sun rose high in the heavens, fiercely, blighting everything in its course. The glare was heightened by the filmy cloud of furnace-like heat that arose out of the baked and parched earth.

"Hell is under this spot. Ye can see the smoke rising from it." said Daddy Grimshaw.

"It's six summers I have lived here and every one of thim the same. The blight comes just when the crop is ready to be tuck in," he added. For three days it blew and then there was a lull. Everything hung dead and lifeless. The corn stalks were burned as if by fire, the late wheat was crisp, the corn roasted black on the ear and the melons, which thirsty Kansians prize as a summer beverage instead of iced drinks, were as if cooked on the shrivelled vines.

Davidson, anxious to appear hopeful, said, "We have not fared so badly. I did not expect to ship much this year and the wheat in shock may turn out well."

A tornado came next, plenty of wind but little water. It was in the evening and they spent the night in the cyclone cave. The huge chimney of their humble dwelling blew down, carrying ruin and devastation with it. The lowly huts of the settlers did not suffer much but the cattle in the march of destruction were killed. "Coos," one of their faithful milch cows, was found almost severed in two, a part of a sewing machine imbedded in her vitals. This, with other debris, had blown from Ness, their distant county seat, which was almost a total ruin. Business blocks, a new fifty-thousand dollar-school building, hotels and dwellings, erected by Eastern speculators to force a boom, all were razed to the ground and many deaths resulted.

"I had hoped to build the frame dwelling this fall, but owing to the failure of the crops, I am afraid we will have to content ourselves with a sod house for the winter," said Davidson. "I could do it by selling some of the steers."

He did not add that he feared that the steers might be needed to save them from starvation.

A new sod house was built nearer the cyclone cave. The chimney must be rebuilt in any event and the cattle have shelter during the winter, they could not live in the fierce prairie winds. The old house was dismantled of its windows, doors and floors, and made weather tight for the cattle. To the new one these with a few conveniences were added. A long low parapet of sod was built to break the force of the wind and all was secure for the winter, which soon came in all its fury.

There was little or no snow. The wind either blew it to the far off mountain peaks or it melted as it reached the ground. The sod house half burrowed under the knoll was warm. There was no wood within seventy miles and they could as well afford to burn silver as coal, but fuel was plenty of a kind. The corn on the ear was thrown into the corral for the pigs. They were of the black, long snouted, razor-back, wild breed, ready to chew up anything from a human being to an ear of corn and they cleared the cobs in their rapacious maws. They were fed at alternate ends of the corral. Whilst Tommy, pole in hand for defense, engaged their attention Math a fresh supply at one end, Davidson would clamber in at the other and fill his bags with the cobs. These with the burnt corn fodder and "cowchips" formed their fuel and engaged the attention of one person constantly to feed the fire. They did not arise with or before the workingman's whistle now, but courted daylight no matter how many wakeful hours intervened between dusk and dawn.

There was no work to do but attend the stock, and the family needed but two meals a day and these were painfully stereotyped, cornmeal and bacon. They seemed but to live on with no object in life but existence. Reading matter, however, from Eastern friends was plentiful, and this kept them in touch with the outer world. Twice a week Davidson went to the cross roads post office and the cheeseman still called for an exchange of supplies.

CHAPTER III

Life was not without its concomitant variety as winter went on apace. Insurance agents, tree peddlers, and speculators made of their house a wayfaring hotel. They were only too pleased to have the dread monotony broken by these casual guests. An itinerant minister, not of their creed, from the Mission Church in Pueblo, preached at the ranch and among the neighbors, once in two weeks. Mrs. Davidson played the organ and led the hymns for the sparse congregation. When services were held elsewhere they took the instrument with them in the wagon to the next place. Then a Roman Catholic Missionary Priest came too. He put up with the Davidsons and asked if he might erect an altar and hold mass there for the three families that lived in dugouts in that vicinity. Davidson had frequently met the zealous and pious man in his travels across the prairies on a little sorrel pony with his saddle bags filled with the orders of his holy office and medicines for the sick and afflicted. They acquiesced. "Anything to help uplift humanity," said Anna. The Grimshaws, whom their mother described as, "Worse nor South-say islanders;" not without incipient rebellion on their part, together with a few adults and their numerous broods were thus, on stated occasions, initiated into the formula of their church; and time went on.

A strange looking being came over the prairie one evening in the twilight. A tall broad-shouldered man, with long curling ringlets and flowing beard of blonde hair. His garb was nondescript and picturesque; he wore no hat, simply a kerchief tied about his neck and in his hand a large shepherds' crook.

"Here comes Schlatter, the divine healer," called Kate, who was at the window.

The stranger made the sign of the cross as he entered the house and held up a small tablet with pencil attached; he apparently was dumb. He asked "for shelter for the night."

The girls roomed together and his host took the settle behind the stove, where he slept the half of the time to replenish the fire. In the morning the stranger invoked a blessing on the meal and all within the house. As he took his coffee he stirred it and looked about anxiously for the sugar they could not afford to use themselves! and did not offer him. After breakfast he again invoked a blessing on the house and its inmates and departed. He had not gone far before Mrs. Davidson came hurriedly for Davison to follow him. "He has taken your full set of red flannels, chest protector and all, that hung on the line in that room," said she.

"He had them on then, he had no bundle when he left," said her husband.

"Cannot you ride and catch him; they are all you have to change in?"

"Poor devil! it is cold, let him have them," said Davidson, watching the rapidly disappearing "Healer."

Anna's health was not good and a new source of anxiety presented itself. One balmy, clear day, Kate said: "The wind is only fitful, let us take a walk like we used to at home. We will go over to the timber claim and see if the wind has left any trees." They dressed with extra care and took a basket with them, with a few large stones in it in case they would be needed to ballast the young trees. On their return the spirit of frugality being strong in Kate, she piled the basket high with "cow chips" which were plentiful in that direction. A team and surrey approached and the gentleman within raised his high silk hat to the ladies.

"What shall I do with the basket?" said Kate, "sotto voce."

"'Drop it, you goose; he has not seen it," replied Anna. But Kate perverse as usual, still held on to it. "Can you tell me, ladies, where Mr. Davidson lives? I was informed at Pueblo that he might accommodate me for the night."

"I am his wife," said Anna, drawing herself up to her full height. "It is but a short distance. I have no doubt but that my husband will be pleased to see you."

The evening was pleasantly spent, with cards, music and conversation. Banker Angell was making a tour of that part of the country to look after the bank's investments in mortgages on the farms. "It is a poor country, hereabouts, sir," he said. "I advise you to get out of it as soon as possible, you are outside of the rain belt, Mr. Davidson," and he looked pityingly at the unconscious ladies. David merely shook his head.

Kate was re-trimming an old hat. "Let me trim it for you," said the banker.

"As if a man knew anything about trimming a hat," joked Kate.

In the morning there were hasty "good-byes" and a "warm invitation to come again." Kate took up the hat and in the velvet bow found a crisp ten dollar bill deftly knotted in. Anna was inclined to be indignant but Kate said, "Not at all. We will use it. We will send to Chicago for a whole ready made wardrobe and we need worry no more. But do not tell David."

Kate did not add that she feared he might want the money for some of the urgent needs of the farm.

Spring came and with it the new born babe, a girl. Fragile and quiet, with a gravity on her tiny, puckered features that angured that the anxieties of the situation were not unknown to her, but that they wore inculcated in her little being from her very conception.

"Let us call her Marguerite, for she is like unto a flower," said Anna, and Davidson assented.

Already the spring turmoil was in full blast. He had little time to think of anything else. Anna was very delicate and Kate assumed all her cares but the infant. Cooking, milking, baking, feeding the poultry, gathering the eggs, butter making, and the chores that the men could not perform. It still rained occasionally, and the draws relieved her from watering the cattle.

The grind went on; Davidson felt they must make a success of it this year. They rose with the first shadow of dawn, working until dusk, when they crawled into bed, exhausted, seldom lighting a lamp. There was little time to read. Anna sometimes would try to alond, when she nursed the puny baby and Kate churned.

David became moody and morose. He would talk of nothing but "the exorbitant rates of freight, grasping corporations, and the necessity of the Government purchasing the railroads. The farmer would then get living prices for his farm products, without the lecherous monopolies sucking the life's blood out of the fruits of his toil." He talked well, and men came miles to hear him after their day's work. But the girls were beginning to dread these rampant flights, verging as they were with some of the most unruly, toward socialism and anarchy. They were on the eve of a national election and party feeling ran high.

"The reapers will be here day after tomorrow," he said one morning.

"So soon," said Anna. "I believe the torrid wave will come before they do. I can see it in the baby. She scarcely seems to breathe."

Davidson muttered something that sounded very like a smothered curse and went out slamming the door.

How the girls hated the coming of that ill-kempt gang, honest toilers of the soil though they were. One of them, even a college professor, who had settled there, partly for his health,, and came tilled with enthusiasm for the irrigation of the southwest. There were no rivers in that section to draw the supply of water from, for the sluices which the settlers laid and after exhausting all his and some of his neighbor's available funds, and some too of Davidson's scanty dollars in the vain endeavor to turn a small stream, thirty miles away, thitherward and in building dams to hold the rainwater, that never fell, he gave up the vain attempt. The girls had never seen him, but heard that he fed the steam thresher as well in the fierce heat, as if he had never heard of anything else.

These men worked hard and were voracious eaters. Bread must be baked in quantities, and unless they wanted to sizzle fried pork for hours they must boil off several shoulders to eat cold.

"If you can attend to the bread, Anna, after I am through churning, I will go for some wild plums and we will make a batch of pies, it will save us other cooking," said Kate.

She was gone some time, the bread was ready for the stove, the pie crust being deftly turned in Anna's nimble fingers.

How did it all happen? Kate heard a slight scream and then a moan; she ran and then stood spellbound at the door.

Anna stood motionless before her babe, one hand still full of the dough uplifted before her face, the other holding the babe as far from her in her cradle as she could. Suspended from the ceiling, from between the muslin folds, hung a huge rattlesnake. It had given the ominous rattle and the work was done. The poor woman stood as if entranced, gazing at the beady eyes and basilisk head of the swaying reptile.

It was but a moment, but that moment seemed a lifetime to Kate, who grasped the forked stick that stood at the door and brought the snake to the floor, his head between the prongs and dispatched it. In that moment it flashed through her mind that Anna had said "there were rattlers about again, she had heard them." They had lodged in the roof of the sod house,

Anna had fainted and Tommy in response to Kate's cries ran for his mother, who was working in one of their fields within hailing distance. They carried her to Led and discovered a tiny puncture in the dough covered hand which they tenderly washed. The poison was already spreading and Kate cauterized the wound under Anna's own direction. They had often together studied the treatment from medical works. Tommy was dispatched for her husband, on their best farm horse, and Kate not knowing where the reapers were at work, was doubtful as to whether she should go to Pueblo for the Doctor or wait for her brother-in-law. She could not leave. Mrs. Grimshaw, who essayed the baking and boiling to completion, insisted on dosing the patient with whiskey until, as Anna herself said, "She could no longer see."

The long day wore on, she grew no better, the poison had spread to her arm and was affecting her system. The opportune arrival of the "cheeseman" on his rounds, seemed providential to the half-crazed watcher. He inspected the arm of the patient and suggested remedies that were at once applied, but privately told Mrs. Grimshaw that "she was too weakly to fight blood poisoning." He went back at once to the Professor, who owned the best horse in the neighborhood, and happened to be at home that day nursing his eyes, burned in the fierce heat of threshing the day before. The Professor went to Hayes, a nearer point, for the Doctor, but neither he nor Davidson arrived before night fall.

The Doctor, a dissolute fellow, an excellent, practitioner when sober, was just finishing off a hard case of drink and seemed helpless. He ordered a few simple applications for the poor patient, who was suffering intensely, and then retired to the kitchen to gorge his abnormal appetite on the cold meat and pies prepared for the threshers on the morrow, and slept.

"H he was only sober enough to take off her arm," sobbed Kate, "perhaps it would save her life."

All night they kept their lone vigil with the dying woman. At intervals she was conscious. She spoke of home, Father, Mother, and friends of her childhood. Then visions of the "dear, dear" old Pennsylvania mountains pictured themselves in her disordered fancy. How beautiful the green trees looked, how fresh the air and how sweet the dew. Ever and anon she dipped her hot hands in the imaginary silvery mountain brook and tried to lave her parched temples with the cooling waters.

Her husband sat as one dazed at the foot of the bed. The babe wailed in its feeble way as though it was conscious of the loss it was about to sustain. Mrs. Grimshaw recited the prayers for the dying, while the Professor kept watch in the doorway.

Suddenly at midnight she sat up; Kate held her head on her shoulder.

"Bring my babe, poor waif, von will not be long after me," she said. "I am glad I can go home. I could not live here. Bury me with my face toward the East, from whence the Son of God will come in all His glory, when the last trump shall sound and the grave give up its dead."

"Good-bye" ____, "God Bless! ____"

"My wife! Say that you forgive me for this," cried the sorrow-stricken husband.

But the voice had ceased, the tired hands were folded across her bosom, the pure spirit had tied to its Maker.

Davidson drove to Pueblo in the early dawn for the casket. "Bring a large plain pine box," said Kate.

"Thim ready made caskets is too small for a grown person," said Mother Grimshaw. "I've helped to lay out a good many in thim since I've been here, and the crowdin' of thim is awful. The coffin makers must think we belong to them 'pigmies,' the little fairy people of Arizony."

Together they dressed her in her pretty grey cashmere gown with the neat white collar and cuffs. Her face was not much discolored, her never-failing smile calm and peaceful.

Davidson returned along four in the afternoon with the large plain pine box in the wagon, while beside it on horseback rode the Priest, who came to pay his last tribute to a loved friend and oft-time hostess.

It was summer; there were no preserving influences at hand for the poor body. She must be buried at nightfall. They took her soft, white, blue-bordered blankets to line the box, and gently laved her between them, covering her with the fleecy folds.

The cheesman had spread the sad story on his rounds, and the settlers came from far and near. As far north as the creek, forty miles away, to Hayes, thirty miles south. People they had never seen, but felt united to through the common bond of neighborhood and sympathy. They came afoot, on horseback and in the prairie vehicle, the high-backed wagon. The men with their swarthy unshaven faces, with great beards, their skins burned a bronze red that stamped them with as distinct a type as the Arabians of the desert. The women, their huge sunbonnets flapping in the wind, the same influence that dried their baked and parchment-like skins, seemed to have warped their lives.

All wore the same listless, dejected air as if death to them was "but the parting of a breath," a laying down of the burden.

Tommy, who had killed the mate of the dread reptile, drawing it from a crevice in the roof and exhibited the rattlers and skins, was listened to eagerly as he told and retold the horrible story. Kate brought the infant to the Priest who performed the simple rite of baptism at the side of the mother's coffin, before they wended their way to the cemetery.

The cortege proceeded to the hillside, as the sun went down, Davidson driving and Kate, Mother Grimshaw and the Priest steadying the box, while the mournful procession followed.

"I am the resurrection and the life, saith the Lord; he that believeth in me, though he were dead, yet shall he live, and whosoever liveth and believeth in me shall never die," read the Priest from the ritual. But the beautiful service fell, like the cold clods on hearts that were dead to its influence.

The beloved remains were lowered into the ground. They heard a shout. A wagon approached over the prairie. It was the Professor waving his hat to attract attention. He asked the assistance of the men to unload some stone slabs which he had quarried himself, some twenty miles away.

"The gophers and coyotes will dig into any grave without these," he said.

They placed the small stones upright about the coffin, and covered the walls thus made with the slabs. Then they united in the Lord's Prayer, the Priest and Mother Grimshaw kneeling beside the grave, and all was over.

The next day the reapers came, and Kate followed the beaten path with a blurring in her ears and a mist before her eyes. Davidson was taciturn, avoiding her and the child, seeming to find his only solace in the work and the men.

The sultryness increased. The sun for days seemed to rise out of the baked earth like a huge ball of fire, shedding scintillating sparks from the disc of its lurid globe as it rose high in the heavens. Rainstorms came up all about them, they could see them at every point on the blank horizon, some mirages, no doubt, but not a drop of water fell on the "Dead Man's Foot." One morning it seemed as if neither men nor cattle could live if the hot wind did not soon subside.

Marguerite lay in her cradle. She had not moaned since the simoon came. Her eyelids fluttered a little when Kate urged her to take her milk. There was a faint tremor and then deathly quiet. She lifted the little form and carried her to the door. It was vain; she was dead. Laying her gently on the bed and covering her over, she went about the work saying again and again, "It is better so. She is with her mother. But oh! my little darling," amid the sobs she could not restrain.

No one would be home until evening. The chores finished, she washed and dressed the tiny mite in her prettiest white dress. She took her mandolin box, lined it with an old white and blue dress of her own, making of it a bassinet in which she laid the babe in her waxen-like purity, an angel now indeed. In the evening they buried her in the same grave with her mother.

The next day Kate told Davidson he must attend to the chores. She took Tommy to Pueblo with the team, returning with a large plain white marble slab with the names of mother and child inscribed on it. The grave was dug into a foot or two and filled with stones as a farther precaution against wild beasts and the headstone set. Kate told the bereaved husband "her work here was complete. She would leave for home the week following."

A team, one morning, drove up to the door and from it emerged Professor Merton, cleanly shaven and with more attention than usual bestowed on his rough-and-ready attire.

"What! Are you going too?" asked Davidson, looking dazed. A blush overspread the professor's tan-beaten features, but there was a merry twinkle in the eyes behind the blue goggles.

"Yes, but not to the Keystone State, where Kate tells me she has secured her old school again, but somewhere never to get out of sight of water again. Driving a street sprinkling cart may satisfy me.

"I have tried for years to sell my place. No one has the money to buy. I had the cattle driven over here and closed the door of the ranch. If there is anything over there you want, help yourself. I will never come back."

The lonely grief stricken man leaned on the gate post, his eyes so blinded with tears he could not see their extended hands.

"I will never leave her," he said pointing to the cemetery. "I brought her here against her will. I will never leave until they lay me beside her."

A professor's chair in mathematics, in a college near Chicago. A pretty vine-covered cottage in full view of Lake Michigan, the professor's home; his wife a cheery faced woman; Merton and Kate with whom the reader is well acquainted; is the sequel of the story of the "Dead Man's Foot."

[The End.]

www.ingramcontent.com/pod-product-compliance
Lightning Source LLC
Chambersburg PA
CBHW032120090426

42743CB00007B/411